W9-CFI-919

THE
Savvy Mom's
BOOK OF
LEGAL FORMS

the *Savvy Mom's* BOOK *of* LEGAL FORMS

EVERYTHING YOU NEED TO PROTECT YOUR FAMILY, HOME, AND FUTURE

CLIFF ROBERSON, LLM, PH.D.

McGraw-Hill

New York   Chicago   San Francisco   Lisbon
London   Madrid   Mexico City   Milan   New Delhi
San Juan   Seoul   Singapore   Sydney   Toronto

The *McGraw·Hill* Companies

1 2 3 4 5 6 7 8 9 0   FGR/FGR   0 9 8 7

ISBN-13: P/N 978-0-07-147928-8 of set
               978-0-07-147927-1

ISBN-10: P/N 0-07-147928-7 of set
               0-07-147927-9

This publication is designed to provide accurate and authoritative information in regard to the subject matter covered. It is sold with the understanding that the publisher is not engaged in rendering legal, accounting, or other professional service. If legal advice or other expert assistance is required, the services of a competent professional person should be sought.

—*From a Declaration of Principles Jointly Adopted by a Committee of the American Bar Association and a Committee of Publishers and Associations*

McGraw-Hill books are available at special discounts to use as premiums and sales promotions, or for use in corporate training programs. For more information, please write to the Director of Special Sales, Professional Publishing, McGraw-Hill, Two Penn Plaza, New York, NY 10121-2298. Or contact your local bookstore.

This book is printed on acid-free paper.

Library of Congress Cataloging-in-Publication Data

Roberson, Cliff
  The savvy mom's book of legal forms : everything you need to protect your family, home, and future / Cliff Roberson.
     p. cm.
  Includes index.
  ISBN 0-07-147928-7 (book) – ISBN 0-07-147929-5 (cd-rom) – ISBN 0-07-147927-9 (set) 1. Forms (Law)– United States–Popular works. I. Title.
KF170.R57 2007
347'.055–dc22

2006102214

Contents

Introduction

This book is a collection of forms, agreements, and contracts that I have developed in my 20-plus years of law practice. As we get older, we learn to work smarter, not harder. One way to do this is to have a library of forms to cover the various situations that generally occur in the everyday running of a home.

It is commonly said, "Why reinvent the wheel?" We should adhere to this maxim. Having the right form provides everyone with a paper record of the contents of any agreement, contract, or statement of intention. Having a library of standard forms means that no reinvention of the wheel is necessary.

Each of the forms in this book has been reviewed or written by an attorney. Depending on the complexity of the situation each covers, you may wish to have your attorney review the completed form. The cost to have a lawyer review a completed form is substantially less than the cost of having it prepared from scratch. In case of doubt, consult an attorney regarding the proper use of any specific form.

The book is designed so that each chapter is semi-independent of the others. This allows you to focus on current problems or needs without having to search the entire book. The book covers most situations and applies in most situations within the United States or elsewhere. The book is not intended as the substitute for personalized professional advice from a knowledgeable attorney. If you need legal help, consult an attorney who is licensed to practice law in your state.

The accompanying CD contains a copy of each form discussed in the book. These forms may be downloaded onto your computer and edited or modified for your personal use. Also contained on the CD are additional information and reference materials (saved in Windows & Microsoft Word and in Adobe Reader format) such as a copy of the Fair Credit Reporting Act and the following publications: Preventing Mail Fraud, Postal Service Identify Theft, Telephone Consumer Fraud, and Stopping Unsolicited Sexually Oriented Mail.

Author's Note: Using the Forms

A Note about the Forms

In the text, the term "form" is used in the broad sense to include all types of standard agreements, form letters, and so on. The terms "agreement" and "contract" are often used interchangeably, and for the most part, the two terms are interchangeable. A contract is a binding agreement. In some cases, however, an agreement may not be binding, in which case it is not a contract. In this book, only binding agreements are discussed. (A nonbinding agreement is merely an unenforceable promise to do something—for example, a promise to have lunch with a friend.)

The advantages of using standard forms include the following:

- *Preventing disputes.* A written agreement that spells out each party's rights and duties is the best method of preventing disputes.
- *Avoiding lawsuits.* By using written agreements, each party is forced to recognize what the agreements really provide. Written agreements help to prevent the types of misunderstandings that usually end up in court.
- *Reducing legal fees.* The forms in this book may often be used to eliminate the need for the assistance of an attorney.
- *Improving records.* The use of written agreements helps provide proof of your activities, which therefore helps you avoid tax and other difficulties in establishing a record.
- *Increasing efficiency.* It is easier and more efficient to complete a standard form than to attempt to draft one from scratch.

General Rules for Completing and Using Forms

In building and using a library of standard forms, certain general rules should be followed. Accordingly, the most important general rules are highlighted and numbered throughout the book. Consider them as cardinal rules to be violated only with great caution.

Rule 1: Read the selected form carefully.   After you have tentatively selected the correct form, read it carefully. Are there any terms, statements, or other materials in the form that do not correspond to the purpose you intend? If so, delete the inappropriate parts or statements. Too often individuals in a hurry select the apparently correct form and use it without carefully examining it. After you have completed the form, reread it. Does it make sense? If not, seek professional advice.

Rule 2: If there is any phrase or statement in the form that you do not understand, don't use the form.   People often use a standard form that is apparently what they need for a transaction without fully understanding all the parts of the form. This is a dangerous practice and can lead to expensive litigation later. If you don't understand a part of the form, find out what it means or delete it before you use the form.

Rule 3: Ensure that the complete terms of the transaction are in the form.   Too often, we use a form as a record of a transaction but do not include the verbal understandings by the parties of essential aspects of the transaction. Omission of the verbal understandings is dangerous. All important aspects of the transaction, including the verbal ones, should be contained in the form. The general law in most states is that the parties to a written agreement may not bring in evidence of verbal agreements that contradict the terms of the written agreement. This principle, known as the Parole Evidence Rule, has caused many problems when all the terms of an agreement are not reduced to writing and signed by both parties.

Rule 4: Date forms on the date they are executed.   Any form that is the record of an agreement or contract should be dated as of the date that the parties complete and sign it. If the form applies to a transaction that is to be completed in the future, the form should still be dated on the date that it is completed and signed. In addition, it should contain a performance date or completion date. As a general rule, contracts are considered as valid and binding on the date that they are signed. It is assumed that any contract that is dated was signed on the date indicated on the contract.

Rule 5: If the standard form does not fit the transaction, modify it.   No forms are set in concrete. If the selected form does not fit your requirements, tailor it to fit the situation. Some legal forms must meet certain requirements. For example, notice to a tenant that rent is past due usually requires a statement of the exact amount of rent that is actually past due. If you are concerned about deleting or changing a portion of a form, obtain legal advice. Obtaining legal assistance at the time the contract is entered into or the notice given is more economical than obtaining it when a problem arises.

Rule 6: Build your own library of forms by keeping a file of the forms you use.   Although this book contains one of the most complete sets of forms available, you should also start your own library because your forms are designed for your particular circumstances. Develop a filing method to prevent the need to hunt through a stack of forms. One method is to make an extra copy of each form that you use and file it in a forms folder. To make forms easier to locate, it is often helpful to build an index of forms by key words.

Signing Agreements
If an agreement is to be binding on you in your personal capacity, then you may just sign your name to the contract. If, however, you are signing on behalf of your corporation or partnership, make sure that your signature indicates that you are signing on the basis of your authority as an officer of the business. Failure to do so may make you personally liable on the contract.

If it is required that the agreement be signed before a notary public (i.e., acknowledged), then do not sign the agreement until you are in the presence of the notary. If the contract is to be completed by mail and you sign the contract first, sign two copies and mail both to the other party. Request that the other party sign one of the copies and return it to you. This procedure provides both parties with a signed copy of the agreement. If you want the other party to sign first, then send two unsigned copies and ask the other party to sign both copies and return them to you. When you receive both copies, sign one and return it to the other party, keeping one copy for yourself.

If last-minute changes are made to the agreement, you may write them in. In that case, make sure the change is readable and is initialed by all parties to the contract.

Using an Attorney
No book involving agreements could possibly cover every situation in our complex world. This book is designed to give you help with the simpler, more straightforward transactions. If the agreement is complex or involves large sums of money, have it reviewed by your attorney before you sign it. The book cannot replace your attorney, but it can help you reduce your legal fees.

1

Family Protection Forms

Forms and Information in This Chapter

Forms marked with an asterisk (*) only appear on the accompanying CD. Forms marked with a dagger (†) appear in part in the book and in whole on the CD.

I.   Forms Related to Children

Form 1-1 Child Care Contract
Form 1-2 Dependent Care Provider's Identification and Certification Form W-10
Web Sites for Finding and Screening Nannies
Form 1-3 Affidavit of Child's Age
Form 1-4 Children Carpool Agreement
Form 1-5 Appointment of Guardian of Minor Children
Form 1-6 Authorization for Child Participation
Form 1-7 Child Travel Authorization
Form 1-8 Declaration of Emancipation of Minor
Form 1-9 Acknowledgment of Paternity of a Child
Form 1-10 Denial of Paternity and Settlement of the Dispute
Form 1-11 Request for Special Education Program

II.   Forms Related to Adoption

Form 1-12 Consent to Adoption of Child by Present Spouse of Child's Natural (Mother) (Father)
Form 1-13 *Consent for Adoption by Unmarried Mother
Form 1-14 *Consent by Unmarried Father
Form 1-15 *Parental Consent to Adoption

I. Forms Related to Children

FORM 1-1   Child care contract.

> The following form may be used to contract with a care provider who will take care of your children in your home.

This Contract for Child Care is made by and between _____ (Name and address of Caretaker) hereinafter referred to as "Caretaker" and _____(Name and address of parent or guardian) hereinafter referred to as "Parent" on _____ (date).

The parties agree for valuable consideration that the Caretaker will provide safe and comfortable child care for the following minor children: _____ (names and ages of minor children to be included in this contract), hereinafter referred to as the "Children"

Terms of Contract

1. The childcare will commence on (date) and will continue until (date) unless the contract is terminated upon ten days' written notice by either party.
2. The Caretaker's duties shall include (list all important duties of the Caretaker):
   a. housecleaning
   b. laundry
   c. shopping
   d. cooking
   e. bathing and dressing the Children
   f. Care of the children when "Parent or Parents" are not present
   g. such other duties as may be assigned by the "Parent"

3. The Caretaker's normal hours of work will be from ____ to ____ on the following days of the week (list days that Caretaker will be at work): [Note: Consult local laws regarding overtime requirements and the maximum number of hours each week that the Caretaker may work if the number of hours exceeds forty hours per week or eight hours per day.]
4. The Caretaker's pay will be ____ per (hour, day, or week) paid (each week or semimonthly). The Caretaker will be paid by 5:00 P.M. each (Monday or on the 1st and 15th of each month). The following taxes will be withheld from the Caretaker's pay: [Example: Social Security and federal, state, and local taxes.]
5. The Caretaker will receive the following benefits: [List benefits, e.g., holidays, meals; number of sick days, vacation days, and personal days (if any), health insurance, life insurance, transportation, etc.]
6. If this contract is terminated by the Parent without good cause, the Caretaker is entitled to _____ weeks' severance pay in addition to all accrued wages and benefits up to the date the contract is terminated. If this contract is terminated by Caretaker or by mutual agreement of the parties, the Caretaker will be paid all accrued wages and benefits, but no severance pay.

FORM 1-1 continued

7. This contract supersedes all prior agreements and understandings between the parties and may only be modified in writing signed by both parties.
8. This contract may not be assigned without the prior consent of both parties.
9. This contract shall be governed by the laws of the State of _____ (name of local state) and the City of _____ (name of local city).
10. This contract is in force when signed by both parties.

Date signed:_____

Signed:

_____   _____
Caretaker   Parent

FORM 1-2 Dependent care provider's identification and certification, IRS Form W-10.

Form **W-10**

(Rev. August 1996)

Department of the Treasury
Internal Revenue Service

Dependent Care Provider's Identification and Certification

Do NOT file Form W-10 with your tax return. Instead, keep it for your records.

Part I	Dependent Care Provider's Identification (See instructions.)	
Please print or type	Name of dependent care provider	**Provider's taxpayer identification number**
	Address (number, street, and apt. no.)	If the above number is a social security number, check here ▶ . . . . . ☐
	City, state, and ZIP code	

Certification and Signature of Dependent Care Provider.—Under penalties of perjury, I, as the dependent care provider, certify that my name, address, and taxpayer identification number shown above are correct.

Please Sign Here	Dependent care provider's signature	Date

Part II	Name and Address of Person Requesting Part I Information (See instructions.)

Name, street address, apt. no., city, state, and ZIP code of person requesting information

General Instructions

Section references are to the Internal Revenue Code.

Purpose of form.—You must get the information shown in Part I from each person or organization that provides care for your child or other dependent if:

1. You plan to claim a credit for child and dependent care expenses on Form 1040 or 1040A, or

2. You receive benefits under your employer's dependent care plan.

If either **1** or **2** above applies, you must show the correct name, address, and taxpayer identification number (TIN) of each care provider on **Form 2441,** Child and Dependent Care Expenses, or **Schedule 2,** Child and Dependent Care Expenses for Form 1040A Filers, whichever applies.

You may use Form W-10 or any of the other sources listed under **Due diligence** below to get this information from each provider.

Penalty for failure to furnish TIN.—TINs are needed to carry out the Internal Revenue laws of the United States. Section 6109(a) requires a provider of dependent care services to give to you a valid TIN, even if the provider is not required to file a return. The IRS uses the TIN to identify the provider and verify the accuracy of the provider's return as well as yours.

A care provider who does not give you his or her correct TIN is subject to a penalty of $50 for each failure unless the failure is due to reasonable cause and not willful neglect. This penalty does not apply to an organization described in section 501(c)(3). See **Tax-exempt dependent care provider** later.

If incorrect information is reported.—You will not be allowed the tax credit or the exclusion for employer-provided dependent care benefits if:

• You report an incorrect name, address, or TIN of the provider on your Form 2441 or Schedule 2, and

• You cannot establish, to the IRS upon its request, that you used due diligence in trying to get the required information.

Due diligence.—You can show due diligence by getting and keeping in your records any one of the following:

• A Form W-10 properly completed by the provider.

• A copy of the provider's social security card or driver's license that includes his or her social security number.

• A recently printed letterhead or printed invoice that shows the provider's name, address, and TIN.

• If the provider is your employer's dependent care plan, a copy of the statement provided by your employer under the plan.

• If the provider is your household employee and he or she gave you a properly completed **Form W-4,** Employee's Withholding

Allowance Certificate, to have income tax withheld, a copy of that Form W-4.

If your care provider does not comply with your request for one of these items, you must still report certain information on your Form 2441 or Schedule 2, whichever applies. For details, see the Form 2441 or Schedule 2 instructions.

Specific Instructions

Part I

The individual or organization providing the care completes this part.

Enter the provider's name, address, and TIN. For individuals and sole proprietors, the TIN is a social security number (SSN). But if the provider is a nonresident or resident alien who does not have and is not eligible to get an SSN, the TIN is an IRS individual taxpayer identification number (ITIN). For other entities, it is the employer identification number. If the provider is exempt from Federal income tax as an organization described in section 501(c)(3), see **Tax-exempt dependent care provider** below.

How to get a TIN.—Providers who do not have a TIN should apply for one immediately. To apply for an SSN, get **Form SS-5,** Application for a Social Security Card, from your local Social Security Administration office. To apply for an ITIN, get **Form W-7,** Application for IRS Individual Taxpayer Identification Number, from the IRS. To apply for an EIN, get **Form SS-4,** Application for Employer Identification Number, from the IRS.

Note: *An ITIN is for tax use only. It does not entitle the individual to social security benefits or change his or her employment or immigration status under U.S. law.*

Tax-exempt dependent care provider.—A provider who is a tax-exempt organization described in section 501(c)(3) and exempt under section 501(a) is not required to supply its TIN. Instead, the provider must complete the name and address lines and write "tax-exempt" in the space for the TIN. Generally, an exempt 501(c)(3) organization is one organized and operated exclusively for religious, charitable, scientific, testing for public safety, literary, or educational purposes, or for the prevention of cruelty to children or animals.

Income tax reporting requirements for dependent care providers.—The individual provider must report on his or her income tax return all income received for providing care for any person. If the provider is a self-employed individual, the income is reported on Schedule C or C-EZ (Form 1040), whichever applies.

Part II

Complete this part only if you are leaving the form with the dependent care provider to return to you later.

Web Sites for Finding and Screening Nannies

Hire Nannies Nationwide

> The Nation's Premier Online Family and Nanny Matching Service
> http://www.Nannies4Hire.com

National Association of Nannies

> Oldest and largest national, not-for-profit, education-focused, professional support organization, run by nannies, for nannies. Run by professional nannies.
> http://www.nannyassociation.com/

Nannyhood and Apple Pie

> As capitalism's "latest recruits," American women may know less than their nannies about loving care.
> http://www.theatlantic.com/doc/200310/tsingloh

Nanny Agency Search for Nannies and Au Pair Nanny Jobs Service

> A nanny agency is a nanny and au pair search and job service, providing employment for nannies and au-pair jobs worldwide.
> http://www.nanny-agency.com

The Bub Hub

> Professional nannies and babysitters provide flexible child care options with agencies providing cover for regular bookings, changing bookings.
> http://www.bubhub.com.au/servicesnannies.shtml

FORM 1-3 Affidavit of child's age.

This form may be used to prove the age of your child.

Affidavit

I, _____ (full name of parent or guardian), hereby certify that I am an adult and of lawful age. I depose, affirm, and swear that I am the (mother/father/legal guardian) of the child _____. I further depose, affirm, and swear that the child _____ (name of child) was born on _____ (date) at _____ (place of birth) and presently resides with me at _____ (address) and is on this date, _____ years _____ months, and days _____.

Signed this _____ day of _____ 20_____

ACKNOWLEDGMENT

State of   )
County of   )

On this date, [list names of person(s) who signed above] personally appeared before me and acknowledged that the above signature(s) are valid and binding.

_____   _____
Notary Public   Date signed

My Commission expires: _____

FORM 1-4 Children carpool agreement.

This form may be used to provide for the transportation of children.

[Date] _____

This agreement is entered into by the below signed parents or legal guardians for the purpose of providing transportation of the named children to _____ (activity, e.g., Girl Scouts meetings) from their respective residences to _____ (address of activity). This agreement will commence on _____ (date) and end on _____ (date).

I

The children covered by this agreement are as follows:

1. _____ (name) whose parents (or guardians) are _____ (names)
   and who reside at _____ (address)
   Pick-up address: _____
   Drop-off address: (same) (or otherwise state address)_____
   Parents' or Guardians' contact telephone numbers: home _____,

FORM 1-4 continued

work _____, cell _____, and other _____

Driver's name _____ Driver's license _____

Insurance Company _____ Policy number _____

Description of vehicle that the driver will use: _____

Name of additional emergency contact in addition to above:

_____ (name) _____ (contact number)

Name and number of Child's doctor _____

2. _____ (name) whose parents (or guardians) are _____ (names)

and who resides at _____ (address)

Pick-up address:_____

Drop-off address: (same) (or otherwise state address)_____

Parents' or Guardians' contact telephone numbers: home _____,

work _____, cell _____, and other _____

Driver's name _____ Driver's license _____

Insurance Company _____ Policy number _____

Description of vehicle that the driver will use: _____

Name of additional emergency contact in addition to above

_____ (name) _____ (contact number)

Name and number of Child's doctor: _____

3. _____ (name) whose parents (or guardians) are _____

(names) and who resides at _____

(address)

Pick-up address:_____

Drop-off address: (same) (or otherwise state address) _____

Parents' or guardians' contact telephone numbers: home _____,

work,_____ cell _____, and other _____

Driver's name _____ Driver's license _____

Insurance company _____ Policy number _____

Description of vehicle that the driver will use:_____

Name of additional emergency contact in addition to above:

_____ (name) _____ (contact number)

Name and number of Child's doctor:_____

FORM 1-4   continued

---

4. _____ (name) whose parents (or guardians) are _____ (names) and who
   resides at _____ (address)
   Pick-up address:_____
   Drop-off address: (same) (or otherwise state address) _____
   Parents' or guardians' contact telephone numbers: home _____,
        work,_____ cell _____, and other _____
   Driver's name   _____ Driver's license _____
        Insurance company _____   Policy number _____
   Description of vehicle that the driver will use:_____

II

General Provisions

1. Persons other than the above named drivers will not drive the children unless written
   permission is given by all parents and guardians.
2. The above parents and guardians will rotate as to driving responsibilities as follows: (Describe
   which parents or guardians will drive on which days.) _____
   _____
3. The children will not be dropped off at a different location without prior arrangement
   by a parent or guardian.
4. Any special arrangements are indicated below (describe any special arrangements): _____
   _____
   _____
5. Each parent or guardian who signs this agreement hereby agrees to use care in driving
   the children and otherwise carry out this agreement to the best of their ability. If a parent or guardian is not fulfilling his or her obligations or there are any problems with any
   child, that person may be asked to leave the carpool.
6. This document is not intended as a legal agreement, but as an agreement that will work
   for the benefit of the children and parents or guardians.

_____   _____
[Signed by parents]   Date

_____   _____
[Signed by parents]   Date

_____   _____
[Signed by parents]   Date

_____   _____
[Signed by parents]   Date

FORM 1-5 Appointment of guardian of minor children.

This form may be used to ensure that your children will have the appropriate guardian should both parents become unable to take care of the children.

We, _____ and _____ are the parents and legal guardians of the following child(ren):

   Name _____   Date of Birth _____

   Name _____   Date of Birth _____

_____ (Name and Address) is hereby appointed to act as guardian of the minor child(ren) stated above upon my inability to so act. If he or she should be unable to or refuses to serve, I/we then appoint _____ _____ (Name and Address) to act as the guardian of the minor children upon my/our inability to act as guardian.

The appointed guardian shall have the following authority:
   (a) to assume physical custody of the minor child(ren).
   (b) to approve medical treatment of any kind or type or to disapprove the same within the legal bounds of the law.
   (c) to designate schooling for the minor children, and access to any and all of their educational records.
   (d) to generally act in the capacity as guardian of the minor.
   (e) to control any property belonging to the minor children under the Uniform Transfer to Minors Act, or the Uniform Gifts to Minors Act or similar statute.
   (f) I designate the guardian or successor guardian to act as custodian for all such custodial property of the children.
   (g) In the event that formal legal proceedings are commenced to establish a guardian for the child, it is my desire that the guardians mentioned herein have priority in appointment. The failure to list an individual as a guardian or successor guardian is intentional.

_____ Signature   _____ Date
_____ Signature   _____ Date

ACKNOWLEDGMENT

State of   )
County of   )
On this date, [list names of person(s) who signed above] personally appeared before me and acknowledged that the above signature(s) are valid and binding.

_____   _____

Notary Public   Date signed

My Commission expires: _____

FORM 1-6 Authorization for child participation.

This form may be used to give written authorization for your child to participate in a school, church, or other organizational activity.

To: (School, church, or organization or person)

This is to confirm that my child, _____, is authorized to participate in:
(list the activities that he or she is permitted to participate in)

This authorization is effective for _____ (date) and under the following conditions. If these conditions are not met, my child may not participate. (List the conditions.)

_____

_____

During this time period, I can be reached at:
Cell phone: _____
Beeper: _____
Other phone: _____
Other phone: _____

If I cannot be reached in any of these ways, I authorize _____ (name and telephone number) to consent to any emergency medical care that may be necessary.

Signed _____ Parent   Date signed _____

FORM 1-7 Child travel authorization.

Before your child or children travel with another person, a child travel authorization is essential. The form below provides the necessary authorization. The specific areas or locations that you consent to allow your child to travel to should be spelled out in detail.

We, _____ (name of one parent), and _____ (name of other parent, if applicable), authorize my/our child, _____, whose birth date is _____, and whose passport number is _____, (insert passport number only for international travel) to travel with _____ (name of person or group) to _____ (travel destinations) during the dates of _____ to _____.

I/we affirm that I/we are the legal guardian and have physical custody of _____ (child) and that there are no custody issues or cases pending in any court.

I/We authorize _____ (name of adult traveling with minor) to make any and all necessary decisions regarding medical care.

FORM 1-7 continued

Parent's name: _____

Address: _____

Day phone: _____

Evening phone: _____

Cell phone: _____

Parent's name: _____

Address: _____

Day phone: _____

Evening phone: _____

Cell phone: _____

Signature: _____

ACKNOWLEDGEMENT

State of   )

County of   )

On this date, [list names of person(s) who signed above] personally appeared before me and acknowledged that the above signature(s) are valid and binding.

_____   _____

Notary Public   Date signed

My Commission expires: _____

FORM 1-8 Declaration of emancipation of minor.

This form may be used for parents to emancipate a minor. In most states the form must be approved by a family court. It is used when a minor child wishes to have complete control over his or her financial affairs. For example, in the 1970s a popular country-and-western singer who was seventeen years old wanted to have control over her singing and public appearance contracts. So she went to court and received approval to enter into contracts as if she were an adult. This form indicates that both parents have agreed. If there is only one parent, modify the declaration as necessary.

DECLARATION OF EMANCIPATION

This is to certify that _____ and _____ (full names), are the parents (or legal guardians) of _____, a minor, who was born on _____ and is presently _____ years of age as of (date) _____. As the parents (or guardians) of the minor, we are the only ones entitled to the full and complete custody of the child.

Effective on this date, we hereby emancipate the minor, and, pursuant to (Statute or as the case may be), we give up or forgo all rights of controlling _____ (minor's name), and all rights to receive his/her earnings.

Signature _____   Date _____

FORM 1-9 Acknowledgment of paternity of a child.

To Whom It May Concern:

Regarding the minor child: _____ (name), a baby (girl)(boy) born on _____ (date) at the _____ Hospital, located in the city and state of _____.

_____ (Name and Address) is the Mother of the above named child, and

_____ (Name and Address) is the Father. Both Mother and Father agree that Mother gave birth to the child and the Father hereby acknowledges paternity of the child.

Dated:_____

_____   Signature of Mother

_____   Signature of Father

FORM 1-9 continued

ACKNOWLEDGMENT

State of   )
County of   )
On this date, [list names of person(s) who signed above] personally appeared before me and acknowledged that the above signature(s) are valid and binding.

_____   _____
Notary Public   Date signed

My Commission expires: _____

FORM 1-10 Denial of paternity and settlement of the dispute.

This form may be used to settle a dispute as to paternity of an unborn child.

[Date] _____

This agreement entered into between _____ (name and address) referred to as the Mother and _____ (name and address) referred to as the Alleged Father.
Both Parties agreed that the issues and facts are as follows:
1. The Mother is _____ months pregnant.
2. The Mother claims that the Alleged Father is the natural father of the unborn child.
3. The Alleged Father denies that he is the natural father of the unborn child.
4. They desire to resolve this dispute without litigation.

The parties agree as follows:
1. Without admitting fatherhood, the Alleged Father will pay to the Mother the sum of $ _____ no later than _____ [date].
2. The Mother agrees that on receipt of the above stated sum of money, she will not bring any proceeding for paternity before any court or administrative agency.
3. By accepting the payment, the Mother herewith releases the Alleged Father from any and all claims related to the paternity and support of the child.
4. If the Alleged Father does not timely pay the full amount stated above, then this agreement shall be of no effect.
5. Any modification to this agreement shall be required to be in writing.

Signature of Mother _____   Date _____

Signature of Alleged Father _____   Date _____

FORM 1-11 Request for special education program.

This form may be used to request that a child be enrolled in a special education program.

(Date) _____

To: (School or special education administrator) _____

_____

Re: Student _____, grade__, teacher _____

1. We are the parents (or guardians) of the above referenced child and we hereby request that the child be enrolled in the following special education program(s): (list program or programs or other services requested).
2. This request is based on the following reasons: (such as the child is having difficulty in reading his/her assignments and it appears that professional assistance is needed).
3. Under the Family Educational Rights and Privacy Act (20 USC 1232g), we hereby request a complete copy of all school records maintained on the child. The files should include reports of all tests or grades, assessments, all notes made by school personnel including teachers and counselors regarding the child, and any other information retained on the child.
4. We also request to be notified as to the action taken upon this request for special education program.

Sincerely,

_____
(Parents) or (Guardians)

II. Forms Related to Adoption

FORM 1-12   Consent to adoption of child by present spouse of child's natural (mother) (father).

This consent form may be used when the spouse who is presently married to the mother or father of a child wishes to adopt the child.

I hereby certify that I, _____, am the natural (mother) (father) of the minor child _____.

The minor child, _____ (name of child) is a (male/female) child and was born on (date). The natural (mother) (father) of the above-named child, _____ is presently married to _____ (name), who wishes to adopt the child.

I hereby consent to the formal adoption of the child by _____, (name and addresses of adopting parent) in accordance with the order of the _____ (Court), made on _____(date).

The child is to be hereafter named and known as _____, and duly and duly adopted and raised as (his)(her) own child.

Signed at _____ (place of execution) on _____ (month, day, and year)

_____
(Signature)

_____   _____
Witnesses

ACKNOWLEDGMENT

State of   )
County of   )

On this date, [list names of person(s) who signed above] personally appeared before me and acknowledged that the above signature(s) are valid and binding.

_____   _____
Notary Public   Date signed

My Commission expires: _____

The following forms, 1-13 through 1-18, only appear on the accompanying CD.

- Form 1-13 Consent for Adoption by Unmarried Mother
- Form 1-14 Consent by Unmarried Father
- Form 1-15 Parental Consent to Adoption
- Form 1-16 Refusal to Consent to Adoption
- Form 1-17 Agreement for Visitation by Natural Parents after Adoption
- Form 1-18 Agreement for Natural Sibling Visitation

III. Forms Covering Other Family Matters

FORM 1-19   Agreement for elder care.

(Date) _____

This Agreement for Elder Care is entered into by _____ (name and address of guardian or person arranging for the care) and _____ (care provider) to provide elder care for _____ (name of person who will receive the care).

Terms of Agreement

1. The elder care will commence on _____ (date).
2. This agreement will continue until _____ (date), unless sooner terminated by _____ days written notice by either party or the death or incapacity of the elder care patient.
3. The elder care will be provided at _____ (address).
4. The days and hours that the care will be provided are as follows: (specify the times and days).
5. The care to be provided under this agreement include the below-listed duties: (list duties of care provider).
6. Medical information:
    a. Primary physician and contact number _____
    b. Insurance coverage is _____
    c. Emergency contact persons and numbers _____
    _____
    _____
7. Salary and payment schedule: (discuss salary and payment schedule)
8. Benefits: (list any benefits)
9. Additional terms of the agreement:

SIGNED:

_____   _____
Contractor for Care   Date

_____   _____
Care Provider   Date

FORM 1-20 Authorization to drive automobile.

I, _____ (name), currently residing at _____ (address),
am the owner of the following described vehicle: _____ (year and make), license
number _____. The vehicle is insured with _____
insurance company under policy number _____. The insurance company's theft or
accident reporting number is _____.

I hereby give _____ (name), driver's license _____, permission to drive
the above-described vehicle. No one else is authorized to operate the vehicle except _____
_____ (if none, indicate so), on the following date(s), for the purpose of _____.

Signed: _____ owner

Date signed: _____.

FORM 1-21 Contract for maid services.

This Contract for housekeeping service is made by and between _____
(name and address of maid service or housekeeping service) hereinafter referred to as
"Employee," and _____
_____ (name and address of home occupant) hereinafter
referred to as "Employer," on _____ (date).

The parties agree for valuable consideration that the Employee will provide housekeeping services for the residence located at: _____
_____
(address).

Terms of Contract
  1. The housekeeping service will commence on (date) and will continue until (date) until
     the contract is terminated by written notice by either party.
  2. The Employee's duties shall include: (list all important duties of the Employee)
       a. housecleaning
       b. laundry
       c. shopping
       d. cooking
       e. such other duties as may be assigned by the "Employer"

FORM 1-21   continued

3. The Employee's normal hours of work will be from _____ to _____ on the following days of the week: (list the days that Employee will be at work). [Note: Consult local laws regarding overtime requirements and the maximum number of hours each week that the Employee may work if the number of hours exceed forty hours per week or eight hours per day.]

4. The Employee's pay will be _____ per (hour, day, or week), paid (each week or semi-monthly). The Employee will be paid by 5:00 p.m. each (Monday or on the 1st and 15th of each month). The following taxes will be withheld from the Employee's pay: (example, Social Security and federal, state, and local taxes).

5. The Employee will receive the following benefits: (list benefits, e.g., holidays, meals; number of sick days, vacation days, and personal days (if any); health insurance, life insurance; transportation, etc.)

6. If this contract is terminated by the Employer without good cause, the Employee is enti- tled to _____ weeks' severance pay in addition to all accrued wages and benefits up to the date the contract is terminated. It this contract is terminated by Employee or by mutual agreement of the parties, the Employee will be paid all accrued wages and benefits, but no severance pay.

7. This contract supersedes all prior agreements and understandings between the parties and may only be modified in writing signed by both parties.

8. This contract may not be assigned without the prior consent of both parties.

9. This contract shall be governed by the laws of the State of _____ (name of local state) and the City of _____ (name of local city).

10. This contract is in force when signed by both parties.

Date signed: _____
Signed:

_____   _____
Employee   Parent

Web Sites for Finding and Screening Housekeeping or Maid Services

The Maids

Find professional maid services and house cleaning services at The Maids Home Services, the professional housekeepers you can trust.
http://www.maids.com/

Home Cleaning Services, Maid Service, Merry Maids

Home cleaning services by Merry Maids provides maid service that is thorough, dependable, and worry-free. Get the details of our customized home cleaning http://www.merrymaids.com/

Molly Maid Quality Maid Service

A site to find household help, be a maid, or own a franchise. http://www.mollymaid.com/

Find local maids for cleaning and housekeeping

Prescreened and customer-rated home professionals to give you peace of mind when hiring a professional. http://www.servicemagic.com/task.Maid-Service.40006.html

FORM 1-22   Notice of name change.

This form may be used to notify individuals, banks, etc., of the change of your name. The form indicates that the change of name resulted from a marriage or a court order allowing the change. In most jurisdictions there is no requirement to obtain legal documents in order to change your name if you are not doing the change to defraud or mislead others.

Date: _____

To: _____

Notice is hereby given that I, formerly known as _____, have changed my legal name and shall hereafter be known as _____.

Reason for change was my marriage to _____ on _____(date). [Delete this paragraph if not applicable.]

My name was changed by court order issued by _____ (name of court) on _____ _____ (date order signed) in case no. _____. [Delete this paragraph if not applicable.]

_____
Signature (New Name)

FORM 1-23 Application for Social Security card.

The SS 5 form may be used to apply for a Social Security card for the first time or to notify the Social Security Administration of a name change.

SOCIAL SECURITY ADMINISTRATION
Application for a Social Security Card

Form Approved
OMB No. 0960-0066

		First	Full Middle Name	Last
1	**NAME** TO BE SHOWN ON CARD			
	FULL NAME AT BIRTH IF OTHER THAN ABOVE	First	Full Middle Name	Last
	OTHER NAMES USED			

2 MAILING ADDRESS Do Not Abbreviate
Street Address, Apt. No., PO Box, Rural Route No.
City | State | ZIP Code

3 CITIZENSHIP (Check One)
☐ U.S. Citizen ☐ Legal Alien Allowed To Work ☐ Legal Alien Not Allowed To Work (See Instructions On Page 2) ☐ Other (See Instructions On Page 2)

4 SEX
☐ Male ☐ Female

5 RACE/ETHNIC DESCRIPTION (Check One Only - Voluntary)
☐ Asian, Asian-American or Pacific Islander ☐ Hispanic ☐ Black (Not Hispanic) ☐ North American Indian or Alaskan Native ☐ White (Not Hispanic)

6 DATE OF BIRTH Month, Day, Year
7 PLACE OF BIRTH (Do Not Abbreviate) City | State or Foreign Country | FCI

8 A. MOTHER'S NAME AT HER BIRTH First | Full Middle Name | Last Name At Her Birth

B. MOTHER'S SOCIAL SECURITY NUMBER (See instructions for 8B on Page 2) ⌶⌶⌶ - ⌶⌶ - ⌶⌶⌶⌶

9 A. FATHER'S NAME First | Full Middle Name | Last

B. FATHER'S SOCIAL SECURITY NUMBER (See instructions for 9B on Page 2) ⌶⌶⌶ - ⌶⌶ - ⌶⌶⌶⌶

10 Has the applicant or anyone acting on his/her behalf ever filed for or received a Social Security number card before?
☐ Yes (If "yes," answer questions 11-13.) ☐ No (If "no," go on to question 14.) ☐ Don't Know (If "don't know," go on to question 14.)

11 Enter the Social Security number previously assigned to the person listed in item 1. ⌶⌶⌶ - ⌶⌶ - ⌶⌶⌶⌶

12 Enter the name shown on the most recent Social Security card issued for the person listed in item 1.
First | Middle Name | Last

13 Enter any different date of birth if used on an earlier application for a card. Month, Day, Year

14 TODAY'S DATE Month, Day, Year
15 DAYTIME PHONE NUMBER ( ) - Area Code | Number

I declare under penalty of perjury that I have examined all the information on this form, and on any accompanying statements or forms, and it is true and correct to the best of my knowledge.

16 YOUR SIGNATURE
17 YOUR RELATIONSHIP TO THE PERSON IN ITEM 1 IS:
☐ Self ☐ Natural Or Adoptive Parent ☐ Legal Guardian ☐ Other (Specify)

DO NOT WRITE BELOW THIS LINE (FOR SSA USE ONLY)

NPN			DOC	NTI	CAN			ITV
PBC	EVI	EVA	EVC	PRA	NWR	DNR		UNIT

EVIDENCE SUBMITTED

SIGNATURE AND TITLE OF EMPLOYEE(S) REVIEWING EVIDENCE AND/OR CONDUCTING INTERVIEW

DATE

DCL | DATE

Form SS-5 (12-2005) ef (12-2005) Destroy Prior Editions Page 5

FORM 1-24   Letter firing a professional.

Send this letter Certified Mail, Return Receipt Requested.

(Date)
(Name and address of professional)

Dear [Name]:
As I stated over the telephone, I am unhappy regarding the manner in which you have handled my interest. Accordingly, your services are hereby terminated. You are not authorized to take any further actions on my behalf.

As you are aware, my file belongs to me, not to you. Please provide me with instructions on when and where I can pick up the file.

Sincerely,

_____

(Signature)

FORM 1-25   Letter to professional association regarding professional services.

Send this letter Certified Mail, Return Receipt Requested.

(Date)
(Name and address of professional association)
Attn: Section on Professional Misconduct

Dear Madam/Sir:
The purpose of this letter is to inform your Association that I am unhappy regarding the manner in which attorney, doctor, CPA, etc. (name) has handled my case. The circumstances are as follows: [include a brief statement of the problem]:

_____

_____

_____

It is requested that your committee conduct an investigation into the actions of Mr./Ms. (name), since it appears that his/her conduct is not in accordance with the state requirement. I will be happy to provide additional information or to testify before your committee regarding this case.

Please keep me advised as to the status of this complaint.
Sincerely,

_____

(Signature)

FORM 1-26   Letter regarding professional fees.

Send this letter Certified Mail, Return Receipt Requested.

(Date)
(Name and address of professional)

Dear (name): _____

As I stated over the telephone, I am unhappy regarding the statement of professional fees which you have presented to me. Your original estimate was less than 50 percent of the amount billed.

Accordingly, I hereby request that you submit this dispute to your professional Association for Arbitration of Fees.

Sincerely,

_____
(Signature)

FORM 1-27   Change of address for U.S. Postal Service.

OFFICIAL MAIL FORWARDING CHANGE OF ADDRESS ORDER — **OFFICIAL USE ONLY**

Please PRINT items 1-10 in blue or black ink. Your signature is required in item 9.

1. Change of Address for: (Read Attached Instructions)
   ☐ Individual (#5)   ☐ Entire Family (#5)   ☐ Business (#6)

2. Is This Move Temporary?   ☐ Yes   ☐ No

Zone/Route ID No.

3. Start Date: (ex. 02/27/06)

4. If TEMPORARY move, print date to discontinue forwarding: (ex. 03/27/06)

Date Entered on Form 3982
M M   D D   Y Y

5a. LAST Name & Jr./Sr./etc.

5b. FIRST Name and MI

Expiration Date
M M   D D   Y Y

6. If BUSINESS Move, Print Business Name

Clerk/Carrier Endorsement

PRINT OLD MAILING ADDRESS BELOW: HOUSE/BUILDING NUMBER AND STREET NAME (INCLUDE ST., AVE., CT., ETC.) OR PO BOX

7a. OLD Mailing Address

7a. OLD APT or Suite

7b. For Puerto Rico Only: If address is in PR, print urbanization name, if appropriate.

7c. OLD CITY

7d. State

7e. ZIP

PRINT NEW MAILING ADDRESS BELOW: HOUSE/BUILDING NUMBER AND STREET NAME (INCLUDE ST., AVE., CT., ETC.) OR PO BOX

8a. NEW Mailing Address

8a. NEW APT/Ste or PMB

8b. For Puerto Rico Only: If address is in PR, print urbanization name, if appropriate.

8c. NEW CITY

8d. State

8e. ZIP

9. Print and Sign Name (see conditions on reverse)
   Print: _____
   ► Sign: _____

10. Date Signed: (ex. 01/27/06)

OFFICIAL USE ONLY

PS FORM 3575 MAY 2006   **Visit usps.com to change your address online or call 1-800-ASK-USPS (1-800-275-8777)**   0506

FORM 1-28 Letter to Secretary of State regarding a corporation.

This form only appears on the accompanying CD.

IV. Do Not Call Registry

The National Do Not Call Registry gives you a choice about whether to receive telemarketing calls at home. Most telemarketers should not call your number once it has been on the registry for 31 days. If they do, you can file a complaint at https://www.donotcall.gov/register/Reg.aspx. You can register your home or mobile phone for free. Your registration will be effective for five years. If you do not have online access to the above Web site, you may register your telephone number by calling 1–888–382–1222.

The first step in registering your telephone is to complete the online form. You may enter up to three phone numbers and your e-mail address. After the registration is complete, you should receive an e-mail from Register@donotcall.gov. To complete the registration, you need to open the e-mail and click on the link to complete your registration. Note: If you share any of these telephone numbers with others, please remember that you are registering for everyone who uses these lines.

The National Do Not Call Registry is managed by the Federal Trade Commission (FTC), the nation's consumer protection agency.

Frequently Asked Questions Regarding the Do Not Call Registry

Q1. *Why would I register my phone number with the National Do Not Call Registry?*

The National Do Not Call Registry gives you an opportunity to limit the telemarketing calls you receive. Once you register your phone number, telemarketers covered by the National Do Not Call Registry have up to 31 days from the date you register to stop calling you.

Q2. *Who manages the National Do Not Call Registry?*

The National Do Not Call Registry is managed by the Federal Trade Commission (FTC), the nation's consumer protection agency. It is enforced by the FTC, the Federal Communications Commission (FCC), and state law enforcement officials.

Q3. *Why was the National Do Not Call Registry created?*

The registry was created to offer consumers a choice regarding telemarketing calls. The FTC's decision to create the National Do Not Call Registry was the culmination of a comprehensive, three-year review of the Telemarketing Sales Rule (TSR), as well as the commission's extensive experience enforcing the TSR over seven years. The FTC held numerous workshops, meetings, and briefings to solicit feedback from interested parties and considered over 64,000 public comments, most of which favored creating the registry. You can review the entire record of the rule review at www.ftc.gov/bcp/rulemaking/tsr/tsrrulemaking/index.htm.

Q4. *How soon after I register will I notice a reduction in calls?*

The telemarketers covered by the National Do Not Call Registry have up to 31 days from the date you register to stop calling you.

Q5. *When I register my phone number, how long until it shows up on the National Do Not Call Registry?*

After you register, your phone number will show up on the registry by the next day. Telemarketers have up to 31 days to get your phone number and remove it from their call lists.

Q6. *What if I change my mind? Can I take my number off the National Do Not Call Registry?*

You can delete your phone number only by calling toll-free 1–888–382–1222 from the telephone number you want to delete. After you contact the registry to delete it, it will be removed from the National Do Not Call Registry by the next day. But telemarketers have up to 31 days to access information about your deletion and add your number back to their call lists, if they choose to.

Q7. *If I registered by phone, will I receive a confirmation?*

No, but you can verify that your number is on the registry online at www.donotcall.gov or by calling the registry's toll-free number (1–888–382–1222) and following the prompts for verifying that your number is on the registry.

Q8. *I received a phone call from someone offering to put my name on the National Do Not Call Registry. Should I let them?*

No. The FTC does not allow private companies or other such third parties to register consumers for the National Do Not Call Registry. Web sites or phone solicitations that claim they can or will register a consumer's name or phone number on the National Do Not Call Registry—especially those that charge a fee—are almost certainly a scam. Consumers may register directly or through some state governments, but never through private companies. For consumers, the National Do Not Call Registry is a free service of the federal government.

Q9. *If I choose to register my phone number, how will my information be used and disclosed?*

The registry collects your phone number and stores it in the National Do Not Call Registry so that telemarketers and sellers covered by the FTC's rules can remove your phone number from their call lists. Telemarketers are required to search the registry every 31 days and delete from their call lists phone numbers that are in the registry. Phone numbers in the registry also may be shared with law enforcement to assure compliance with federal and state law. For information about the privacy of your information, check the FTC's privacy policy at www.ftc.gov/ftc/privacy.

Q10. *Can I register my cell phone on the National Do Not Call Registry?*

Yes, you may place your personal cell phone number on the National Do Not Call Registry. The registry has accepted cell phone numbers since it opened for registrations in June 2003. There is no deadline to register a home or cell phone number on the registry.

You may have received an e-mail telling you that your cell phone is about to be assaulted by telemarketing calls as a result of a new cell phone number database; however, that is not the case. FCC regulations prohibit telemarketers from using automated dialers to call cell phone numbers. Automated dialers are standard in the industry, so most telemarketers don't call consumers on their cell phones without their consent.

Q11. *Can I register all my family and friends?*

You should register only your own telephone numbers.

Q12. *I have more than three personal telephone numbers. How can I register all of those numbers?*

You may register up to three telephone numbers at one time on the National Do Not Call Registry Web site. You will receive a separate confirmation e-mail for each number you wish to register online. You must open each e-mail and click on the link in each one to complete the registration process. If you have more than three personal telephone numbers, you will have to go through the registration process more than once to register all of your numbers. There is a limit on the number of phone numbers you can register in this manner.

You can register only one phone number each time you call the National Do Not Call Registry, and you must call from the phone number you wish to register.

Q13. *What happens if I register more than one number at a time online?*

You will get an e-mail for each number you register online. You need to open each e-mail and click on the link in each e-mail within 72 hours to register those numbers.

Q14. *Can I register my business phone number or a fax number?*

The National Do Not Call Registry is only for personal phone numbers. Business-to-business calls and faxes are not covered by the National Do Not Call Registry.

Q15. *How long does my phone number stay registered?*

Your phone number will remain on the registry for five years from the date you register (unless you choose to take it off the registry or your phone number is disconnected). If you register online, you may want to print the Web page for your records when your registration is accepted.

Q16. *How can I find out when my registration expires?*

Your registration will expire five years from your registration date. You may want to print the Web page with your registration date for your records.

Q17. *I moved and got a new phone number. Do I need to register the new number?*

Yes.

Q18. *Do I need to take my old phone number off the list when I get a new number?*

No. You can if you would like to, but the system will automatically remove most numbers that are disconnected and reassigned.

Q19. *What happens if my phone number is disconnected and then reconnected?*

If your number is disconnected and then reconnected, you may need to re-register. In addition, there are actions that you or your telephone company might take that could cause your registered phone number to become unregistered—even if your service has not been interrupted (such as changing calling plans or other services, or changing the billing name on the account). To verify that your number is in the registry, go to www.donotcall.gov or call 1–888–382–1222 (TTY 1–866–290–4236). Each time you re-register, telemarketers will have 31 days to take your number off their call lists.

Q20. *If my area code changes, do I need to re-register?*

If the phone companies change the three-digit area code for your home or mobile phone number, you do not have to re-register it with the National Do Not Call Registry. The number with the new area code will be registered for you during the 90-day period when both the old and new area codes work. This is known as the Permissive Dialing Period.

Q21. *Do I need to delete registration of my number with the old area code?*

No. You do not need to delete the registration of your phone number with the old area code. An automated process will remove it after 90-day Permissive Dialing Period.

Q22. *Why does the registry need my e-mail address?*

When you use the registry's Web site to put a phone number on the National Do Not Call Registry, the registry collects your e-mail address to confirm your request. They will send you an e-mail and you will need to click on the link in the e-mail within 72 hours to finalize your registration. They also collect your e-mail address when you request to verify your registration online so they can e-mail you a response to your verification request. They will store your e-mail address in a secure manner, separate from your telephone number. The registry will not share your e-mail address with telemarketers.

Q23. *Can I register online if I do not have an active e-mail address?*

No. The online registration process requires an active e-mail address. If you register online, they will send you an e-mail message with a link in it. You need to click on the link in the e-mail within 72 hours to finalize your registration. If you do not have an e-mail address, you can register by phone (1–888–382–1222).

Q24. *Can I reply to the e-mail I got when I was registering?*

No. The e-mail address is a one-way mail service. It cannot accept incoming e-mails. You must click on the link within the e-mail within 72 hours to finalize your registration.

Q25. *What if my e-mail address changes after I register? Will I still be able to verify my registration on the national registry?*

Yes, you will be able to use your new e-mail address to verify your phone number online.

Q26. *I called to register my phone number, but the message said my phone number could not be verified. Why not?*

When you call to register a phone number, you are asked to enter the number you are calling from. The system tries to match the number you enter to "Automatic Number Identification" or ANI, which is like caller ID for the telephone network. A small percentage of U.S. phones do not have ANI. If your phone doesn't, the system will have trouble locating your phone number. You can register your phone number on the National Do Not Call Registry Web site at www.donotcall.gov.

Q27. *I called to register my phone number, but the message said that the phone number I was calling from did not match the phone number I entered. What happened?*

To register, you must call from the phone you want to register. For example, you cannot register your home phone number by calling from work.

Also, people in certain communities—such as senior living centers or university residences—have phone numbers that are hidden by a PBX (private branch exchange) telephone system and cannot be matched by the National Do Not Call system. If you live in such a community, you can register your phone number on the National Do Not Call Registry Web site at this URL: www.donotcall.gov.

Q28. *I received an e-mail from Register@donotcall.gov, but I don't get a "Registration Complete" message when I try to click on the link. What should I do?*

You may not be able to click on the link in your e-mail from Register@donotcall.gov, or it may take you to a page that says "Registration Incomplete." You can complete your registration by using the cut and paste functions to insert the link in the e-mail into the "address" line on your Web browser. You must cut and paste the entire link. It is very long—possibly more than one line of text. You cannot retype the link.

Q29. *If I register my number on the National Do Not Call Registry, will it stop all telemarketing calls?*

No. Placing your number on the National Do Not Call Registry will stop most telemarketing calls, but not all. Because of limitations in the jurisdiction of the FTC and FCC, calls from or on behalf of political organizations, charities, and telephone surveyors would still be permitted, as would calls from companies with which you have an existing business relationship, or those to which you've provided express agreement in writing to receive their calls.

Q30. *Are calls from political organizations or calls soliciting for charities covered?*

Political solicitations are not covered by the TSR at all, since they are not included in its definition of "telemarketing." Charities are not covered by the requirements of the national registry. However, if a third-party telemarketer is calling on behalf of a charity, a consumer may ask not to receive any more calls from, or on behalf of, that specific charity. If a third-party telemarketer calls again on behalf of that charity, the telemarketer may be subject to a fine of up to $11,000.

Q31. *What about telephone surveys?*

If the call is really for the sole purpose of conducting a survey, it is not covered. Only telemarketing calls are covered—that is, calls that solicit sales of goods or services. Callers purporting to take a survey but also offering to sell goods or services must comply with the National Do Not Call Registry.

Q32. *My number is on the National Do Not Call Registry. After I bought something from a company, a telemarketer representing that organization called me. Is this a violation?*

No. By purchasing something from the company, you established a business relationship with the company. As a result, even if you put your number on the National Do Not Call Registry, that company may call you for up to 18 months after your last purchase or delivery from it, or your last payment to it, unless you ask the company not to call again. In that case, the company must honor your request not to call. If they subsequently call you again, they may be subject to a fine of up to $11,000.

An established business relationship with a company also will be created if you make an inquiry to the company or submit an application to it. This kind of established business relationship exists for three months after the inquiry or application. During this time, the company can call you.

If you make a specific request to that company not to call you, however, then the company may not call you, even if you have an established business relationship with that company.

Q33. *Are telemarketing calls from overseas covered?*

Yes. Any telemarketers calling U.S. consumers are covered, regardless of where they are calling from. If a company within the U.S. solicits sales through an overseas professional telemarketer, that U.S. company may be liable for any violations by the telemarketer. The FTC can initiate enforcement actions against such companies.

Q34. *I'm happy to have the choice to limit telemarketing contacts, but there are some telemarketing calls I don't mind receiving. Is there a way to allow only certain companies to call?*

Yes. If you give a company your written permission to call you, they may do so even if you have placed your number on the National Do Not Call Registry.

Q35. *If I don't want to put my number on the National Do Not Call Registry, can I still stop telemarketers from calling?*

Yes. Even if you do not register with the National Do Not Call Registry, you can still prohibit individual telemarketers from calling by asking them to put you on their company's Do Not Call list.

Q36. *What is the relationship between the state Do Not Call lists and the National Do Not Call Registry in terms of coverage?*

The National Do Not Call Registry requirements are at least as stringent as most state laws. Most unwanted telemarketing calls will be covered by the National Do Not Call Registry. States also can continue to enforce their laws, which will not be limited by the FTC. However, the FCC's requirements impact some state laws. For information on the FCC's rule, visit www.fcc.gov.

Q37. *When can I file a Do Not Call complaint?*

If your number has been on the National Do Not Call Registry for at least 31 days and you receive a call from a telemarketer that you believe is covered by the National Do Not Call Registry, you can file a complaint at the registry's

Web site at www.donotcall.gov or by calling the registry's toll-free number at 1–888–382–1222 (for TTY, call 1–866–290–4236). To file a complaint, you must know either the name or the telephone number of the company that called you and the date the company called you.

Q38. *How do I file a Do Not Call complaint? What do I need to file a complaint?*

You can file your complaint on the registry's Web site, www.donotcall.gov, using the File a Complaint page. You must know either the name or the phone number of the company that called you. You also must provide the date that the company called you and your registered phone number. You may provide your name and address, but it's not required for you to submit a complaint. You also may call the registry's toll-free number (1–888–382–1222) to file a complaint (for TTY, call 1–866–290–4236).

Q39. *What happens to my complaint?*

Do Not Call complaints will be entered into the FTC's Consumer Sentinel system, a secure online database available to more than 1,000 civil and criminal law enforcement agencies. While the FTC does not resolve individual consumer problems, your complaint will help the registry investigate the company and could lead to law enforcement action.

Q40. *What if I get a telemarketing call but can't get the telemarketer's name or phone number?*

For law enforcement officials to take action on your complaint, they need either the telemarketer's name or phone number, as well as the date of the call. If you want to report a Do Not Call violation, please get that information.

Q41. *Where can I get more information?*

If you have questions or complaints regarding the Do Not Call Registry, please contact the FTC by e-mail at dncconsumerinquiry2@ftc.gov, or by mail at:

National Do Not Call Registry
Attn: DNC Program Manager
Federal Trade Commission
600 Pennsylvania Avenue, N.W.
Washington, DC 20580

The FTC works for the consumer to prevent fraudulent, deceptive, and unfair business practices in the marketplace and to provide information to help consumers spot, stop, and avoid them. To file a complaint or to get free information on consumer issues, visit www.ftc.gov or call toll-free 1–877-FTC-HELP (1–877–382–4357); TTY: 1–866–653–4261. The FTC enters Internet, telemarketing, identity theft, and other fraud-related complaints into Consumer Sentinel, a secure online database available to hundreds of civil and criminal law enforcement agencies in the U.S. and abroad.

File a Complaint

To file a complaint now, your phone number must have been on the registry for 31 days.

To file a complaint, you need the date you got the call and either the name or telephone number of the company that called you.

Reminder. Even if your number is registered, companies with which you do business may continue to call you. So may charities, political organizations, and telephone surveyors.

The voluntary complaint form is designed to improve public access to the FTC Do Not Call Complaint Registry. The estimated time of completion is two minutes. Under the Paperwork Reduction Act, as amended, an agency may not conduct or sponsor, and a person is not required to respond to, a collection of information unless it displays a valid OMB control number. The OMB control number for this collection is 3084–0047.

V. Forms Related to Powers of Attorney

A power of attorney allows another person to act in your place. For example, say you want an individual to sell some real property (land) that you own. If you give that individual a power of attorney, then he or she has the power to sell your property. A person in the military service often gives his or her spouse a power of attorney when the military person is serving overseas so the spouse can take care of matters for him or her. Since you are giving someone the authority to act in your name, in most cases a special power of attorney is recommended. A special power of attorney would be one that authorizes the individual to do only the listed actions for you.

FORM 1-29 General power of attorney (long form).

I

I, _____ [name of person giving the power of attorney] _____ of [city and state] hereby appoint _____ [name of person to whom the power is given] of _____ [city and state], as my true and lawful attorney in fact for me and in my name, place, and stead for my use and benefit:

To perform or exercise any act, right, power, duty, or obligation that I have or may acquire the right, power, duty, and capacity to exercise or perform;

To engage in and transact any lawful business for me and in my name;

To sign, endorse, execute, acknowledge, deliver, receive, and possess any contracts, agreements, notes, options, covenants, deeds, bills of sale, trust deeds, leases, mortgages, assignments, insurance policies, bonds, checks, drafts, any commercial paper, receipts, evidences of debt, warehouse receipts, security agreements, liens, and any other such instrument in writing whatsoever and kind as may be necessary in the exercise of the rights and powers granted herein;

To lease, purchase, trade, exchange and acquire, to bargain for, contract, and agree to lease, purchase, acquire and take, possess any real or personal property whether tangible or intangible, on any terms and conditions as such attorney-in-fact shall deem proper;

To improve, repair, maintain, manage, insure, rent, lease, sell, release, convey, mortgage, subject to lien, and in any manner deal with all or any part of any real or personal property, intangible and tangible, whatsoever, or any interest which I may own or may hereafter acquire for me and in my name under such terms and conditions as the attorney-in-fact deems appropriate and proper;

II

I grant to my attorney-in-fact the full power and authority to do and perform all and every act and thing required and proper to be done in the exercise of any of the rights and powers granted herein as fully as I might do.

III

This instrument is to be construed and interpreted as a general power of attorney. The failure to enumerate a specific item, power, or authority does not restrict nor limit my attorney-in-fact from doing them.

IV

The rights, powers, and authority granted to my attorney-in-fact shall be effective on the date this document is signed and delivered to the attorney-in-fact and shall remain in effect unless sooner canceled by me until _____ [date].

Dated: _____   Signature:_____

FORM 1-29 continued

ACKNOWLEDGMENT

State of   )
County of   )

On this date, [list names of person(s) who signed above] personally appeared before me and acknowledged that the above signature(s) are valid and binding.

_____   _____

Notary Public   Date signed

My Commission expires: _____

FORM 1-30   General power of attorney (short form).

I, [name of person giving the power of attorney] _____, of [city and state] _____ hereby appoint [name of person to whom the power is given] _____ of [city and state] _____, as my true and lawful attorney-in-fact for me and in my name, place, and stead for my use and benefit:

To perform or exercise any act, right, power, duty or obligation that I have or may acquire the right, power, duty, and capacity to exercise or perform.
I grant to my attorney-in-fact the full power and authority to do and perform all and every act and thing required and proper to be done in the exercise of any of the rights and powers granted herein as fully as I might do.

This instrument is to be construed and interpreted as a general power of attorney. The failure to enumerate a specific item, power, or authority does not restrict nor limit my attorney-in-fact from doing them.

The rights, powers, and authority granted to my attorney-in-fact shall be effective on the date this document is signed and delivered to the attorney-in-fact and shall remain in effect unless sooner canceled by me until [date].

Dated: _____   [Signature] _____

ACKNOWLEDGMENT

State of   )
County of   )

On this date, [list names of person(s) who signed above] personally appeared before me and acknowledged that the above signature(s) are valid and binding.

_____   _____

Notary Public   Date signed
My Commission expires: _____

FORM 1-31   Special power of attorney.

I, [name of person giving the power of attorney], of [city and state] hereby appoint [name of person to whom the power is given] of [city and state], as my true and lawful attorney-in-fact for me and in my name to act in my capacity to do any and all of the following:

[List special duties or powers that the attorney-in- fact is empowered to do on behalf of the principal.]

_____

_____

_____

This instrument is to be construed and interpreted as a special power of attorney.

The rights, powers, and authority granted to my attorney-in-fact shall be effective on the date this document is signed and delivered to the attorney-in-fact and shall remain in effect unless sooner canceled by me until [date].

Dated: _____   [Signature] _____

ACKNOWLEDGMENT

State of   )
County of   )

On this date, [list names of person(s) who signed above] personally appeared before me and acknowledged that the above signature(s) are valid and binding.

_____   _____

Notary Public   Date signed
My Commission expires: _____

FORM 1-32 Special power of attorney (from one spouse to another).

I, [name of person giving the power of attorney], of [city and state] hereby appoint by [husband or wife], [name of person to whom the power is given] of [city and state], as my true and lawful attorney-in-fact for me and in my name to act in my capacity to do any and all of the following:

[List special duties or powers that the attorney-in-fact is empowered to do on behalf of the principal.] _____

_____

_____

This instrument is to be construed and interpreted as a special power of attorney.

The rights, powers, and authority granted to my attorney-in-fact shall be effective on the date this document is signed and delivered to the attorney-in-fact and shall remain in effect unless sooner canceled by me until [date] _____.

Dated: _____   [Signature]: _____

ACKNOWLEDGMENT

State of   )
County of   )

On this date, [list names of person(s) who signed above] personally appeared before me and acknowledged that the above signature(s) are valid and binding.

_____   _____
Notary Public   Date signed

My Commission expires: _____

FORM 1-33   Special power of attorney (from husband and wife to another)

We, [name of one spouse] _____, and [name of other spouse] _____, husband and wife of [city and state] _____, hereby appoint [name of person to whom the power is given] _____ of [city and state] _____, as our true and lawful attorney-in-fact for us and in our names to act in our capacity to do any and all of the following: [List special duties or powers that the attorney-in-fact is empowered to do on behalf of the principal.] _____

_____

_____

This instrument is to be construed and interpreted as a special power of attorney.

The rights, powers, and authority granted to our attorney-in-fact shall be effective on the date this document is signed and delivered to the attorney-in-fact and shall remain in effect unless sooner canceled by us until [date].

Dated: _____   [Signed by one spouse] _____

Dated: _____   [Signed by other spouse] _____

ACKNOWLEDGMENT

State of   )
County of   )

On this date, [list names of person(s) who signed above] personally appeared before me and acknowledged that the above signature(s) are valid and binding.

_____   _____

Notary Public   Date signed
My Commission expires: _____

FORM 1-34   Renunciation of power of attorney.

To: All persons

The power of attorney in which I, [name] _____ was appointed as the attorney-in-fact for _____ is hereby renounced. I renounce all right and claim to act as attorney-in-fact for [name of principal] _____.

Dated: _____

Signature: _____

FORM 1-35   Durable power of attorney.

Warning to Person Executing This Document

This document is an important legal document. It creates a durable power of attorney. Before executing this document, you should know the following information:

1. This document may provide the person you designate as your attorney-in-fact with broad powers to dispose, sell, convey, and encumber your real and personal property.
2. These powers will exist for an indefinite period of time unless you limit their duration in this document. These powers will continue to exist notwithstanding your subsequent disability or incapacity.
3. You have the right to revoke or terminate this durable power of attorney at any time.

I [name of person giving the power of attorney] _____, of [city and state] _____ hereby appoint [name of person to whom the power is given] _____ of [city and state] _____, as my true and lawful attorney-in-fact for me and in my name to act in my capacity to do any and all of the following: [List special duties or powers that the attorney-in-fact is empowered to do on behalf of the principal.] _____

_____

_____

This instrument is to be construed and interpreted as a durable power of attorney, and any subsequent incapacity of the principal shall not affect this power of attorney.

The rights, powers, and authority granted to my attorney-in-fact shall be effective on the date this document is signed and delivered to the attorney-in-fact and shall remain in effect unless sooner canceled by me until [date] _____.

Dated: _____

Signature: _____

FORM 1-35 continued

ACKNOWLEDGMENT

State of   )
County of   )

On this date, [list names of person(s) who signed above] personally appeared before me and acknowledged that the above signature(s) are valid and binding.

_____   _____

Notary Public   Date signed

My Commission expires: _____

FORM 1-36 Notification of revocation of power of attorney.

To: All persons

The power of attorney in which I, [name], appointed _____ as the attorney-in-fact for me _____ [date] is hereby revoked. I have revoked all rights and claims of _____ to act as attorney-in-fact for me.

Dated: _____
Signature: _____

VI. Forms Related to Marriage and/or Living Together

The following forms only appear on the accompanying CD.

- Form 1-37 *Premarital Agreement
- Form 1-38 *Living Together Agreement
- Form 1-39 *Property Sharing Agreement
- Form 1-40 *Agreement to Keep Property Separate
- Form 1-41 *Reconciliation Agreement
- Form 1-42 *Separation Agreement

2

Medical Protection Forms

Forms and Information in This Chapter

I. Forms Related to Medical Care of a Child

II. Forms Related to Other Medical Issues

III. Living Wills

I. Forms Related to Medical Care of a Child

FORM 2-1   Authorization for medical care of minor child.

> This form may be used to authorize medical care of a minor child when the minor child is temporarily in the custody of another person.

I, _____, am the (Father/Mother) (legal guardian) of _____ (Child), who is at present in the custodial care of _____ _____ (Name/Names).

I hereby lawfully authorize _____ (Name) to make any arrangements necessary for the appropriate medical or surgical care of the above-named child and confer all required consents in connection therewith to the above-named child.

This medical care authorization will cease to be effective at that point in time when (Child) is released from the custodial care of (Name).

Dated: _____

_____
Signature of Parent

FORM 2-2   Authorization for hospital to discharge child to relative.

> This form may be used to authorize a relative to check a child out of the hospital.

Date:_____
To:_____ (hospital name)
Re: Minor Patient:_____.

As the parent (or legal guardian) of the above-named minor patient, I hereby authorize the hospital to release or discharge the minor patient into the temporary care and custody of _____ (name and address of relative), who is the _____ (relationship, e.g., aunt) of the patient. This release is for the purpose of returning the child directly to my custody.

_____
Signature of Mother

_____
Signature of Father

Receipt of Child
I, _____, (Name of Relative) acknowledge that I have assumed custody of the above named minor patient and will deliver the child directly to its parents (or legal guardian).

FORM 2-3   Parent's consent for medical treatment of minor.

This form may be used by parents to consent to the medical treatment of a minor.

I, _____ (Full Name), am the (Father/Mother) of _____, a minor, born _____ (Date). I have been fully informed by Dr. _____ (Physician) of the hazards and possible consequences, as well as the alternative methods of treatment, involved in treating the (name of minor) for (medical problem).

I hereby consent to such treatment by such Physician.

Signature _____   Date _____

Witness _____   Date _____

Consent of Minor

I, _____ (name of minor), have read the above consent form signed by my (Father/Mother) and hereby join with (Him/Her) in the consent.

I have been informed of the hazards and possible consequences involved in the treatment.

Signature _____   Date _____

Witness _____   Date _____

FORM 2-4   Emergency medical treatment for minor, authorization to school.

I, _____ (name and address), am the (father/mother/legal guardian) of _____, a minor, date of birth _____, who attends (name of school and address).

In the event all reasonable attempts by authorized school personnel to contact me at (phone number) or to contact (other parent/guardian) at (phone number) have been unsuccessful, I give my consent for:

- The administration of any treatment deemed necessary by _____ (name of preferred physician) or _____ (name of preferred dentist), or, in the event the appropriate preferred practitioner is not available, by another licensed physician or dentist; and
- The transfer of the minor to _____ (name of preferred hospital) or any hospital reasonably accessible.

This authorization does not cover major surgery unless the medical opinions of two other licensed physicians concurring in the necessity for such surgery are obtained prior to the performance of such surgery.

FORM 2-4 continued

The following information must be given to any hospital or practitioner not having access to the minor's medical history:

Allergies: _____

_____

Date of last tetanus shot: _____

Physical impairments: _____

_____

Other facts to which physician or hospital should be alerted: _____

_____

Signature _____   Date _____

II. Forms Related to Other Medical Issues

FORM 2-5 Surgery authorization and consent.

To: _____ (Patient's name)

Admitting physician(s):

_____ (name)

_____ (name)

Supervising physician or surgeon for this surgery or special procedure is: _____

Right to Be Informed of Risks of Operation or Procedure

The hospital maintains personnel and facilities to assist the physician(s) and surgeon(s) in their performance of various surgical operations and other special diagnostic and therapeutic procedures. These operations and procedures may all involve risks of unsuccessful results, complications, injury or even death, from both known and unforeseen causes, and no warranty or guarantee is made as to result or cure.

1. You have the right to be informed of these risks as well as the nature and purpose of the operation or procedure, and the available alternative methods of treatment and their risks and benefits.
2. You also have the right to be informed whether your physician has any independent medical research or economic interests related to the performance of the proposed operation or procedure.

FORM 2-5 continued

3. This form is not intended as a substitute for such explanations, which are provided by the supervising physician(s) or surgeon(s).
4. Except in cases of emergency, operations or procedures are not performed until the patient has had the opportunity to receive this information.
5. You have the right to consent to or refuse any proposed operation or procedure at any time prior to its performance.

Physicians or Surgeons to Perform Operation or Procedure

Your physician(s) and surgeon(s) have recommended the operations or procedures set forth below.

On your authorization and consent, the operations or procedures, together with any different or further procedures which in the opinion of the supervising physician(s) or surgeon(s) may be indicated due to any emergency or previously unforeseen circumstances, will be performed on you.

The operations or procedures will be performed by the supervising physician(s) or surgeon(s) named above [or, in the event of any emergency causing his, her, or their absence, qualified substitute supervising physician(s) or surgeon(s) to be selected by your admitting physician] together with associates and assistants, including but not limited to, anesthesiologists, pathologists, and radiologists with _____ (Name of Hospital) medical staff privileges.

The persons in attendance for the purpose of performing specialized medical services such as, but not limited to, anesthesia, radiology, or pathology are not agents or employees of the hospital or your supervising physician(s) or surgeon(s) but are independent contractors, and therefore are your agents or employees.

Disposition of Body Member, Organ, or Tissue

The hospital is authorized to use discretion in disposing of any member, organ or other tissue removed from my person during the below-named operations or procedures, except: _____ _____ (list any exceptions).

Blood Transfusion

If your physician determines that there is a reasonable possibility that your may need a blood transfusion as a result of the surgery or procedure to which you are consenting, your physician will inform you of this and will provide you with information concerning the benefits and risks of the various options for blood transfusion, including predonation by yourself or others. The transfusions of blood or blood products involve certain risks, including the transmission of infectious hepatitis, Human Immunodeficiency Virus, or other diseases or blood impairments, and that you have a right to consent or refuse consent to any transfusion.

FORM 2-5   continued

ACKNOWLEDGMENT

Your signature below constitutes your acknowledgment that you have read and agreed to the above provisions and that the operations or procedures set forth below have been adequately explained to you by the supervising physician(s) or surgeon(s) and that you have received and understood all of the information you desire concerning the operations or procedures, and that you authorize and consent to the performance of the operations or procedures including, but not limited to, the administration and maintenance of anesthesia and the performance of services including radiology and pathology.

_____   Date: _____
Signature of Patient or Person Authorized to Consent for Patient

_____   Date: _____

(If not the Patient, please provide the relationship to Patient): _____

_____   Date: _____
Witness

FORM 2-6   Consent for test to detect HIV infection.

I,_____ (Name), voluntarily give my consent to _____ (Name of Hospital), to be tested to see whether I have been infected with the Human Immunodeficiency Virus (HIV), which is thought to cause Acquired Immune Deficiency Syndrome (AIDS).

I understand that this test is not a test for AIDS but only for the presence of HIV. I understand that being HIV infected does not mean that I have AIDS. Not everyone who is HIV infected will get AIDS.

I understand a negative test result means that I probably do not have HIV infection. However, I understand in some cases the test may fail to detect that a person is infected with HIV when the person really is infected. I understand it may take several weeks or months or more before my blood will show signs of HIV infection, but during that time I can infect other people. Therefore, if I test negative, I may need to be retested at a later time to confirm I have not been infected. I also understand if I test negative now, I can still become infected in the future.

FORM 2-6 continued

I understand a positive test result means I probably have the HIV virus and that I should consider myself able to infect other people. However, I also understand in some cases the test results may indicate the person tests positive for HIV when the person actually is negative for the HIV virus.

I understand that all reasonable efforts to provide confidentiality and/or anonymity to the extent provided by law will be made. However, I understand that the results of the test will be kept in my medical record. The test results, as medical record information, will be regarded as confidential, and _____ (Name of Hospital) and my physician will not disclose these test results to unauthorized third parties without my express written authorization. However, the results will be available to physicians and other health care providers.

I have had the opportunity to discuss the HIV test and understand that before I decide to take the test I may ask any questions I have about the nature of the test, its expected benefits and risks, and any alternatives to the test. I understand that if I refuse this test, my exposure to the HIV will remain unknown and my ability to infect others with the virus will also remain unknown.

I have been informed that if the test is positive, a physician will provide counseling for follow-up care and for precautions against transmitting this infection.

I acknowledge that I have been given the information I need to decide whether to take the HIV test and have had my questions concerning the test answered. I agree that I freely give my consent for my blood to be tested for HIV infection. I understand that I may withdraw this consent at any time prior to having my blood drawn.

Signature of patient _____ Date _____

Witness _____ Date _____

FORM 2-7   Authorization for release of medical records.

This form may be used to authorize the release of medical records or other medical information that a hospital may have on you or a member of your family.

(Date) _____

To: (Name of hospital) _____

Re: (name of patient, dates of hospitalization, birth date, and Social Security number) I am the (patient/parent of the minor patient/legal guardian of the minor patient). You are hereby authorized to furnish medical information and medical records in your possession concerning the above referenced (former) patient to: (list persons or institutions to whom the medical records may be released): _____

_____

_____

[If only certain records or information is to be released, insert the following paragraph:] [The medical records and information to be released pertain only to the (back injury suffered on June 4, 20__) (hospital stay during the period May 1 to May 6, 20__)].

The information and records released may be used only for the following purposes (list purposes). Any other use of the medical information and records is not authorized without my specific written consent.

This authorization is effective immediately and shall be valid until (date), unless revoked by me.

_____   Date _____
Signed

III. Living Wills

The "living will" concept developed from the "right to die" cases of the 1970s and the ability of medical science to sustain life. Medical advancements have created a "new class" of patients, those unable to breathe without the aid of mechanical respirators and without mental facilities, i.e., the "living dead." A living will is not an actual will, but a letter of instruction to your physician not to sustain your life with extraordinary measures when there is no hope for recovery. As of 2005, there were forty-three states and the District of Columbia that had living will laws. Several other states are considering legislation to permit living wills.

Most state statutes are very similar to the Texas Act, which provides:

> Any competent adult person may, at any time, execute a directive for the withholding or withdrawal of life-sustaining procedures in the event of a terminal condition. The directive shall be signed by the declarant in the presence of two witnesses not related to the declarant by blood or marriage and who would not be entitled to any portion of the estate of the declarant.

"Declarant" means the person who has executed or issued a directive under this act. "Attending physician" means the physician who has primary responsibility for the treatment and care of the patient. "Terminal condition" means an incurable condition caused by injury, disease, or illness, which, regardless of the application of life-sustaining procedures, serves only to postpone the moment of death of the patient.

While a living will provides the health care professional with the authority to stop treatment in hopeless cases, the doctor may ignore it and continue his or her treatment of you. The decision on whether to execute a living will is an individual choice that each patient should make.

There are two associations involved in the "right to die" movement. Some of the services that they provide include keeping a registered copy of your will and providing you with a mini-will for your wallet and specialized publications on the right to die. The two organizations are listed below:

Concern for Dying
250 West 57th Street
New York, NY 10107
Telephone: (212) 246–6962

Society for the Right to Die
250 West 57th Street
New York, NY 10107
Telephone: (212) 246–6973

The living will provisions are not to be construed to condone, authorize, or approve mercy killing, or to permit any affirmative or deliberate act or omission to end life, other than to permit the natural process of dying. No heath care person may require as a condition of proving medical services that a patient execute a living will.

Requirements for Living Will

The requirements for a valid living will or right to die document vary in each state. The general rules include the following:

1. The declaration must be signed by the declarant in the presence of two witnesses, neither of whom are related to the declarant (person signing the will).
2. The witnesses must not be entitled to any benefit from the estate or will of the declarant.
3. The witnesses must sign the document as witnesses.
4. The witnesses also must not have any direct financial responsibility for the declarant's medical care, or an employee of any health care facility in which the declarant is a patient.

*[The preceding four requirements are taken from Delaware's Death with Dignity Act.]**

5. The document is valid for a limited period of time. For example, in California the document is valid for only five years.
6. Some states require that the document be signed and witnessed before a notary public.
7. The directive or living will may be revoked at any time by the declarant, without regard to his or her mental state or competency, by any of the following methods: by destruction of the document, by written revocation, and by verbal expression.
8. Any attempted revocation is not effective until communicated to the attending physician.
9. No life insurance policy shall be impaired or invalidated in any manner by the withholding or withdrawal of life-sustaining procedures from an insured, qualified patient.

---

*Death with Dignity Act, 16 Del. Code 2503(b).

FORM 2-8 California living will.

Directive to Physicians

Directive made this day of _____ 20__.

I, _____, being of sound mind, willfully and voluntarily make known my desire that my life shall not be artificially prolonged under the circumstances set forth below, and do hereby declare as follows:

1. If at any time I should have an incurable injury, disease, or illness certified to be a terminal condition by two physicians, and where an application of life-sustaining procedures would serve only to artificially prolong the moment of my death, and where my physician determines that my death is imminent whether or not life-sustaining procedures are utilized, I direct that such procedures be withheld or withdrawn, and that I be permitted to die naturally.
2. In the absence of my ability to give directions regarding the use of such life-sustaining procedures, it is my intention that this directive shall be honored by my family physician as the final expression of my legal right to refuse medical or surgical treatment and to accept the consequences from such refusal.
3. If I have been diagnosed as pregnant and that diagnosis is known to my physician, this directive shall have no force or effect during the course of my pregnancy.
4. I have been diagnosed and notified at least 14 days ago as having a terminal condition by _____, M.D., whose address is _____ _____, and whose telephone number is _____. I understand that if I have not filled in the physician's name and address, it shall be presumed that I did not have a terminal condition when I made out this directive.
5. This directive shall have no force or effect five years from this date.
6. I understand the full import of this directive, and am emotionally and mentally competent to make this directive.

(Signed)_____

The declarant has been personally known to us and we believe him or her to be of sound mind. Witnessed this _____ day of ____, 20__.

Witness _____

Witness _____

City of _____, County of _____, State of California

FORM 2-9 Florida living will.

To my family, my clergyperson, my physician and health care provider, and my attorney:

If the time comes when I am no longer able to take part in decisions for my own future, this DECLARATION shall stand as the expression of my wishes. I recognize that death is as much a reality as birth, growth, and maturity. If there is no reasonable expectation of my recovery from physical or mental disability, I desire and wish to be allowed to die and not be kept alive by artificial means or heroic measures, but wish only that drugs be mercifully administered to me for terminal suffering, even if they hasten the moment and time of my death.

Recognizing that my wishes place a heavy burden of responsibility upon you, I therefore make and sign the following declaration with the intention of sharing this responsibility and this decision with you and of mitigating any feeling of guilt that you may have:

Declaration

The Declaration made this _____ day of 20__, I willfully and voluntary make known my desire that my dying shall not be artificially prolonged under the circumstances set forth below, and I do hereby declare:

If at any time I should have a terminal condition and if my attending physician has determined that there can be no recovery from such condition and that my death is imminent, I direct that life-prolonging procedures be withheld or withdrawn when the application of such procedures would serve only to prolong artificially the process of dying, and that I be permitted to die naturally with only the administration of medication or the performance of any medical procedure deemed necessary to provide me with comfort care or to alleviate pain.

In the absence of my ability to give directions regarding the use of such life-prolonging measures and procedures, it is my intention that this declaration be honored by my family and physician as the final expression of my legal right to refuse medical or surgical treatment and to accept the consequences for such refusal.

I understand the full import of this declaration, and I am emotionally and mentally competent to make this declaration.

_____
Testator

The declarant, also known as the testator, is known to me, and I believe him or her to be of sound mind.

Witnessed this day of _____ 20__

Witness: _____   Witness: _____

3

Financial Protection Forms

Forms and Information in This Chapter

Forms marked with an asterisk (*) only appear on the accompanying CD. Forms marked with a dagger appear in part in the book and in whole on the CD.

I. Forms Related to Credit

V.   Forms Related To Tax Issues

VI.   Forms Related to Assignments of Debt

I. Forms Related to Credit

Checklist for Negotiating a Loan

The Loan Agreement

Most banks and finance companies have their own loan agreements or letters of understanding that contain their financial arrangements. Before you sign them, read all of the agreements carefully. Make sure you understand them and that you have no questions about them. Some of the essential terms you should know and that should be clearly set forth in the agreements are the following:

1. When will the loan proceeds be available?
2. When is the interest payable?
3. When is the principal payable?
4. How is the interest rate calculated?
5. Is there a penalty if you repay the loan early?
6. Are there provisions to extend the term of the loan, to renew the loan, or to convert the loan to a different type?
7. What are the reporting requirements?
8. What are the restrictions on the use of the loan proceeds?
9. What are the restrictions on incurring other debts, selling major assets, or changing business lines?
10. Under what circumstances can the bank or finance company declare the loan in default and demand immediate payment?

11. What events can trigger a default?
12. What are the insurance provisions?
13. Who is required to insure any collateral?
14. What are the restrictions on the use of any property used as collateral?
15. Can the financial institution accelerate the due date of the loan payments or principle?

    And above all else:

16. What is the total cost of the loan?
17. Are there other loan fees, commitment fees, placement fees, points, and so on, that will be charged in addition to the interest rate?

FORM 3-1   Disclosure of credit information.

This letter may be used to have a credit reporting agency send the business's credit report to a potential vendor in order to establish a credit account with the vendor. Send it Certified Mail, Return Receipt Requested.

Date: _____

To: _____

Re: Credit file of: _____, SSN: _____

Dear Madam/Sir:

I hereby request a complete disclosure of my credit file, to include the sources of any information in my file and the names and addresses of any parties who have received any credit information on me or my credit report. This request is made pursuant to the Federal Fair Credit Reporting Act.

_____
Signature

_____
Printed name

_____
Address

_____
Telephone number

FORM 3-2 Authorization to release credit information.

Date: _____

To [creditor]: _____

Address: _____

Dear Madam/Sir:

I have a credit account with your company. I hereby authorize the release of my credit information and request that a report of my credit history with your company be forwarded to the below-listed credit reporting agencies. [name and addresses of credit reporting agencies]

_____

_____

_____

_____

Sincerely,

_____

Signature

_____

Address

FORM 3-3 Adverse credit information request.

Date: _____

To [business denying credit application]: _____

Address: _____

Dear Madam/Sir:

I applied for credit with your company. My credit application was denied. Accordingly, under the provisions of the Federal Fair Credit Reporting Act, I hereby request a full and complete disclosure of the reasons for the denial, including the sources of any adverse credit information received from any person, company, business, and so on.

Signature: _____

Printed name: _____

Address: _____

Telephone number: _____

FORM 3-4   Request to correct credit information.

Date: _____

To [creditor reporting agency]: _____

Address: _____

Re: Credit report of _____, SSN _____

In reviewing a copy of my credit report received from your agency I discovered the following error(s) [List erroneous information here]: _____

_____

_____

_____

Please be advised that the above information is incorrect, and pursuant to the provisions of the Federal Fair Credit Reporting Act, demand is hereby made on you to correct the said information. I also request that this letter be made a part of my credit report and transmitted with any credit reports disseminated on me.

Sincerely,

_____

Signature

_____

Printed name

_____

Address

_____

Telephone number

FORM 3-5 Collection letter.

This form may be used in an attempt to collect a debt.

Date: _____

To [Name and address of debtor]: _____

Re: Your debt

Dear [name of debtor] _____:

Under the terms of our agreement, you were to pay me the sum of _____ by _____ (date). Since I have not received that payment, your account is delinquent.

[(Alternate paragraph.) You are currently several payments behind on the above- referenced account.]

Unless this account is current within the next _____ days, I will be required to take formal action to collect the past due amount.

You are hereby advised that if payment is not received, suit in small claims court may be commenced against you forthwith and without further notice for the amount indicated above, together with prejudgment interest. Instead of small claims court, this matter may instead be referred to our attorney.

As I am sure you are aware, if this matter goes to suit, all court costs, process server's fees, sheriff's fees, attorney fees where permitted, and other postjudgment costs will be added to the amount that you already owe.

You can avoid the unnecessary inconvenience and added expenses of a lawsuit by making immediate payment within five days.

Sincerely,

_____

Signature

FORM 3-6 Collection letter (automobile).

This form may be used to collect past due sums associated with the sale of your automobile.

Date: _____

To [name and address of debtor]: _____

_____

Re [describe automobile]: _____

_____

Dear [name of debtor] _____

At the time I sold you the above-referenced automobile, you promised to make weekly payments of _____. Presently you are delinquent in the amount of _____.

Unless payment is received within __ days, your delinquent account formal collection action will be commenced.

If it is necessary to bring legal action against you, the action may result in levies against your property or other assets after judgment. In addition, the automobile may be repossessed.

You are hereby further advised that if payment of _____ is not received within _____ days of the date of this letter, suit in small claims court may be commenced against you forthwith and without further notice for the amount indicated above, together with prejudgment interest. Instead of small claims court, this matter may be referred to our attorney.

As I am sure you are aware, if this matter goes to suit, all court costs, process server's fees, sheriff's fees, attorney fees where permitted, and other postjudgment costs will be added to the amount that you already owe.

You can avoid the unnecessary inconvenience and added expenses of a lawsuit by making immediate payment to us within _____ days.

Sincerely,

_____

Signature

FORM 3-7   Final notice before legal action.

Date: _____

To [name and address of debtor]: _____

_____

Re: Your past due account

Dear [name of debtor] _____:

I have made numerous requests for payment on your long overdue account. The balance is currently $ _____.

Since you have failed to pay this account, I am by copy of this letter forwarding the account to my attorney. You may, however, still avoid legal action if you contact me within the next _____ days and make satisfactory arrangements for payment.

This is your final opportunity to avoid legal action.

Sincerely,

_____

Signature

FORM 3-8   Notice of disputed account balance.

Date: _____

To [creditor, address]: _____

Notice is hereby given that your invoice or statement of [date] is incorrect for the following reasons:

___Payment of [date] not reflected on statement.

___The goods have been returned.

___The price listed for the goods is incorrect.

___The goods listed on the statement have not been received.

___Goods were not ordered and are being held for your instructions regarding return.

___Other: _____

The correct balance on the statement should be: $____

Sincerely,

_____

Signature

FORM 3-9   Request for information on account balance.

Date: _____

To [creditor, address] _____

_____

Notice is hereby given that regarding your invoice or statement of [date], I feel that it may be incorrect. In order that I may verify the correctness of the account, please provide me with the below-requested items or information:

___Copies of the purchase orders received from me.

___List of goods claimed to have been shipped to me.

___Any debt memoranda that are outstanding.

___Other: _____.

When I have received the above information, I will audit the account and provide you with my conclusions.

Sincerely,

_____

Signature

FORM 3-10   Settlement of disputed account balance.

Date: _____.

By this agreement between, [name of Creditor], Creditor, and [name of Debtor], Debtor, resolve and forever settle and adjust the below-listed claim. Both parties agree that there is a bona fide dispute regarding the amount due the Creditor on this account.

Accordingly, the parties agree that Debtor shall pay to Creditor the sum of $_____ no later than [date] _____ as payment in full on the below-described account or claim.

Should Debtor fail to pay the agreed sum by the above-listed date, then Creditor has the right to pursue the full amount claimed and is no longer under obligation to take the agreed sum as payment in full. If Debtor pays the agreed amount on or prior to the above-listed date, Creditor will accept the payment as payment in full.

This agreement covers the below-described account [describe the account or claim in this space]: _____

_____

This agreement shall be binding on all parties involved, their assigns, successors, and personal representatives.

Sincerely,

_____

Signature

FORM 3-11   Direction to pay.

This letter may be used to direct your debtors to pay the proceeds due you to a third party. This may be used as part of a financing plan for the purchase of goods or products.

Date: _____

To: _____

Re: [list account number or description of debt] _____

_____

You are hereby directed to pay to [name of person who will receive the payment], Assignee, all sums of money currently due me as the result of:

[describe the account in question]

_____

_____

Accordingly, all payments to be made under the above-described account should be addressed to the named Assignee until you receive other directions.

_____

Assignor

FORM 3-12   Increase in credit limit request.

This letter may be used to request an increase in credit limits with a company.

Date: _____

To: _____

Re: Account of _____

We are reviewing our plans for the forthcoming year. It appears that we may be placing increased orders with your company. To prevent any problems, we are requesting an increase in our credit limit. As you will note, we have been ordering products from your company for the past __ years, and we have always paid in full and on time.

Thank you for your consideration in this matter. We look forward to hearing from you.

Sincerely,

_____

Signature

FORM 3-13 Settlement of disputed account balance.

This settlement agreement may be used when the parties settle a disputed account balance.

Date: _____

By this agreement between them, _____ [name of Creditor], Creditor, and _____ [name of Debtor], Debtor, resolve and forever settle and adjust the below-listed claim. Both parties agree that there is a bona fide dispute regarding the amount due the Creditor on this account. Accordingly, the parties agree that the Debtor shall pay to the creditor the sum of $_____ no later than _____ [date] as payment in full on the described account or claim.

Should Debtor fail to pay the agreed sum by the above-listed date, then Creditor has the right to pursue the full amount claimed and is no longer under obligation to take the agreed sum as payment in full. If Debtor pays the agreed amount on or prior to the above-listed date, Creditor will accept the payment as payment in full.

This agreement covers the following account: [describe the account or claim in this space.]

_____

_____

_____

This agreement shall be binding on all parties involved, their assigns, successors, and personal representatives.

Sincerely,

_____
Creditor

_____
Debtor

FORM 3-14   Payment on specific account.

This letter may be used to direct payment to a specific account when you have more than one account with a company. Send letter as Certified Mail, Return Receipt Requested.

Date: _____

To: _____

Dear _____,

Enclosed is a check in the amount of $_____. This payment is to be applied to the following accounts only: _____

_____

Invoice no. _____

Payment due date: _____

Amount to credit: _____

Please ensure that the above amounts are credited to the correct accounts.

Sincerely,

_____

Signature

FORM 3-15   Request for credit chargeback.

If goods were ordered and paid for in advance by credit card, this letter may be used to notify the credit card company of your desire for a chargeback. Send letter Certified Mail, Return Receipt Requested.

Date: _____

To: _____

Re: Credit chargeback; [card number and name as listed on the card] _____

Dear Madam/Sir:

On _____ [date] a charge was placed on the above-referenced account in a transaction with _____ [name of business]. Please do not honor that charge, or if it has been honored, please reverse the charge. This request is made for the following reason [state reasons such as: the merchandise was defective; the merchandise was not as ordered; etc.]:

_____

_____

Thank you for your assistance in this matter.

Sincerely,

_____   _____

Signature   Address

FORM 3-16 Denial of debt.

This form may be used when you receive a bill that you did not incur or do not owe. Send as Certified Mail, Return Receipt Requested.

[Date] _____

To (company issuing the bill) _____

Re: your bill in the amount of _____; copy attached.

This is to notify you that the above-referenced statement is incorrect in that:

__ I never incurred the charges listed.

__ The balance was paid on _____ (date) and a copy of the receipt or cancelled check is enclosed.

__ Your records are in error for the following reasons:

Please advise me when corrective action has been taken.

Sincerely,

_____

Signature

FORM 3-17 Request to stop debt harassment.

This form may be used when you are being harassed by a collection company. Send as Certified Mail, Return Receipt Requested.

Date: _____

To (company): _____

Re: (describe the debt) _____

_____

_____

Please stop contacting me by telephone or mail regarding the above-referenced debt. Any further contact will be considered as harassment and I will enforce my legal rights in this regard.

Sincerely,

_____

FORM 3-18 Mail fraud report.

U.S. Postal Inspection Service
Mail Fraud Report

See Privacy Act Statement on Page 3

Complainant Information

Your Name	SSN*	Year of Birth*

Address

City	State	ZIP Code®	Country

Home Phone No. *(Include area code)*	Work Phone No. *(Include area code)*	E-Mail

*These two fields are optional, but the information may be helpful to Postal Inspectors tracking your complaint. Also, penalties may increase when certain crimes target particular age groups.

Complaint Filed Against

Company Name	Person's Name and Title

Address

City	State	ZIP Code	Country

Home Phone No. *(Include area code)*	Work Phone No. *(Include area code)*	E-Mail

Fax No. *(Include area code)*	Web Address

Details of Mail Fraud Complaint

Did you lose money? ☐ Yes. If so, how much? _____   ☐ No

What was the advertised cost of the offer?

How did you pay? *(Check one)*   ☐ Postal Money Order   ☐ Electronic Transfer   ☐ Debit Card | Date of Payment
☐ Cash   ☐ Check   ☐ Other Money Order   ☐ Credit Card   ☐ Telephone Bill

Find the general category below that describes your area of concern and check the specific item. *(Check one only)*

Advance Payment
☐ Loan
☐ Credit Repair/Debt Consolidation
☐ Credit Card
☐ Student Loan
☐ Mortgage

☐ **Chain Letter**

☐ **Charity Fraud**

Education
☐ School
☐ Degree

Employment
☐ Postal Job
☐ Overseas Job
☐ Work at Home *(Such as envelope stuffing)*
☐ Distributorship/Multilevel Marketing

False Bill or Notice
☐ Office Supplies
☐ Directory Solicitation
☐ Subscription/Periodical
☐ Classified Ad
☐ Taxes

☐ **Harassment** *(Merchandise ordered in your name without your consent.)*

Investment
☐ Real Estate
☐ Gems, Coins, Precious Metals
☐ Securities

Lottery *(You pay to play.)*
☐ Domestic
☐ Foreign

Medical Quackery
☐ Weight Loss
☐ AIDS Cure
☐ Cancer Cure
☐ Sexual Aid

Merchandise or Service
☐ Failure to Pay
☐ Failure to Provide
☐ Misrepresentation of Product/Service

☐ Nigerian Fraud

Personals
☐ Mail-Order Bride
☐ Dating Service
☐ False Divorce Decree

☐ Prize or Sweepstakes

☐ Sexually Oriented Advertisement

☐ Vacation or Travel

On what date did you receive the solicitation?

FORM 3-18　continued

How were you contacted? *(Check one)*

☐ U.S. Mail™　　☐ Newspaper　　☐ Radio/TV　　☐ Internet　　☐ Fax
☐ Telephone　　☐ Magazine　　☐ In Person　　☐ E-Mail　　☐ Other

If by mail, do you have the envelope it was mailed in?	Does the envelope have a permit number instead of a stamp?
☐ Yes　　☐ No	☐ Yes. Permit No.: _____　☐ No

Does the envelope have a postage meter number instead of a stamp?	How did you respond to the offer?
☐ Yes. Meter No.: _____　☐ No	☐ U.S. Mail　☐ Telephone　☐ Internet　☐ E-Mail　☐ Fax

Do you have a mailing receipt from your response? *(Such as for certified, insured, or Express Mail)*

☐ Yes. Mail Receipt No.: _____　　☐ No

To what address did you mail your response?

What did you receive?

How did it differ from what you expected?

Do you have the item?	How was it delivered?
☐ Yes　　☐ No	☐ U.S. Mail™　　☐ Private Courier　　☐ In Person

Have you contacted the company or person about the complaint?

☐ Yes. Date: _____　　☐ No. Why?　☐ Delivery Attempted, Returned Endorsed "Moved, Left No Address"　☐ Disconnected Telephone
☐ Unanswered Telephone　☐ Unlisted Telephone
☐ Address Unavailable

Legitimate businesses appreciate feedback. Check the offer for the delivery time frame, usually 6 to 8 weeks, and then contact the company. Please wait 2 weeks after contacting them before sending us this form. When a delivery time is not specified, a Federal Trade Commission rule mandates fulfillment within 30 days, unless you applied for first-time credit with the company.

Additional Information

Print Your Name　　　　　　　　　　　　　　　　　　　Today's Date

Thank you for completing this form. Please mail it with copies *(not originals)* of any bills, receipts, advertisements, canceled checks (front and back) or correspondence related to your report to the address below.

The U.S. Postal Inspection Service is a federal law enforcement agency. Postal Inspectors gather facts and evidence to determine whether a violation has occurred under the Mail Fraud or False Representation Statutes. While the Postal Inspection Service can't guarantee that you'll recover money lost to fraud, the information can help alert Inspectors about new fraud schemes and prevent others from being victimized.

Postal Inspectors base mail fraud investigations on the number, substance, and pattern of complaints received from the public; therefore, we ask you to keep all original documents relating to your complaint, including the solicitation, any mailing envelopes, and canceled checks. Under our Consumer Protection Program, Postal Inspectors may contact individuals or businesses on your behalf to request that complaints be resolved. We will contact you if more information is needed.

Postal Inspectors caution that, once you've been targeted in a fraud scheme, your name may be passed along to other con artists, so beware of future solicitations. If you know of others who believe they were victimized in a fraud scheme, we recommend that you encourage them to submit a Mail Fraud Report as well.

Avoid being a victim: Postal Inspectors recommend that, before completing a business transaction, contact the Chamber of Commerce, Better Business Bureau, or county or state Office of Consumer Affairs in the area where the firm is located to get any information available on the company. If you have Internet access, you can get information from the Better Business Bureau online at: *www.bbb.org*, and from the individual state Attorneys General Consumer Protection Divisions at *www.naag.org*. Also, check the Postal Inspection Service Web site at: *www.usps.com/postalinspectors* for more information on fraud schemes that involve the use of the mail.

Remember: If a deal sounds too good to be true, it probably is!

Please return this form to your postmaster, or mail to this address:

INSPECTION SERVICE SUPPORT GROUP
222 S RIVERSIDE PLAZA STE 1250
CHICAGO IL 60606-6100

FORM 3-18 continued

> **Privacy Act Statement:** Your information will be used to support investigations of criminal, civil, or administrative matters. Collection is authorized by 39 USC 401 and 404; and 18 USC 3061.
>
> Providing the information is voluntary, but if not provided, we may not investigate your complaint. We may only disclose your information as follows: in relevant legal proceedings; to law enforcement when the USPS or requesting agency becomes aware of a violation of law; to a congressional office at your request; to entities or individuals under contract with USPS; to entities authorized to perform audits; to labor organizations as required by law; to federal, state, local or foreign government agencies regarding personnel matters; to the Equal Employment Opportunity Commission; to the Merit Systems Protection Board or Office of Special Counsel; to the public, news media, trade associations, or organized groups for USPS public interest purposes; to a federal, state, local or foreign prison, probation, parole, or pardon authority or to any other agency involved with the maintenance, transportation, or release of a person held in custody; and to a foreign country to the extent necessary to assist such country in apprehending or returning a fugitive to its jurisdiction

FORM 3-19 Notice of billing error rights with a telephone company.

This form only appears on the accompanying CD.

II. Forms Related to Credit Cards and Checks

FORM 3-20   Notice of lost or stolen credit card.

Date: _____

To: [credit card company, address] _____

_____

Re: Lost or stolen credit card; [card number and name as listed on the card] _____

_____

The above-referenced credit card has been lost or stolen. The last authorized purchase made
with this card was on _____ (date) in the amount of _____ with (name
of business) _____.

Accordingly, please cancel the card, do not authorize any additional charges against the
account, and provide me with a replacement.

Sincerely,

_____

Signature of card holder

_____

Address of card holder

FORM 3-21   Request for credit chargeback.

Date: _____

To: [credit card company, address] _____

Re: Credit chargeback; [card number and name as listed on the card] _____

Dear Sir/Madam:

On _____ [date] a charge was placed on the above-referenced account on a transaction with _____ [name of business]. Please do not honor that charge, or if it has
been honored, please reverse the charge. This request is based on the following reason [State
reasons, such as, the merchandise was defective or the merchandise was not as ordered, etc.]:

_____

_____

Thank you for your assistance in this matter.

Sincerely,

_____   _____

Signature of card holder   Address

FORM 3-22   Notice of dishonored check.

Notice

Date: _____

To: _____

The undersigned is the payee of a check you wrote for $ _____. The check was refused by your bank because of insufficient funds, and the payee demands payment.

If you fail to pay the payer the full amount of the check in cash within _____ days after this notice is mailed, you could be sued and held responsible to pay at least all of the following:

   1. The amount of the check.

   2. Damages.

   3. The cost of mailing this notice.

Upon receipt of good replacement funds, the check will be returned to you. You may wish to contact a lawyer to discuss your legal rights and responsibilities.

Amount due: check amount $ _____; check return fee $ _____

Total due: $ _____

Sincerely,

_____

Signature

FORM 3-23   Notice of dishonored check (stop payment).

Notice

Date: _____

To: _____

The undersigned is the payee of a check you wrote for $ _____. The check was not paid because you stopped payment, and the payee demands payment. You may have a good faith dispute as to whether you owe the full amount. If you do not have a good faith dispute with the payee and fail to pay the payer the full amount of the check in cash within _____ days after this notice is mailed, you could be sued and held responsible to pay at least all of the following:

   1. The amount of the check.

   2. Damages.

   3. The cost of mailing this notice.

FORM 3-23 continued

If the court determines that you do have a good faith dispute with the payee, you will not have to pay the damages and mailing cost mentioned above. If you stopped the payment because you have a good faith dispute with the payee, you should try to work out your dispute with the payee. You can contact the payee's attorney at the below-listed address.

You may wish to contact a lawyer to discuss your legal rights and responsibilities.

Amount due: Check amount $ _____; check return fee $ _____

Total due: $ _____

Sincerely,

_____

Signature

FORM 3-24 Check stop-payment order.

Date: _____

To: [bank, address] _____

_____

Please stop payment on the check below. This stop-payment order remains in effect until you receive other written instructions. If the check below has already been paid, please advise me immediately.

Date of check: _____

Account number involved: _____

Name of payee: _____

Amount of check: _____

Check number: _____

You may debit my account for the stop-payment fee.

Sincerely,

_____

Signature

FORM 3-25 Bank collection—dishonored check.

Date: _____

To: [bank address] _____

_____

Dear Sir/Madam:

The enclosed dishonored check is placed with you for collection. Any funds collected should, after deducting your standard charges, be credited to our account.

Date of check: _____

Name of maker: _____

Amount of check: _____

Check number: _____

Drawee bank: _____

Account number: _____

Sincerely,

_____

Signature

_____

Account name

_____

Account number

III. Forms Related to Promissory Notes

FORM 3-26 Promissory note (time).

For good and valuable consideration, the undersigned promises to pay to the order of _____, the sum of _____ dollars ($ _____). All principal and earned interest shall be due and payable on _____, 20 __. Time is of the essence. Interest shall be at the annual rate of __% on the unpaid balance.

The failure to make full payment with all accrued interest on the above-stated due date shall constitute a default on the note, and the defaulted note will be turned over for collection.

In the event of default, the undersigned shall be responsible to pay attorney fees, collection costs, and other fees associated with collection of the note.

FORM 3-26 continued

All parties to the note waive presentment, demand, notice of nonpayment, protest, and notice of protest. Parties also agree to remain fully bound on the note notwithstanding the release of any party or an extension or modification in the terms of the note. The undersigned parties shall be jointly and severally liable under this note.

Signed under seal this _____ day of ____, 20 __.

_____

_____

Signatures of both parties

FORM 3-27 Promissory note (demand).

For good and valuable consideration, the undersigned promises to pay to the order of _____ the sum of _____ dollars ($____). The unpaid principal and any earned interest are due and immediately payable upon demand of the holder of this note. Interest shall be at the annual rate of __% on the unpaid balance.

The failure to make full payment with all interest due within __ days after demand shall constitute a default on the note, and the defaulted note will be turned over for collection.

In the event of default, the undersigned shall be responsible to pay attorney fees, collection costs, and other fees associated with collection of the note.

This note may be prepaid in whole or in part, without penalty.

All parties to the note waive presentment, demand, notice of nonpayment, protest, and notice of protest. Parties also agree to remain fully bound on the note notwithstanding the release of any party or an extension or modification in the terms of the note. The undersigned parties shall be jointly and severally liable under this note.

Signed under seal this _____ day of ____, 20 __.

_____

_____

Signatures of parties

FORM 3-28   Promissory note (installment).

For good and valuable consideration, the undersigned promises to pay to the order of _____ the sum of _____ dollars ($_____). Interest shall be at the annual rate of _____ % on the unpaid balance.

The principal with interest shall be paid in ___ installments of $ _____ each, with the first installment due on _____, 20 ___, and the same amount on the same day of each month thereafter until the principal and earned interest are fully paid. Payments shall be first applied to earned interest and then the balance to the principal.

The note shall be fully payable including earned interest upon the demand of any holder in the event that the undersigned defaults on any payment due by _____ days of its due date or upon death, insolvency, or bankruptcy of the undersigned.

In the event of default, the undersigned shall be responsible to pay attorney fees, collection costs, and other fees associated with collection of the note.

All parties to the note waive presentment, demand, notice of nonpayment, protest, and notice of protest. Parties also agree to remain fully bound on the note notwithstanding the release of any party or an extension or modification in the terms of the note. The undersigned parties shall be jointly and severally liable under this note.

Signed under seal this _____ day of _____, 20 ___.

_____

_____

Signature of parties

FORM 3-29   Promissory note (with balloon payment).

For good and valuable consideration, the undersigned promises to pay to the order of _____ the sum of _____ dollars ($_____). Interest shall be at the annual rate of ___ % on the unpaid balance.

The principal with interest shall be paid in _____ installments of _____ each, with the first installment due on _____, 20 ___, and the same amount on the same day of each month thereafter for the next _____ consecutive months.

The remaining balance with accrued but unpaid interest shall be fully paid on or before _____, 20 ___.

Payments shall be first applied to earned interest and then the balance to the principal.

The note shall be fully payable including earned interest upon the demand of any holder in the event that the undersigned defaults on any payment due by ___ days of its due date or upon death, insolvency, or bankruptcy of the undersigned.

In the event of default, the undersigned shall be responsible to pay attorney fees, collection costs, and other fees associated with collection of the note.

FORM 3-29   continued

All parties to the note waive presentment, demand, notice of nonpayment, protest, and notice of protest. Parties also agree to remain fully bound on the note notwithstanding the release of any party or an extension or modification in the terms of the note. The undersigned parties shall be jointly and severally liable under this note.

Signed under seal this ____ day of _____, 20 __.

_____

_____

Signature of the parties.

FORM 3-30   Notice of default on promissory note.

Date: _____

To: [name and address of debtor] _____

Notice is hereby given that you are in default under your promissory note of [date note was entered into]. The below payments are due and owing:

Payment due date: _____   Amount due: $ _____

Your total arrears: $ _____

Accordingly, demand is hereby made for full payment of the balance due of $ _____ unless the above-noted past due payments are received within the next _____ days. If payment is not forthcoming, I will forward this note to my attorneys for legal action.

Sincerely,

_____

Signature

IV. Forms Related to Other Credit Issues

FORM 3-31 Bill of sale (with encumbrances).

This bill of sale may be used by the buyer as proof of purchase of products.

For good and valuable consideration, and the payment of the sum of $ __, receipt of which is hereby acknowledged, the Seller hereby sells and transfers to the Buyer the following described personal property:

[Describe the property here.] _____

_____

The Seller warrants to Buyer and its assigns and successors that Seller, except as noted below, has good and marketable title to said property and the full authority to sell and transfer the property free of all liens, encumbrances, liabilities, and adverse claims of every nature and description whatsoever. Except as noted below, the said property is sold and transferred free of all liens, encumbrances, liabilities, and adverse claims of every nature and description whatsoever.

The said property is sold subject to a certain security interest, lien, or encumbrance on said property in the favor of _____ (lien holder) with a balance owed thereon of $ __. Buyer agrees to assume and promptly pay said secured debt and indemnify and hold Seller harmless from any claim arising thereon.

Seller further warrants to Buyer that, except for claims arising out of the above encumbrance, Seller will fully defend, protect, indemnify, and hold harmless the Buyer and Buyer's lawful successors and assigns from any other adverse claim thereto.

Except as noted above, the goods are sold in "as is condition" and where presently located.

Signed under seal and accepted this _____ day of ____, __.

_____

Seller

_____

Address

FORM 3-32   Bill of sale (quitclaim).

This bill of sale may be used by the buyer as proof of purchase of products. Note that with this bill of sale, there are no warranties of title.

For good and valuable consideration, and the payment of the sum of $ _____, receipt of which is hereby acknowledged, the Seller hereby sells and transfers with quitclaim covenants to the Buyer the following described personal property:

[Describe the property here.] _____

_____

The Seller hereby sells and transfers only such rights, title, and interest as Seller may hold. The said property is sold subject to such prior liens, encumbrances, and adverse claims, if any, that may exist, and Seller hereby disclaims any and all warranties thereto.

Except as noted above, the goods are sold in "as is condition" and where presently located.

Signed under seal and accepted this _____ day of ____, __.

_____

Seller

_____

Address

FORM 3-33   Bill of sale (warranty).

This bill of sale may be used by the buyer as proof of purchase of products.

For good and valuable consideration, and the payment of the sum of $_____, receipt of which is hereby acknowledged, the Seller hereby sells and transfers to the Buyer the following described personal property:

[Describe the property here.] _____

_____

The Seller warrants to Buyer and its assigns and successors that Seller has good and marketable title to said property and the full authority to sell and transfer the property free of all liens, encumbrances, liabilities, and adverse claims of every nature and description whatsoever. The said property is sold and transferred free of all liens, encumbrances, liabilities, and adverse claims of every nature and description whatsoever.

Seller further warrants to Buyer that Seller will fully defend, protect, indemnify, and hold harmless the Buyer and Buyer's lawful successors and assigns from any adverse claim thereto.

Except as noted above, the goods are sold in "as is condition" and where presently located.

Signed under seal and accepted this _____ day of ____, __.

_____   _____

Seller   Address

FORM 3-34 Pledge of personal property.

Frequently, individuals who have no established line of credit need to offer collateral to secure an open purchase account. That may be accomplished by a pledge of personal property or stock. Note: Personal property is any property that is not considered real property.

For good and valuable consideration of [describe the debt, e.g., the loan of $1,000], [name of debtor/pledger], the Pledger/Debtor, delivers to and pledges with [name of person who is receiving the property], the Pledgee, as collateral security in the following property, [Describe property being pledged.]: _____

_____, Collateral.

The Pledger/Debtor and Pledgee warrant that or agree to:

1. He or she is the owner of the collateral and that it is free of any liens, encumbrances, security interests, or mortgages except as noted herein.

2. The Pledgee may assign, sell, or transfer his or her interest in the Debt and may transfer the pledged property to any third party who is assigned, sold, or transferred interest in the Debt.

3. On a default of any obligation for which the security interest is granted, or the breach of any term of this security agreement, the secured party may declare all obligations immediately due and payable and shall have all the remedies of a secured party as set forth in the Uniform Commercial Code as enacted in Debtor's state. These rights are to be considered as cumulative and not necessarily successive with any other right or remedy.

4. Debtor will maintain insurance on the collateral as the secured party may require, with the secured party named as loss payee. In addition the Debtor will pay any personal property tax, excise, or other tax or levy that may be imposed on the collateral during the life of this agreement.

5. In the event of default, Debtor shall be responsible to pay attorney fees, collection costs, and other fees associated with enforcement of this agreement.

6. This agreement is binding upon, and inures to the benefit of the parties, their successors, assigns, and personal representatives.

7. This agreement shall also be in default upon the death, insolvency, or bankruptcy of any party who is obligated under this agreement or on the material decrease in the value of the collateral.

8. Pledger understands that upon foreclosure the pledged property may be sold at public auction or private sale. In the event that sale price of the property is less than the amount owing, after expenses of sale, the Pledger shall be liable for any deficiency.

Signed under seal this _____ day of _____, 20 __ .

_____   _____
Pledger/Debtor   Pledgee

FORM 3-35   Notice of default on settlement agreement.

Date: _____

To: [name and address of debtor] _____

Dear [name of debtor] _____:

This is to advise you that you are in default of the monthly payments for _____.
Accordingly, unless the account is current within 20 days after you receive this letter, I intend
to file a notice of default with the court and to take action necessary to collect the balance due
under the settlement agreement we entered into on _____ (date).

Sincerely,

_____

Signature

_____

Title

FORM 3-36   Receipt for payment in full.

Date: _____

To: [name and address of debtor] _____

_____

The undersigned Creditor hereby acknowledges the receipt of $ ____ from [debtor]. This sum
is accepted as payment in full for the below-described account.

[Describe account here.] _____

_____

Signed: _____

Creditor

FORM 3-37 Release of all claims (installment payments).

Date: _____

FOR AND IN CONSIDERATION of the sum of _____ Dollars and No Cents ($ _____) which will be paid as follows: $ _____ on the execution of this document and the balance paid in _____ monthly installments of $ _____ and the final monthly installment of $ _____ with the monthly installments commencing on _____, 20 __; and with each succeeding monthly installment due on the _____ of each succeeding month until paid with the final installment of $ _____ due on _____, 20 __; the undersigned, _____, his/her assigns, successors, and any other in privity with the undersigned, do HEREBY RELEASE AND FOREVER DISCHARGE [name of person being released] _____ and their agents, employees, employers, principals, partners, and all others in privity with said, Releases (agreeing parties) of and from any and all claims, demands, rights, liens, damages, injuries, losses, contracts, covenants, suits, causes of action, expenses, judgments, orders and liabilities of any kind and nature, whether now known or unknown, suspected or unsuspected, foreseen or unforeseen, and whether or not concealed and hidden, which may have existed or may not have existed, or which can, may, or shall hereafter exist, or which have accrued or may hereafter accrue, on account of, or in any way relating to the accident or other incident, which occurred on or about _____, 20 __, in the City of _____, between _____ and an employee of _____, which accident allegedly gave rise to the claims of _____ against the agreeing parties.

It is understood and agreed by all parties and the undersigned does hereby state that this is a full and final Release in accord with its terms, applying to all unknown, unanticipated, and unsuspected injuries, damages, claims, and expenses as set forth above, arising out of said accident, as well as to those now known or disclosed.

It is understood and agreed, and the undersigned does hereby state that reliance is placed wholly upon his judgment, belief, and knowledge as to the nature, cause, extent, and duration of any injuries and damages; and that no statement with regard thereto made by the Releases has in any way influenced the making of this compromise settlement and the execution of this Release.

It is understood and agreed that this offer and/or compromise shall not be deemed or construed as an admission of liability as to any of the agreeing parties.

The undersigned does hereby expressly represent to the releases that no medical liens are involved and there is no claim for reimbursement being made by any governmental agency or other third party and no third party has asserted any right to claim any proceeds of this settlement. Such representations have been relied upon by the releases herein and are deemed to be a material element of this settlement.

Having read and understood the terms of this Release of All Claims, and in witness whereof, the undersigned have hereunto set his/her hand this _____ day of _____, 20 __.

_____   _____

_____   _____

Signature(s) of person being released   Signature(s) of other party

---

FORM 3-38   Release of all claims (lump-sum payment).

FOR AND IN CONSIDERATION of the sum of _____ Dollars ($____) which will be paid as follows: $____ by certified check or money order within 15 days after this signed document is received by _____, the undersigned _____, his (her) assigns, successors, and any other in privity with the undersigned, do HEREBY RELEASE AND FOREVER DISCHARGE [person being released from claim] and their agents, employees, employers, principals, partners, and all others in privity with said Releases (agreeing parties) of and from any and all claims, demands, rights, liens, damages, injuries, losses, contracts, covenants, suits, causes of action, expenses, judgments, orders and liabilities of any kind and nature, whether now known or unknown, suspected or unsuspected, foreseen or unforeseen, and whether or not concealed and hidden, which may have existed or may not have existed, or which can, may, or shall hereafter exist or which have accrued or may hereafter accrue, on account of, on in any way relating to the [describe incident, e.g., car accident].

The undersigned does hereby state that this is a full and final Release in accord with its terms, applying to all unknown, unanticipated, and unsuspected injuries, damages, claims and expenses as set forth above, arising out of the above incident, as well as to those now known or disclosed.

It is understood and agreed, and the undersigned does hereby state that reliance is placed wholly upon his and his attorney's judgment, belief, and knowledge as to the nature, cause, extent, and duration of any injuries and damages; and that no statement with regard thereto made by the Releases has in any way influenced the making of this compromise settlement and the execution of this Release.

It is understood and agreed that this offer and/or compromise shall not be deemed or construed as an admission of liability as to any of the agreeing parties.

Having read and understood the terms of this Release of All Claims, and in witness whereof, the undersigned has hereunto set their hands this _____ day of ____, 20 __.

_____

Signature of person releasing claim

FORM 3-39 Notice of rescission.

A notice of rescission is used to cancel a contract or other legal obligation where you have an option to cancel it. It is a formal notice that you are exercising your rights to cancel the obligation.

Date: _____

To: [company, address] _____

Re: Rescission of contract with your company dated [date] _____

Dear Sir/Madam:

You are hereby notified that I am exercising my rights to rescind the contract entered into with your company on [date] _____. Accordingly, please cancel said contract and return my deposit of $_____. Please note that under the provisions of the Federal Truth in Lending Act, I have three days to cancel the said contract and this rescission is pursuant to that right.

In addition, you are requested to cancel any lien against our property within ten days as required by law.

Sincerely,

_____

Signature of card holder

_____

Address

FORM 3-40 Compromise.

Compromise is used to settle a debt for less than the amount owed, provided the amount agreed to is paid within a certain date. For example, an individual owes you $10,000 and the debt is past due. Rather than sue him or her in court, you may be willing to accept an immediate payment of $8,000 as payment in full and discharge the obligation.

Date: _____

For good and valuable consideration, [name of Creditor], Creditor, and [name of Debtor] Debtor, hereby agree to compromise and discharge the indebtedness owed to the Creditor by the Debtor according to the following terms:

1. The Debtor acknowledges that the sum of the present debt due the Creditor is $_____.

2. The Creditor agrees to accept the sum of $_____ as payment in full and agrees to discharge, release, and accept as satisfaction of all monies presently due.

FORM 3-40 continued

3. Agreement of the Creditor to accept a lesser sum is binding only if payment by the Debtor is made within _____ days of the signing of this agreement.

4. If Debtor fails to pay the agreed sum within _____ days of the signing of this agreement, the Creditor shall have the right to pursue his/her claim for the full amount.

5. In the event of default, the defaulting parties agree to pay reasonable attorney fees and costs.

6. The agreement shall be binding on parties, their heirs, assigns, successors, and personal representatives.

Signed this _____ day of _____, 20 __.

Creditor _____   Debtor _____

FORM 3-41 Agreement to assume obligation.

For good and valuable consideration, the _____ Creditor and _____ Debtor and _____ the Undersigned enter into this agreement, whereby all parties acknowledge and agree to the below terms, facts and conditions:

1. Debtor currently owes to Creditor the sum $ _____ (Debt), which sum is currently due and payable.

2. Undersigned agrees unconditionally and irrevocably to assume and fully pay the Debt and guarantees to Creditor the prompt payment of the Debt on terms as set forth below, and to fully indemnify and save harmless both Creditor and Debtor from any loss thereof.

3. The terms of the Debt repayment are as follows [insert terms]: _____
   _____

4. This agreement does not release or discharge the Debtor's obligations to the Creditor regarding the Debt. The Creditor will, however, forbear in commencing collection action as long as the Undersigned promptly makes the payments as outlined above. In the event of default, Creditor will have full rights, jointly and severally, against both the Debtor and the undersigned for any sums owed on the Debt.

5. This agreement extends only to the Debt described above [describe the Debt]. _____
   _____

6. In the event of default, the Undersigned and/or the Debtor shall be responsible to pay attorney fees, collection costs, and other fees associated with collection of the note.

7. This agreement is binding upon and inures to the benefit of the parties, their successors, assigns, and personal representatives.

Signed under seal this _____ day of _____, 20 __.

_____   _____
Guarantor   Guarantor

FORM 3-41 continued

Creditor

ACKNOWLEDGMENT

State of   )

County of   )

On this date, [list names of person(s) who signed above] personally appeared before me and acknowledged that the above signature(s) are valid and binding.

Notary Public

My Commission expires: _____

FORM 3-42 Security agreement.

For good and valuable consideration of [describe the debt, e.g., the loan of $1,000], [name of Debtor] _____, the Debtor, grants to [name of person who is receiving the security interest] _____ the Secured Party, and his/her successors, and assigns a security interest as per the Uniform Commercial Code, Article 9, in the following property, [describe property covered by security interest] _____ _____, which also includes all after-acquired property of a like nature and description and proceeds and products thereof, Collateral.

The security interest is granted to secure payment and performance on the following obligations now or hereinafter owed Secured Party from Debtor:

The Debtor makes the below acknowledgments:

1. He/She is the owner of the collateral, and that it is free of any liens, encumbrances, security interests, or mortgages except as noted herein.

2. The collateral will be kept at the following address and shall not be moved or relocated without written consent of Secured Party: [address where collateral will be kept] _____ _____

3. Debtor will execute the necessary financing statements as are reasonably required by Secured Party to perfect the security interest in accordance with state law and the Uniform Commercial Code.

4. On a default of any obligation for which the security interest is granted, or the breach of any term of this security agreement, the secured party may declare all obligations immediately due and payable and shall have all the remedies of a secured party as set forth in the Uniform Commercial Code as enacted in Debtor's state. These rights are to be considered as cumulative and not necessarily successive with any other right or remedy.

FORM 3-42   continued

> 5. Debtor will maintain insurance on the collateral as the secured party may require, with the secured party named as loss payee.
>
> 6. In the event of default, Debtor shall be responsible to pay attorney fees, collection costs, and other fees associated with enforcement of this agreement.
>
> 7. This agreement is binding upon and inures to the benefit of the parties, their successors, assigns, and personal representatives.
>
> 8. This agreement shall also be in default upon the death, insolvency, or bankruptcy of any party who is obligated under this agreement or on the material decrease in the value of the collateral.
>
> Signed under seal this _____ day of _____, 20 __.
>
> _____
>
> Debtor
>
> _____
>
> Secured Party

FORM 3-43   Pledge of personal property.

> For good and valuable consideration of [describe the debt, e.g., the loan of $1,000], [name of Pledger/Debtor] _____, the Pledger/Debtor, delivers to and pledges with [name of person who is receiving the property] _____, the Pledgee, as collateral security in the following property: [describe property being pledged], _____
> _____, Collatoral.
>
> The Pledger/Debtor and Pledgee warrant that or agree to:
>
> 1. He/She is the owner of the collateral and that it is free of any liens, encumbrances, security interests, or mortgages except as noted herein.
>
> 2. The Pledgee may assign, sell, or transfer his/her interest in the Debt and may transfer the pledged property to any third party who is assigned, sold, or transferred interest in the Debt.
>
> 3. On a default of any obligation for which the security interest is granted, or the breach of any term of this security agreement, the secured party may declare all obligations immediately due and payable and shall have all the remedies of a secured party as set forth in the Uniform Commercial Code as enacted in Debtor's state. These rights are to be considered as cumulative and not necessarily successive with any other right or remedy.
>
> 4. Debtor will maintain insurance on the collateral as the secured party may require, with the secured party named as loss payee. In addition the Debtor will pay any personal property tax, excise, or other tax or levy that may be imposed on the collateral during the life of this agreement.

FORM 3-43 continued

5. In the event of default, Debtor shall be responsible to pay attorney fees, collection costs, and other fees associated with enforcement of this agreement.

6. This agreement is binding upon and inures to the benefit of the parties, their successors, assigns, and personal representatives.

7. This agreement shall also be in default upon the death, insolvency, or bankruptcy of any party who is obligated under this agreement or on the material decrease in the value of the collateral.

8. Pledgor understands that upon foreclosure the pledged property may be sold at public auction or private sale. In the event that sale of the property is less than the amount owing, after expenses of sale, the Pledger shall be liable for any deficiency.

Signed under seal this _____ day of _____, 20 __.

Pledger/Debtor _____   Pledgee _____

ACKNOWLEDGMENT

State of   )

County of   )

On this date, [list names of person(s) who signed above] personally appeared before me and acknowledged that the above signature(s) are valid and binding.

_____

Notary Public

My Commission expires: _____

FORM 3-44 Indemnification agreement.

An indemnification agreement is used when there is a legal dispute and it is unclear as to whom payment or other duties are owed to. For example, you owe an individual $500 and the individual has died. A bank is attempting to collect the debt. You will want the bank to agree that if a court determines that someone other than the bank should have been paid, the bank will reimburse you. Another example is where you are part owner of a business and you wish to no longer be associated with the business. You would want the remaining owners to agree to indemnification as a condition of continuing the business in the same name.

FORM 3-44   continued

Date: _____

This indemnification agreement is made and entered on [date] _____ by and between [first party] _____, First Party, and [second party] _____, Second Party.

WHEREAS the undersigned parties have agreed to resolve certain disputes which have arisen between them; and

WHEREAS each party wishes the other to indemnify and hold the first party harmless from any and all costs and expenses which have arisen or may arise as a result of their prior relationship;

NOW THEREFORE, in consideration of the premises set forth herein and intending to be legally bound, the parties hereto agree as follows:

[First party] and affiliates hereby jointly and severally agree to indemnify and hold harmless [second party] and any affiliate of his/hers from every liability, claim, action, cause of action, judgment, loss, expense, or cost whatsoever (including but not limited to reasonable attorney's fees and court costs) arising from or in any way related to or resulting from:

(A) Any and all business relationships entered into between the Parties from the beginning of time to the date of these presents; and

(B) Any materially inaccurate representation made by either Party pursuant to their recent agreement; and

(C) [List any other items parties want to be indemnified from]: _____

_____

IN WITNESS WHEREOF the undersigned have hereunto set their hands

this _____ day of ____, 20 __.

First Party _____   Second Party _____

FORM 3-45   Arbitration agreement (binding).

> To prevent legal proceedings involving disputes between parties, an arbitration agreement is often recommended.

The undersigned parties hereby acknowledge that there is a conflict, dispute, or controversy between the parties as follows: [Briefly describe dispute.] _____

_____

The parties hereby agree to resolve this conflict, dispute, or controversy and any future disputes, conflicts, or controversies between them by binding arbitration.

The arbitration will be conducted according to the rules of the American Arbitration Association for the City of _____, which rules and procedures for arbitration are

FORM 3-45 continued

incorporated herein by reference, and the decision or award made by the arbitrator shall be final, binding, and conclusive upon each of the parties and enforceable in a court of law.

SIGNED this _____ day of ____, __.

ACKNOWLEDGMENT

State of   )

County of   )

On this date, [list names of person(s) who signed above] _____ _____
_____ personally appeared before me and acknowledged that the above signature(s) are valid and binding.

_____

Notary Public

My Commission expires: _____

FORM 3-46 Arbitration agreement (nonbinding).

The undersigned parties hereby acknowledge that there is a conflict, dispute, or controversy between the parties as follows: [Briefly describe dispute.] _____
_____

The parties hereby agree to attempt to resolve this conflict, dispute, or controversy and any future disputes, conflicts, or controversies between them by nonbinding arbitration.

The arbitration will be conducted according to the rules of the American Arbitration Association for the City of _____, which rules and procedures for arbitration are incorporated herein by reference. The decision or award made by the arbitrator shall be advisory only and not binding or conclusive upon either of the parties.

SIGNED this _____ day of _____, __.

ACKNOWLEDGMENT

State of   )

County of   )

On this date, [list names of person(s) who signed above] _____
_____ personally appeared before me and acknowledged that the above signature(s) are valid and binding.

_____   _____

Notary Public   Date signed

My Commission expires: _____

FORM 3-47 Release of all claims (installment payments).

This agreement may be used to settle a dispute with a vendor regarding the purchase of goods and/or payment on said goods.

FOR AND IN CONSIDERATION of the sum of $ _____ Dollars and No Cents ($ _____) which will be paid as follows: $ _____ on the execution of this document and the balance paid in _____ monthly installments of $_____ and the final monthly installment of $__, with the monthly installments commencing on _____, 20 __; and with each succeeding monthly installment due on the ____ of each succeeding month until paid with the final installment of $_____, due on ____, 20 __; the undersigned, _____, his or her assigns, successors, and any other in privity with the undersigned, do HEREBY RELEASE AND FOREVER DISCHARGE [name of company being released] _____ and their agents, employees, employers, principals, partners, and all others in privity with said Releases (agreeing parties) of and from any and all claims, demands, rights, liens, damages, injuries, losses, contracts, covenants, suits, causes of action, expenses, judgments, orders, and liabilities of any kind and nature, whether now known or unknown, suspected or unsuspected, foreseen or unforeseen, and whether or not concealed and hidden, which may have existed or may not have existed, or which can, may, or shall hereafter exist or which have accrued or may hereafter accrue, on account of, or in any way relating to the delivery of goods on or about _____, 20 __, in the City of _____, between _____ and an employee of ___ _____, which delivery allegedly gave rise to the claims of _____ against the agreeing parties.

It is understood and agreed by all parties, and the undersigned does hereby state, that this is a full and final Release in accord with its terms, applying to all unknown, unanticipated, and unsuspected injuries, damages, claims, and expenses as set forth above, arising out of said transaction, as well as to those now known or disclosed.

It is understood and agreed, and the undersigned does hereby state, that reliance is placed wholly upon his or her judgment, belief, and knowledge as to the nature, cause, extent, and duration of any injuries and damages; and that no statement with regard thereto made by the Releases has in any way influenced the making of this compromise settlement and the execution of this Release.

It is understood and agreed that this offer and/or compromise shall not be deemed or construed as an admission of liability as to any of the agreeing parties.

The undersigned does hereby expressly represent to the Releases that no other liens are involved and there is no claim for reimbursement being made by any governmental agency or other third party, and no third party has asserted any right to claim any proceeds of this settlement. Such representations have been relied upon by the Releases herein and are deemed to be a material element of this settlement.

FORM 3-47 conintued

> Having read and understood the terms of this Release of All Claims, and in witness whereof, the undersigned have hereunto set his or her hand this _____ day of ____, 20 __.
>
> Signature(s) of person(s) releasing the claim.
>
> _____   _____

FORM 3-48 Release of all claims (lump-sum payment).

This form may be used to settle claims between a vendor and a buyer.

> FOR AND IN CONSIDERATION of the sum of _____ Dollars ($__) which will be paid as follows: $ _____ by certified check or money order within 15 days after this signed document is received by _____, the undersigned, _____, his or her assigns, successors, and any other in privity with the undersigned, do HEREBY RELEASE AND FOREVER DISCHARGE [company being released from claim] and their agents, employees, employers, principals, partners, and all others in privity with said Releasees (agreeing parties) of and from any and all claims, demands, rights, liens, damages, injuries, losses, contracts, covenants, suits, causes of action, expenses, judgments, orders, and liabilities of any kind and nature, whether now known or unknown, suspected or unsuspected, foreseen or unforeseen, and whether or not concealed and hidden, which may have existed or may not have existed, or which can, may, or shall hereafter exist or which have accrued or may hereafter accrue, on account of, or in any way relating to the [describe activity, e.g., purchase of goods during the months of _____].
>
> The undersigned does hereby state that this is a full and final Release in accord with its terms, applying to all unknown, unanticipated, and unsuspected injuries, damages, claims, and expenses as set forth above, arising out of the above activity, as well as to those now known or disclosed.
>
> It is understood and agreed, and the undersigned does hereby state that reliance is placed wholly upon him or her and his or her attorney's judgment, belief, and knowledge as to the nature, cause, extent, and duration of any injuries and damages; and that no statement with regard thereto made by the Releases has in any way influenced the making of this compromise settlement and the execution of this Release.
>
> It is understood and agreed that this offer and/or compromise shall not be deemed or construed as an admission of liability as to any of the agreeing parties.
>
> Having read and understood the terms of this Release of All Claims, and in witness whereof, the undersigned has hereunto set his or her hand this _____ day of ____, 20 __.
>
> _____   _____
>
> Signature(s) of person(s) releasing claim

FORM 3-49 Revocation of guaranty.

This agreement may be used to revoke a guaranty of debt.

To: _____ [Creditor]

Please consider this formal notice of the termination of our guaranty of [date] on behalf of [debtor]. Effective on receipt of this notice, we will not be obligated under the guaranty for any future credit extended to [debtor].

Please advise us as to the present amount due and also notify us when that balance has been paid.

Please confirm below receipt and acknowledgment of this revocation of guaranty by return acknowledgment below.

Sincerely,

_____   _____

Guarantor   Guarantor

ACKNOWLEDGED: Date _____ Present Balance $ _____

_____

Creditor

FORM 3-50 Subordination agreement (full).

As an alternate method of obtaining financing for products, the buyer may be able to use a subordination agreement to ensure that the seller of the products would have a security interest in other property. For example, a buyer has real property that has a mortgage on it. If the buyer can obtain consent from the mortgage holder to allow the mortgagor to take a lower priority, the seller would have a first right to levy on the real property should the buyer fail to pay his or her accounts with the seller.

For good and valuable consideration, the Undersigned hereby subordinates any and all claims or other rights to monies due as now or hereinafter owed the Undersigned from [debtor] _____, Debtor, to any and all claims as may now or hereinafter be due [creditor] _____, Creditor.

This subordination shall be unconditional, irrevocable, and unlimited both as to the amount or duration and notwithstanding whether the respective claims against Debtor are now or hereinafter secured or unsecured in whole or in part, and notwithstanding any other rights to priority as may exist. In addition, the Undersigned shall forbear from collecting any monies due on its claim until all claims due Creditor from Debtor have been fully paid.

This agreement is binding upon and inures to the benefit of the parties, their successors, assigns, and personal representatives.

IN WITNESS WHEREOF the undersigned have hereunto set their hands this _____ day of _____, 20 __ .

_____   _____
Undersigned   Creditor

FORM 3-51 Federal Trade Commission complaint form.

The following form may be used to submit a complaint to the Federal Trade Commission (FTC). The form may be completed and submitted online at www.rn.ftc.gov/pls/dod/wsp;cq$. Note: Do not use this form for complaints pertaining to ID theft. There is a separate form for this in Chapter 4.

FORM 3-51   FTC consumer complaint form.

FTC
Consumer
Complaint Form

OMB #3084-0047

Use this form to submit a complaint to the Federal Trade Commission (FTC) Bureau of Consumer Protection about a particular company or organization. This form also may be used to submit a complaint to the FTC concerning media violence. The information you provide is up to you. However, if you do not provide your name or other information, it may be impossible for us to refer, respond to, or investigate your complaint or request. To learn how we use the information you provide, please read our Privacy Policy.

While the FTC does not resolve individual consumer problems, your complaint helps us investigate fraud, and can lead to law enforcement action. The FTC enters Internet, telemarketing, identity theft and other fraud-related complaints into Consumer Sentinel®, a secure, online database available to hundreds of civil and criminal law enforcement agencies worldwide.

We use secure socket layer (SSL) encryption to protect the transmission of the information you submit to us when you use our secure online forms. The information you provide to us is stored securely.

IMPORTANT:
* If you want to file a complaint about a violation of National Do Not Call Registry or register your telephone number on the Registry, Please go to www.donotcall.gov
* If you want to file a report about Identity Theft, please use our Identity Theft Complaint Form.
* If you want to file a complaint about an online transaction that involves a foreign company, please use our econsumer.gov complaint form.

If you have a specific complaint about **unsolicited commercial e-mail** (spam), use the form below. You can forward spam directly to the Commission at SPAM@UCE.GOV without using the complaint form.

How Do We Reach You?

First Name:

Last Name:

Age Range:

Street Address:

City:

State or Province:

Country:

FORM 3-51   continued

Complaint Form   Page 2 of 3

                                                              ☞ **"Click" Arrow for**
                                   Choices

Zip Code or   [   ]
Postal Code:
E-Mail Address: [   ]
Home Phone: (   )[   ]   *(Area Code)(Phone Number)*
                    (Numbers Only)
Work Phone: (   )[   ] **Ext.**[   ] *(Area Code)(Phone Number)(Extension)*
                    (Numbers Only)
Social Security   -   -   *Enter Only For Complaints Relating to the Accuracy of*
Number: *Your Credit Report*
                    (Numbers Only)

Tell Us Your Complaint...

Subject of Your
Complaint:

Name of Company
You Are Complaining
About:

Check If Company   ☐
Name Is Unknown:

Name of Product You
Are Complaining
About:

Street Address:

City:

State or Province:

Country:

Zip Code or Postal
Code:

Company Web Site:

Company E-Mail   [   ]
Address:

Phone Number: (   )[   ]   **Ext.**[   ] *(Area Code)(Phone Number)*
                        (Extension)
                        (Numbers Only)

How Did the Company
Initially Contact You?

How Much Did the   *(Numbers Only)*

FORM 3-51 continued

Complaint Form

Company Ask You to Pay?

How Much Did You Actually Pay the Company?   *(Numbers Only)*

How Did You Pay the Company?

Did You File a Dispute with the Credit Bureau?

Did You File a Dispute with the Credit Bureau More Than 45 Days Ago?

REPRESENTATIVE OR SALESPERSON First Name:

Last Name:

Date Company Contacted You: **(MM/DD/YYYY)**

Explain Your Problem: (Please limit your complaint to 2000 characters.):

Paperwork Reduction Statement: This form is designed to improve public access to the FTC Bureau of Consumer Protection Consumer Response Center, and is voluntary. Through this form, consumers may electronically register a complaint with the FTC. We estimate that it will take, on average, 5 minutes to complete the form. Under the Paperwork Reduction Act, as amended, an agency may not conduct or sponsor, and a person is not required to respond to, a collection of information unless it displays a currently valid OMB control number. That number is 3084-0047, which also appears in the upper right-hand corner of the first page of this form

FORM 3-52 Release of all claims.

In consideration of the payment of $_____, I, [name of individual with a claim] _____, hereby expressly release and discharge [your name] _____ from all claims and causes of action that I ever had, now have, or may have in the future, known or unknown, or that of any person claiming through me may have or have against [your name] _____ that was caused by or arising out of [describe incident]: _____

_____

_____

I hereby acknowledge receipt of the payment of $_____.

It is my intent that this release be binding on my heirs, legal representatives, assigns, and my wife.

Dated: _____

_____

Signature of person with claim

FORM 3-53 Joint release (husband and wife).

We, _____ and _____, husband and wife, of _____ [city and state], hereby execute this release of liability with the express intention and specific purpose to extinguish the obligations as herein set forth.

In consideration of $ _____ [spell out amount] dollars, receipt of which is hereby acknowledged, we, for ourselves, our assigns, legal representatives, and anyone claiming through us release and discharge [name of person being released] _____ of [city and state] _____, and his/her heirs, assigns, legal representatives, from all claims and causes of action that we or either of us ever had, now have, or may have in the future, known or unknown, or that any person claiming through us or either of us may have or claim to have against [person being released] _____ or his/her heirs, assigns, or legal representatives created or caused by or arising out of [description of incident]: _____

_____

We have read this release, understand its terms and their legal significance, and have voluntarily executed the release.

Dated: _____   Husband: _____

Dated: _____   Wife: _____

V. Forms Related to Tax Issues

FORM 3-54   Change of address for federal income tax purposes.

Form **8822**

(Rev. December 2005)

Department of the Treasury
Internal Revenue Service

Change of Address

▶ **Please type or print.**

▶ **See instructions on back.**   ▶ **Do not attach this form to your return.**

OMB No. 1545-1163

Part I   **Complete This Part To Change Your Home Mailing Address**

Check **all** boxes this change affects:

1 ☐ Individual income tax returns (Forms 1040, 1040A, 1040EZ, 1040NR, etc.)
   ▶ If your last return was a joint return and you are now establishing a residence separate
   from the spouse with whom you filed that return, check here . . . . ▶ ☐

2 ☐ Gift, estate, or generation-skipping transfer tax returns (Forms 706, 709, etc.)
   ▶ For Forms 706 and 706-NA, enter the decedent's name and social security number below.

▶ Decedent's name   ▶ Social security number

3a Your name (first name, initial, and last name) | **3b** Your social security number

4a Spouse's name (first name, initial, and last name) | **4b** Spouse's social security number

5   Prior name(s). See instructions.

6a Old address (no., street, city or town, state, and ZIP code). If a P.O. box or foreign address, see instructions. | Apt. no.

6b Spouse's old address, if different from line 6a (no., street, city or town, state, and ZIP code). If a P.O. box or foreign address, see instructions. | Apt. no.

7   New address (no., street, city or town, state, and ZIP code). If a P.O. box or foreign address, see instructions. | Apt. no.

Part II   **Complete This Part To Change Your Business Mailing Address or Business Location**

Check **all** boxes this change affects:

8 ☐ Employment, excise, income, and other business returns (Forms 720, 940, 940-EZ, 941, 990, 1041, 1065, 1120, etc.)
9 ☐ Employee plan returns (Forms 5500, 5500-EZ, etc.)
10 ☐ Business location

11a Business name | **11b** Employer identification number

12   Old mailing address (no., street, city or town, state, and ZIP code). If a P.O. box or foreign address, see instructions. | Room or suite no.

13   New mailing address (no., street, city or town, state, and ZIP code). If a P.O. box or foreign address, see instructions. | Room or suite no.

14   New business location (no., street, city or town, state, and ZIP code). If a foreign address, see instructions. | Room or suite no.

Part III   **Signature**

Daytime telephone number of person to contact (optional) ▶ (   )

Sign Here

Your signature   Date | If Part II completed, signature of owner, officer, or representative   Date

If joint return, spouse's signature   Date | Title

For Privacy Act and Paperwork Reduction Act Notice, see back of form.   Cat. No. 12081V   Form **8822** (Rev. 12-2005)

FORM 3-55 Request for copy of tax return.

If you are missing a copy of a past federal income tax return, the below IRS form may be used to request the needed form.

Form **4506**	**Request for Copy of Tax Return**	
(Rev. November 2005)	▶ Do not sign this form unless all applicable lines have been completed. Read the instructions on page 2.	OMB No. 1545-0429
Department of the Treasury Internal Revenue Service	▶ Request may be rejected if the form is incomplete, illegible, or any required line was blank at the time of signature.	

Tip: You may be able to get your tax return or return information from other sources. If you had your tax return completed by a paid preparer, they should be able to provide you a copy of the return. The IRS can provide a **Tax Return Transcript** for many returns free of charge. The transcript provides most of the line entries from the tax return and usually contains the information that a third party (such as a mortgage company) requires. See **Form 4506-T,** Request for Transcript of Tax Return, or you can call 1-800-829-1040 to order a transcript.

1a Name shown on tax return. If a joint return, enter the name shown first.	**1b** First social security number on tax return or employer identification number (see instructions)
2a If a joint return, enter spouse's name shown on tax return	**2b** Second social security number if joint tax return

3 Current name, address (including apt., room, or suite no.), city, state, and ZIP code

4 Previous address shown on the last return filed if different from line 3

5 If the tax return is to be mailed to a third party (such as a mortgage company), enter the third party's name, address, and telephone number. The IRS has no control over what the third party does with the tax return.

Caution: *If a third party requires you to complete Form 4506, **do not** sign Form 4506 if lines 6 and 7 are blank.*

6 **Tax return requested** (Form 1040, 1120, 941, etc.) and all attachments as originally submitted to the IRS, including Form(s) W-2, schedules, or amended returns. Copies of Forms 1040, 1040A, and 1040EZ are generally available for 7 years from filing before they are destroyed by law. Other returns may be available for a longer period of time. Enter only one return number. If you need more than one type of return, you must complete another Form 4506. ▶ _____
  Note. *If the copies must be certified for court or administrative proceedings, check here.* . . . . ☐

7 **Year or period requested.** Enter the ending date of the year or period, using the mm/dd/yyyy format. If you are requesting more than eight years or periods, you must attach another Form 4506.

  ___/___/_____   ___/___/_____   ___/___/_____   ___/___/_____

  ___/___/_____   ___/___/_____   ___/___/_____   ___/___/_____

8 **Fee.** There is a $39 fee for each return requested. **Full payment must be included with your request or it will be rejected.** Make your check or money order payable to "United States Treasury." Enter your SSN or EIN and "Form 4506 request" on your check or money order.

  a Cost for each return . . . . $ **39.00**
  b Number of returns requested on line 7 . . . .
  c Total cost. Multiply line 8a by line 8b . . . . $

9 If we cannot find the tax return, we will refund the fee. If the refund should go to the third party listed on line 5, check here . . . ☐

Signature of taxpayer(s). I declare that I am either the taxpayer whose name is shown on line 1a or 2a, or a person authorized to obtain the tax return requested. If the request applies to a joint return, **either** husband or wife must sign. If signed by a corporate officer, partner, guardian, tax matters partner, executor, receiver, administrator, trustee, or party other than the taxpayer, I certify that I have the authority to execute Form 4506 on behalf of the taxpayer.

		Telephone number of taxpayer on line 1a or 2a ( )
Sign Here	▶ **Signature** (see instructions)	Date
	▶ **Title** (if line 1a above is a corporation, partnership, estate, or trust)	
	▶ **Spouse's signature**	Date

For Privacy Act and Paperwork Reduction Act Notice, see page 2.   Cat. No. 41721E   Form **4506** (Rev. 11-2005)

FORM 3-56   Request for innocent spouse relief and innocent spouce statement.

This form only appears on the accompanying CD.

FORM 3-57   Questionnaire for nonrequesting spouse,

This form only appears on the accompanying CD.

VI. Forms Related to Assignments of Debt

Assignments of debts are generally used when the creditor wants his or her money immediately. In some cases it is used to secure a loan or an open charge account. For example, someone owes you a sum of money. You need money now to pay your taxes or your child's college tuition. Debts owed to you by others are considered as assets. To obtain the money now, you can assign the debt to someone else in exchange for a lesser sum of money or you can use it as security for a loan.

FORM 3-58 Assignment of life insurance policy as collateral.

One method of obtaining financing for an item is the assignment of certain assets belonging to the buyer. This agreement may be used to assign a life insurance policy as collateral.

For good and valuable consideration, the undersigned hereby assigns and transfers, subject to the restrictions below, all rights, title, and interest in and to the life insurance policy No. _____ with the _____ [insurance company] on the life of _____.

The undersigned Assignor warrants that he or she is the owner of the said life insurance policy and that he or she has full rights and full authority to make this assignment and transfer. The undersigned also warrants that the rights and benefits assigned hereunder are free and clear of any liens, encumbrances, adverse claims, or interest. In addition, the Assignor also warrants that he or she has no knowledge of any disputes or defenses thereon.

It is expressly agreed by both parties that the following specific rights are included in this agreement:

1. This assignment is made, and the policy is to be held, as collateral security for any and all liabilities of Assignor to Assignee, either now existing, or that may arise between the Assignor and Assignee.

2. In the event of death of the insured prior to the payment of any debts described in paragraph 1 above, the Assignee has the right to recover the remaining portion of the debts to include all interest, late penalties, and other authorized charges.

3. In the event that any payments of the debts are in default by at least 30 days, the Assignee has the right to surrender the policy to the insurance company and collect the remaining portion of the debts to include all interest, late penalties, and other authorized charges.

4. The Assignee is under no obligation to pay any premium on the said policy. Any premiums paid by the Assignee will be added to and become a part of the liabilities secured.

This assignment shall be binding upon and inure to the benefit of the parties, their successors, assigns, and personal representatives.

Signed under seal this _____ day of ____, __.

_____
Assignor

FORM 3-58   continued

ACKNOWLEDGMENT

State of   )

County of   )

On this date, [list names of person(s) who signed above] _____ personally appeared before me and acknowledged that the above signature(s) are valid and binding.

_____

Notary Public

My Commission expires: _____

FORM 3-59   Assignment of money due.

> One method of obtaining financing for large items is the assignment of certain assets belonging to the buyer. This agreement may be used to assign money due.

For good and valuable consideration, the undersigned hereby unconditionally and irrevocably assigns and transfers all rights, title, and interest in and to all monies due from [name of debtor] _____ to [Assignee] _____ and his or her successors and assigns.

The undersigned Assignor warrants that the said account is correct and due in the amount stated, and that he or she has not received payment for the same or any part thereof, and that he or she has full rights and full authority to make this assignment and transfer. The undersigned also warrants that the rights and benefits assigned hereunder are free and clear of any liens, encumbrances, adverse claims, or interest. In addition, the Assignor also warrants that he or she has no knowledge of any disputes or defenses thereon. The account is sold without warranty or guaranty of collection and without recourse to the undersigned Assignor in the event of nonpayment. Assignee may prosecute collection of any receivable in his or her own name.

This assignment shall be binding upon and inure to the benefit of the parties, their successors, assigns, and personal representatives.

Signed under seal this _____ day of ____, __.

_____

Assignor

FORM 3-59   continued

ACKNOWLEDGMENT

State of   )

County of   )

On this date, [list names of person(s) who signed above] _____ personally appeared before me and acknowledged that the above signature(s) are valid and binding.

_____   _____

Notary Public   Date signed

My Commission expires: _____

FORM 3-60   Assignment of note.

> In some situations, when an individual needs to obtain financing for merchandise, an assignment of a negotiable note may be appropriate.

The undersigned, [person assigning the note], the "Assignor," for good and valuable considerations given by [person to whom the note is being assigned], the "Assignee," to assigned note debtor including any renewals, extensions, or refinancing of all or any part thereof and any and all other liabilities of assigned note debtor or Assignor to the Assignee, direct or indirect, absolute or contingent, due or to become due, now existing, or hereafter arising and howsoever evidenced (all herein called the "Liabilities"), hereby assigns, pledges, transfers, and delivers to the Assignee the following:

1. All of its right, title, and interest along with any and all profits, money, or funds due or to become due to Assignor of whatsoever description or character presently or hereafter derived from the certain promissory note, executed on or about [date note executed] _____ by [name of person who is the debtor on the note] _____, the Assigned Note Debtor, and any extensions or renewals thereof (herein called the "assigned note"), wherein the Assigned Note Debtor agrees to pay to the Assignor the sum of _____ Dollars ($____) pursuant to the terms and conditions as are more specifically set forth therein.

2. All damages, money, and consideration of any kind or character to which Assignor may now or hereafter be entitled and arising out of or derived from proceedings now or hereafter instituted by or against the Assigned Note Debtor in any Federal or State Court, under any bankruptcy or insolvency laws or under any laws relating to assignments for the benefit of creditors, to compositions, extensions, or adjustments of indebtedness, or to any other relief of debtors or otherwise.

Assignor further represents, warrants, and agrees as follows:

1. That he or she has full legal right and authority to execute and carry out the terms of this instrument; and that as of the date of the execution of this instrument, Assignor is

FORM 3-60 continued

not in default in the performance of any of the obligations existing with respect to the Assigned Note.

2. That the Assignee shall not be liable to any person or persons for damages sustained in connection with the Assigned Note or such other contract into which the Assignor may have entered in connection therewith.

3. That Assignor will execute and deliver any additional instruments which the Assignee deems necessary to carry out the purport and tenor of this instrument and to better secure the payment of the Liabilities.

This Assignment is binding upon and inures to the benefit of Assignee and any holder of any of the Liabilities and is binding upon the Assignor.

IN WITNESS WHEREOF, Assignor has executed this Assignment of Note on _____, 20__ at [place where signed] _____.

Signed and acknowledged in the presence of:

_____   _____

Assignor   Assignee

ACKNOWLEDGMENT RECIEPT

The undersigned, the Assigned Note Debtor, hereby acknowledges receipt of a copy of the foregoing Assignment of Note and agrees to pay all income, issues, and profits from the Assigned note directly to the Assignee.

Assigned Note Debtor _____

Date: _____

FORM 3-61 Assignment of a secured note.

One method of obtaining financing for goods is the assignment of certain assets belonging to the buyer. This agreement may be used to assign a secured note.

For good and valuable consideration, receipt of which is hereby acknowledged, on [date], I assigned all my interest, title, ownership, and benefit in the below-described promissory note [Describe the note here.]: _____

Attached is the original of the said promissory note, assigned to: [person to whom account is being assigned, including address] _____.

FORM 3-61   continued

The Assignor irrevocably authorizes Assignee to ask for, demand, collect, and give a receipt for money that is due or may become due on the said note, without any previous demand or notice except as required by the terms of the attached note.

The Assignor hereby assigns to the Assignee all of the Assignor's rights to the below-described security interest: [List the item, property, or account that secures the note.] _____
_____ to secure performance under the terms of the attached note. In the event default as described in the security agreement occurs, the Assignee has the right, authority, and power to take the actions permitted to be taken by the Assignor. For this purpose, the Assignee is appointed the attorney in fact of the Assignor to enforce the terms of the security agreement and the attached note.

WITNESSED this _____ day of _____, ____.

_____   _____

Assignor   Assignee

ACKNOWLEDGMENT

State of   )
County of   )

On this date, [list names of person(s) who signed above] personally appeared before me and acknowledged that the above signature(s) are valid and binding.

_____   _____

Notary Public   Date signed

My Commission expires: _____

FORM 3-62   Assignment of an unsecured note.

One method of obtaining financing for goods is the assignment of certain assets belonging to the buyer. This agreement may be used to assign an unsecured note.

For good and valuable consideration, receipt of which is hereby acknowledged, on [date], I assigned all my interest, title, ownership, and benefit in the below-described promissory note [describe the note here]: _____
_____

Attached is the original of the said promissory note, assigned to: [person to whom account is being assigned, including address] _____.

FROM 3-61   continued

The Assignor irrevocably authorizes Assignee to ask for, demand, collect, and give a receipt for money that is due or may become due on the said note, without any previous demand or notice except as required by the terms of the attached note.

WITNESSED this _____ day of ____, ____.

_____
Assignor

ACKNOWLEDGMENT

State of   )

County of   )

On this date, [list names of person(s) who signed above] _____ personally appeared before me and acknowledged that the above signature(s) are valid and binding.

_____   _____
Notary Public   Date signed

My Commission expires: _____

FORM 3-63   Assignment of a bank account.

For good and valuable consideration, receipt of which is hereby acknowledged, on [date], I assigned all my interest and benefit in the following bank account No. _____ in the name of the assignor in [name and address of bank] to: [person to whom account is being assigned, including address]

The Assignor irrevocably authorizes Assignee to ask for, demand, collect, and give a receipt for money in such bank account, without any previous demand or notice.

WITNESSED this _____ day of ____, 20 __.

Assignor _____   Assignee _____

ACKNOWLEDGMENT

State of   )

County of   )

On this date, [list names of person(s) who signed above] _____ personally appeared before me and acknowledged that the above signature(s) are valid and binding.

_____   _____
Notary Public   Date signed

My Commission expires: _____

FORM 3-64 Assignment of stock certificates.

For good and valuable consideration, receipt of which is hereby acknowledged, on [date], I assigned all my interest and benefit in the following stock certificates [describe number of shares, type of stock, e.g., Class A Common Stock] of _____ [corporation], which are represented by certificate number(s) _____ to:[person to whom shares are being assigned, including address] _____

_____

I warrant that the certificate is genuine and to my knowledge is valid, and that I have the legal right to transfer it.

I appoint the Assignee as my attorney in fact to effect a transfer of the assigned shares on the books of the _____ [corporation] with full power of substitution.

WITNESSED this _____ day of ____, 20 __.

Assignor _____   Assignee _____

ACKNOWLEDGMENT

State of   )

County of   )

On this date, [list names of person(s) who signed above] _____ personally appeared before me and acknowledged that the above signature(s) are valid and binding.

_____   _____

Notary Public   Date signed

My Commission expires: _____

FORM 3-65 Assignment of Insurance Claim

For good and valuable consideration, the undersigned hereby unconditionally and irrevocably assigns and transfers all rights, title and interest in and to the insurance claim on insurance policy No. ____ with the [insurance company], to wit the claim that is based on the following incident/event: [Describe the incident/event, e.g., automobile accident which occurred on 2/3/1994 involving a 2004 Ford pickup, license number KKL 342.] _____

_____

_____

The undersigned Assignor warrants that he/she is the owner of the said insurance policy and that he/she has full rights and full authority to make this assignment and transfer. The undersigned also warrants that the claim assigned hereunder is free and clear of any liens, encumbrances, adverse claims, or interest. In addition, the Assignor also warrants that he/she has no knowledge of any disputes or defenses thereon.

This assignment shall be binding upon and inure to the benefit of the parties, their successors, assigns, and personal representatives.

Signed under seal this _____ day of ____, 20 __.

Assignor _____

FORM 3-66   General assignment for the benefit of creditors.

An additional situation where an assignment of debt is used is when your creditors are pressing you for payment. To prevent the creditors from taking legal action against you, they may agree to accept an assignment of any debts owed to you to your creditors.

For good and valuable consideration, the undersigned hereby unconditionally and irrevocably assigns and transfers unto _____ all rights, title, and interest in and to the following property: _____

This assignment is based on the Assignor's financial condition and is to be considered as an assignment for the benefit of creditors. This agreement is made with the hope of avoiding legal proceedings. The creditors who accept this assignment will share in those assets of Assignor that are not exempt by law, without preference or priority except as required by law.

The undersigned warrants that he/she has full rights and full authority to make this assignment and transfer. The undersigned also warrants that the rights and benefits assigned hereunder are free and clear of any liens, encumbrances, adverse claims, or interest except as noted.

This assignment shall be binding upon and inure to the benefit of the parties, their successors, assigns, and personal representatives.

The Assignee shall collect all income, interest, debts, etc., of the property and distribute the proceeds as follows:

1.   payment of expenses of administering this assignment;

2.   payment of priority, preferred, and secured claims in the priority as established by law; and

3.   payment of unsecured claims on a pro rata basis.

The Assignee will not be liable to any unknown creditors or any creditor who failed to receive notice of this assignment. Assignee will not make any payments to creditors who do not accept this assignment unless so ordered by a court or approved by the Assignor.

No bond shall be required of the Assignee.

Signed under seal this _____ day of _____, 20 __.

Assignor _____

Accepted: _____

Date: _____

Assignee _____

Accepted by the below-listed creditors:

Signature of creditors accepting: _____

Date accepted: _____

4

Identify Theft Protection

Forms and Information in This Chapter

Form 4-1 FTC ID Theft Affidavit
Form 4-2 ID Theft Victim Information

Introduction

In 1998 the federal government passed 18 U.S.C. 1028, "The Identity Theft and Assumption Deterrence Act of 1998," which made identity theft a federal crime. Since then all states have passed laws related to identity theft. If you are the victim of this crime, there are two Web sites you need to read; the Federal Trade Commission's (FTC) site at http://www.ftc.gov/ftc/privacy.htm and the Identity Theft Resource Center (ITRC) at http://www.idtheftcenter.org.

Both Web sites are a one-stop national resource to learn about the crime of identity theft. They provide detailed information to help you protect yourself from identity theft and tell you the steps to take if it occurs. Both are comprehensive reference centers—for consumers, businesses, law enforcement, and the media—with access to specific laws, contact information, and resources from state and federal government agencies.

As noted on the FTC site, identity theft is a serious crime. How does it happen? Identity theft occurs when someone uses your personal information without your permission to commit fraud or other crimes. While you can't entirely control whether you will become a victim, there are steps you can take to minimize your risk.

Identity Theft Resource Center

The Identity Theft Resource Center (ITRC) is a nonprofit, nationally respected program dedicated exclusively to identity theft. It provides consumer and victim support and advises governmental agencies, legislators, and companies about this evolving and growing crime. According to the ITRC, identity theft is a crime in which an imposter obtains key pieces of information such as Social Security and driver's license numbers and uses it for his or her own personal gain. You may browse the ITRC Web site at http://www.idtheftcenter.org. Some of their more popular pages are scam alerts, assistance on lost or stolen wallets, victim issues, victim impact studies, and identity theft in the workplace. They also provide for speaking engagements and opportunities to assist media, students, legislators, law enforcement, and governmental agencies in their research.

The ITRC notes on the Web site that identity theft is a difficult crime. It not only affects us financially but also emotionally. In identity theft cases, the burden of proving innocence rests on the shoulders of the victim. The ITRC recommends that you be assertive yet controlled.

The ITRC recommends that you start with their Victim Guide 100, a victim action guide, and FS 106, an organizing guide. Insist on police reports. Insist that credit card companies send you copies of applications and credit slips and the paperwork that links your name to the imposter. If one person at a company won't help you, talk with a supervisor. They recommend you always talk with a fraud investigator, not a customer service representative. Note: Their victim's guide may be downloaded from their Web site.

According to the ITRC, identity theft is a complex problem. You will not be able to work on clearing your name as fast as you'd like. Companies move slowly, partly to protect you. Most imposters are never found, let alone arrested or convicted. This is often not the fault of law enforcement, but rather the nature of the crime. So, work with the police, help them out when you can, but let them investigate. Work on clearing your name and getting your life back to normal.

You may contact the ITRC offices via telephone (858) 693-7935 or e-mail them (itrc@idtheftcenter.org) for direct victim assistance. There are also ITRC-trained victim counselors in many areas around the country. Since state laws vary, please be sure to start victim or consumer e-mail requests with the name of your city and state.

What to Do If You Think Your Identity Has Been Stolen

What are the first steps I should take if I'm a victim of identity theft?
If you are a victim of identity theft, take the following four steps (as recommended by the FTC) as soon as possible and keep a record with the details of your conversations and copies of all correspondence:

1. Place a fraud alert on your credit reports, and review your credit reports.

2. Close the accounts that you know, or believe, have been tampered with or opened fraudulently.
3. File a report with your local police or the police in the community where the identity theft took place.
4. File a complaint with the Federal Trade Commission.

Fraud Alerts

Fraud alerts can help prevent an identity thief from opening any more accounts in your name. Contact the toll-free fraud number of any of the three consumer reporting companies below to place a fraud alert on your credit report. You only need to contact one of the three companies to place an alert. The company you call is required to contact the other two, which will place an alert on their versions of your report too.

Equifax: 1-800-525–6285
www.equifax.com
P.O. Box 740241, Atlanta, GA 30374-0241

Experian: 1-888-EXPERIAN (397-3742)
www.experian.com
P.O. Box 9532, Allen, TX 75013

TransUnion: 1-800-680-7289
www.transunion.com
Fraud Victim Assistance Division, P.O. Box 6790, Fullerton, CA 92834-6790

Once you place the fraud alert in your file, you're entitled to order free copies of your credit reports, and, if you ask, only the last four digits of your Social Security number will appear on your credit reports. Once you get your credit reports, review them carefully. Look for inquiries from companies you haven't contacted, accounts you didn't open, and debts on your accounts that you can't explain. Check that information to make sure your Social Security number, address(es), name or initials, and employers are correct. If you find fraudulent or inaccurate information, get it removed. See Correcting Fraudulent Information in Credit Reports to learn how. Continue to check your credit reports periodically, especially for the first year after you discover the identity theft, to make sure no new fraudulent activity has occurred.

What Is a Fraud Alert?

There are two types of fraud alerts: an initial alert and an extended alert.

An initial alert stays on your credit report for at least 90 days. You may ask that an initial fraud alert be placed on your credit report if you suspect you have been or are about to be a victim of identity theft. An initial alert is appropriate if your wallet has been stolen or if you've been taken in by a "phishing" scam. When you place an initial fraud alert on your credit report, you're entitled to one free credit report from each of the three nationwide consumer reporting companies.

An extended alert stays on your credit report for seven years. You can have an extended alert placed on your credit report if you've been a victim of identity theft and you provide the consumer reporting company with an "identity theft report." When you place an extended alert on your credit report, you're entitled to two free credit reports within 12 months from each of the three nationwide consumer reporting companies. In addition, the consumer reporting companies will remove your name from marketing lists for prescreened credit offers for five years unless you ask them to put your name back on the list before then.

To place either of these alerts on your credit report, or to have them removed, you will be required to provide appropriate proof of your identity: That may include your Social Security number, name, address, and other personal information requested by the consumer reporting company.

When a business sees the alert on your credit report, they must verify your identity before issuing you credit. As part of this verification process, the business may try to contact you directly. This may cause some delays if you're trying to obtain credit. To compensate for possible delays, you may wish to include a cell phone number, where you can be reached easily, in your alert. Remember to keep all contact information in your alert current.

What Is an Identity Theft Report?

An identity theft report may have two parts:

Part One is a copy of a report filed with a local, state, or federal law enforcement agency, like your local police department, your State Attorney General, the FBI, the U.S. Secret Service, the FTC, and the U.S. Postal Inspection Service. There is no federal law requiring a federal agency to take a report about identity theft; however, some state laws require local police departments to take reports. When you file a report, provide as much information as you can about the crime, including anything you know about the dates of the identity theft, the fraudulent accounts opened, and the alleged identity thief.

Part Two of an identity theft report depends on the policies of the consumer reporting company and the information provider (the business that sent the information to the consumer reporting company). That is, they may ask you to provide information or documentation, in addition to that included in the law enforcement report, which is reasonably intended to verify your identity theft. They must make their request within 15 days of receiving your law enforcement report, or, if you already obtained an extended fraud alert on your credit report the date you submit your request to the credit reporting company for information blocking. The consumer reporting company and information provider then have 15 more days to work with you to make sure your identity theft report contains everything they need. They are entitled to take five days to review any information you give them.

For example, if you give them information 11 days after they request it, they do not have to make a final decision until 16 days after they asked you for that information. If you give them any information after the 15-day deadline, they can reject your identity theft report as incomplete; then you will have to resubmit your identity theft report with the correct information.

You may find that most federal and state agencies, and some local police departments, offer only "automated" reports, reports that do not require a face-to-face meeting with a law enforcement officer. Automated reports may be submitted online or by telephone or mail.

If you have a choice, do not use an automated report. The reason? It's more difficult for the consumer reporting company or information provider to verify the information. Unless you are asking a consumer reporting company to place an extended fraud alert on your credit report, you probably will have to provide additional information or documentation when you use an automated report.

Close Your Tampered Accounts

Call and speak with someone in the security or fraud department of each company. Follow up in writing, and include copies (NOT originals) of supporting documents. It's important to notify credit card companies and banks in writing. Send your letters by certified mail, return receipt requested, so you can document what the company received and when. Keep a file of your correspondence and enclosures.

When you open new accounts, use new Personal Identification Numbers (PINs) and passwords. Avoid using easily available information like your mother's maiden name, your birth date, the last four digits of your Social Security number, your phone number, or a series of consecutive numbers.

If the identity thief has made charges or debits on your accounts, or on fraudulently opened accounts, ask the company for the forms to dispute those transactions:

- For charges and debits on existing accounts, ask the representative to send you the company's fraud dispute forms. If the company doesn't have special forms, use the sample letter to dispute the fraudulent charges or debits. In either case, write to the company at the address given for "billing inquiries," NOT the address for sending your payments.

• For new unauthorized accounts, ask if the company accepts the ID Theft Affidavit. If not, ask the representative to send you the company's fraud dispute forms. If the company already has reported these accounts or debts on your credit report, dispute this fraudulent information.

Once you have resolved your identity theft dispute with the company, ask for a letter stating that the company has closed the disputed accounts and has discharged the fraudulent debts. This letter is your best proof if errors relating to this account reappear on your credit report or you are contacted again about the fraudulent debt.

File a Report with the Police

Get a copy of the police report or, at the very least, the number of the report. It can help you deal with creditors who need proof of the crime. If the police are reluctant to take your report, ask to file a "Miscellaneous Incidents" report, or try another jurisdiction, like your state police. You also can check with your state Attorney General's Office to find out if state law requires the police to take reports for identity theft. Check the blue pages of your telephone directory for the phone number or check www.naag.org for a list of State Attorneys General.

What Do I Do If the Local Police Won't Take a Report?

There are efforts at the federal, state, and local level to ensure that local law enforcement agencies understand identity theft, its impact on victims, and the importance of taking a police report. However, we still hear that some departments are not taking reports. The following tips may help you to get a report if you're having difficulties:

• Furnish as much documentation as you can to prove your case. Debt collection letters, credit reports, your notarized ID Theft Affidavit, and other evidence of fraudulent activity can help demonstrate the seriousness of your case.

• Be persistent if local authorities tell you that they can't take a report. Stress the importance of a police report; many creditors require one to resolve your dispute. Remind them that consumer reporting companies will automatically block the fraudulent accounts and bad debts from appearing on your credit report, but only if you can give them a copy of the police report.

- If you're told that identity theft is not a crime under your state law, ask to file a Miscellaneous Incident Report instead.
- If you can't get the local police to take a report, try your county police. If that doesn't work, try your state police.

Some states require the police to take reports for identity theft. Check with the office of your State Attorney General (location and address may be obtained from www.naag.org) to find out if your state has this law.

File a Complaint with the FTC

By sharing your identity theft complaint with the FTC, you will provide important information that can help law enforcement officials across the nation track down identity thieves and stop them. The FTC can refer victims' complaints to other government agencies and companies for further action, as well as investigate companies for violations of laws the agency enforces.

You can file a complaint with the FTC using the online complaint form; or call the FTC's Identity Theft Hotline, toll-free: 1-877-ID-THEFT (438-4338); TTY: 1-866-653-4261; or write Identity Theft Clearinghouse, Federal Trade Commission, 600 Pennsylvania Avenue, NW, Washington, DC 20580.

How Do I Prove That I'm an Identity Theft Victim?

Applications or other transaction records related to the theft of your identity may help you prove that you are a victim. For example, you may be able to show that the signature on an application is not yours. These documents also may contain information about the identity thief that is valuable to law enforcement. By law, companies must give you a copy of the application or other business transaction records relating to your identity theft if you submit your request in writing. Be sure to ask the company representative where you should mail your request. Companies must provide these records at no charge to you within 30 days of receipt of your request and your supporting documents. You also may give permission to any law enforcement agency to get these records or ask in your written request that a copy of these records be sent to a particular law enforcement officer.

The company can ask you for:

- Proof of your identity. This may be a photocopy of a government-issued ID card, the same type of information the identity thief used to open or access the account, or the type of information the company usually requests from applicants or customers.
- A police report and a completed affidavit, which may be the ID Theft Affidavit or the company's own affidavit.

Should I Apply for a New Social Security Number?

Under certain circumstances, the Social Security Administration may issue you a new Social Security number—at your request—if, after trying to resolve the problems brought on by identity theft, you continue to experience problems.

Consider this option carefully. A new Social Security number may not resolve your identity theft problems and may actually create new problems. For example, a new Social Security number does not necessarily ensure a new credit record, because credit bureaus may combine the credit records from your old Social Security number with those from your new Social Security number. Even when the old credit information is not associated with your new Social Security number, the absence of any credit history under your new Social Security number may make it more difficult for you to get credit. And finally, there's no guarantee that a new Social Security number wouldn't also be misused by an identity thief.

Reporting Identity Theft

If you believe you have been the victim of identity theft, you may use the online form accessible at http://www.consumer.gov/idtheft/con_file.htm or call the Federal Trade Commission. The information you provide is up to you. However, if you don't provide your name or other information, it may be impossible for the FTC to refer, respond to, or investigate your complaint or request.

Filing a Complaint

You can file a complaint with the FTC using the online complaint form at https://rn.ftc.gov/pls/dod/widtpubl$.startup?Z_ORG_CODE = PU03; by calling the FTC's Identity Theft Hotline, toll-free: 1-877-ID-THEFT (438-4338); TTY: 1-866-653-4261; or by writing to the Identity Theft Clearinghouse, Federal Trade Commission, 600 Pennsylvania Avenue, NW, Washington, DC 20580.

The only thing you need to file with the FTC is your complaint. Do not send the FTC your completed ID Theft Affidavit, your police report, your credit reports, financial information, or any other documents relating to your case. If a law enforcement agency decides to open an investigation of your case, they will contact you directly and let you know what documents they need.

The FTC serves as the federal clearinghouse for complaints by victims of identity theft. While the FTC does not resolve individual consumer problems, your complaint helps them investigate fraud and can lead to law enforcement action. The FTC enters Internet, telemarketing, identity theft, and other fraud-related complaints into Consumer Sentinel, a secure, online database available to hundreds of civil and criminal law enforcement agencies worldwide.

If you file online at the FTC Web site, the FTC uses secure socket layer (SSL) encryption to protect the transmission of the information you submit when you use their secure online forms. The information you provide to them is stored securely.

Creating a ID Theft Affidavit

A group of credit grantors, consumer advocates, and attorneys at the Federal Trade Commission developed an ID Theft Affidavit to make it easier for fraud victims to report information. While many companies accept this affidavit, others require that you submit more or different forms. Before you send the affidavit, contact each company to find out if they accept it.

It will be necessary to provide the information in this affidavit anywhere a new account was opened in your name. The information will enable the companies to investigate the fraud and decide the outcome of your claim. If someone made unauthorized charges to an existing account, call the company for instructions.

This affidavit has two parts:
- Part One—the ID Theft Affidavit—is where you report general information about yourself and the theft.
- Part Two—the Fraudulent Account Statement—is where you describe the fraudulent account(s) opened in your name. Use a separate Fraudulent Account Statement for each company you need to write to.

When you send the affidavit to the companies, attach copies (NOT originals) of any supporting documents (for example, driver's license or police report). Before submitting your affidavit, review the disputed account(s) with family members or friends who may have information about the account(s) or access to them. Complete this affidavit as soon as possible.

Many creditors ask that you send it within two weeks. Delays on your part could slow the investigation. Be as accurate and complete as possible. You may choose not to provide some of the information requested. However, incorrect or incomplete information will slow the process of investigating your claim and absolving the debt. Print clearly.

When you have finished completing the affidavit, mail a copy to each creditor, bank, or company that provided the thief with the unauthorized credit, goods, or services you describe. Attach a copy of the Fraudulent Account Statement with information only on accounts opened at the institution to which you are sending the packet, as well as any other supporting documentation you are able to provide.

Send the appropriate documents to each company by certified mail, return receipt requested, so you can prove that it was received. The companies will review your claim and send you a written response telling you the outcome of their investigation. Keep a copy of everything you submit.

If you are unable to complete the affidavit, a legal guardian or someone with power of attorney may complete it for you. Except as noted, the information you provide will be used only by the company to process your affidavit, investigate the events you report, and help stop further fraud. If this affidavit is requested in a lawsuit, the company might have to provide it to the requesting party.

FORM 4-1 FTC ID theft affidavit.

As noted earlier, this form may be completed online and then printed so it can be forwarded to the necessary law enforcement persons and/or businesses. If you prefer, you may copy the following form for completion.

First Name: _____

Last Name: _____

Street Address: _____

Apt. or Suite No.: _____

City: _____

State/Province: _____

Zip: _____

Country: _____

Home Phone: _____   _____   _____
                 Area Code   Phone Number   Ext.

Social Security Number: ___-__-____

E-mail Address:_____ (i.e., anyone@myisp.com)

Tell Us About Your Problem

1. Types of Identity Theft You Have Experienced.

ID Theft occurs when someone uses your name or other identifying information for their personal gain. Please check the types of ID theft you were a victim of. (Check as many as apply.)

❑ Credit Cards   ❑ Securities or Other Investments

❑ Checking or Savings Accounts   ❑ Internet or E-Mail

❑ Loans   ❑ Government Documents or Benefits

❑ Phone or Utilities   ❑ Other

Did suspect use the Internet to open the account or purchase the goods or services?

❑ Yes   ❑ No   ❑ Don't Know

FORM 4-1   continued

2. Describe Your Complaint Here.

_____

_____

_____

Please give us information about the identity theft, including, but not limited to, how the theft occurred, who may be responsible for the theft, and what actions you have taken since the theft. Please include a list of companies where fraudulent accounts were established or your current accounts were affected. Please limit your complaint to 2,000 characters.

3. Details of the Identity Theft.

When did you notice that you might be a
victim of identity theft?   _____ (MM/DD/YYYY)

When did the identity theft first occur?
(i.e., when was the first account opened?)   _____ (MM/DD/YYYY)

How many accounts (credit cards, loans,
bank accounts, cellular phone accounts,
etc.) were opened or accessed?   _____

How much money, if any, have you had to
pay?   _____ (Numbers Only)

How much money, if any, did the identity thief obtain from companies in your
name?   _____ (Numbers Only)

What other problems, if any, have you experienced as a result of the identity theft?

No Other Harm Suffered
Civil Suit Filed or Judgement Entered Against You
Criminal Investigation, Arrest or Conviction
Denied Credit or Other Financial Services
Denied Employment or Loss of Job

4. The Identity Thief.

Please provide any information you may have about the identity thief, including his or her name, and any addresses or phone numbers the identity thief may have used.

First Name: _____

Last Name: _____

Street Address: _____

Apt. or Suite No.: _____

City: _____

FORM 4-1   continued

State/Province: _____

Zip _____

Country: _____

Phone Number: _____   _____

               Area Code   Phone Number (Numbers Only)

E-mail Address (i.e., anyone@myisp.com): _____

Your relationship to the identity thief: _____

5. Contacts.

Please indicate which of the following steps, if any, you have already taken to deal with the identity theft.

For which of the following credit bureaus, have you: (check all that apply)

Called to report the fraud?:

    ❑ Equifax   ❑ Experian   ❑ Trans Union   ❑ Other   ❑ None

Put a "fraud alert" on your report?:

    ❑ Equifax   ❑ Experian   ❑ Trans Union   ❑ Other   ❑ None

Ordered your credit report?:

    ❑ Equifax   ❑ Experian   ❑ Trans Union   ❑ Other   ❑ None

Problem with Credit Bureau?:

    ❑ Equifax   ❑ Experian   ❑ Trans Union   ❑ Other

Have you contacted the police?

        ❑ Yes   ❑ No

If yes, please provide police department name: _____

Department State: _____

Report Number?   ❑ Yes   ❑ No

If yes, please provide report number: _____

6. Problems with Companies.

Do you have any problems with the companies, credit bureaus, or organizations you are dealing with concerning your identity theft problems? If so, identify each company, credit bureau, or organization, provide its location and/or telephone number, if you have it, and tell us briefly what the problem is.

NOTE: If you checked the problem box for any of the three credit bureaus in the section above, please include those credit bureaus here.

FORM 4-1   continued

Company 1

Company Name: _____

City: _____

State/Province: _____

Country: _____

Phone Number: _____   _____   ____

                       Area Code   Phone Number   Ext.

Have you notified
this company?   ❑ Yes   ❑ No

Have you sent written
notifications to this company?   ❑ Yes   ❑ No

Company 2

Company Name: _____

City: _____

State/Province: _____

Country: _____

Phone Number: _____   _____   ____

                       Area Code   Phone Number   Ext.

Have you notified
this company?   ❑ Yes   ❑ No

Have you sent written
notifications to this company?   ❑ Yes   ❑ No

Company 3

Company Name: _____

City: _____

State/Province: _____

Country: _____

Phone Number: _____   _____   ____

                       Area Code   Phone Number   Ext.

Have you notified
this company?   ❑ Yes   ❑ No

Have you sent written
notifications to this company?   ❑ Yes   ❑ No

FORM 4-2 ID theft victim information.

This form is generally attached to the ID Theft Affidavit.

---

(1) My full legal name is _____
            (First) (Middle) (Last) (Jr., Sr., III)

(2) (If different from above) When the events described in this affidavit took place, I was known as _____
            (First) (Middle) (Last) (Jr., Sr., III)

(3) My date of birth is _____ (day/month/year)

(4) My Social Security number is _____

(5) My driver's license or identification card state and number are _____
_____

(6) My current address is _____
City _____ State ____ Zip Code ____

I have lived at this address since _____ (month/year)

(8) (If different from above) When the events described in this affidavit took place, my address was _____ City _____ State ____
Zip Code ____

(9) I lived at the address in Item 8 from _____ (month/year) until _____ (month/year)

(10) My daytime telephone number is _____
My evening telephone number is _____

ID Theft Affidavit

Name _____ Phone number _____

How the Fraud Occurred

(Check all that apply for items 11–17)

(11) I did not authorize anyone to use my name or personal information to seek the money, credit, loans, goods or services described in this report.

(12) I did not receive any benefit, money, goods or services as a result of the events described in this report.

(13) My identification documents (for example, credit cards; birth certificate; driver's license; Social Security card; etc.) were stolen/lost on or about _____ (day/month/year)

(14) To the best of my knowledge and belief, the following person(s) used my information (for example, my name, address, date of birth, existing account numbers, Social Security number, mother's maiden name, etc.) or identification documents to get money, credit, loans, goods or services without my knowledge or authorization:

FORM 4-2   continued

Name (if known) _____   Name (if known) _____

Address (if known) _____   Address (if known) _____

Phone number(s) (if known) _____   Phone number(s) (if known) _____

Additional information (if known)   Additional information (if known)

(15)   I do NOT know who used my information or identification documents to get money, credit, loans, goods or services without my knowledge or authorization.

(16)   Additional comments: (For example, description of the fraud, which documents or information were used or how the identity thief gained access to your information.)

_____

_____

_____

_____

(Attach additional pages as necessary.)

Name _____ Phone number _____

Victim's Law Enforcement Actions

(17)   (check one) I ❏ am ❏ am not willing to assist in the prosecution of the person(s) who committed this fraud.

(18)   (check one) I ❏ am ❏ am not authorizing the release of this information to law enforcement for the purpose of assisting them in the investigation and prosecution of the person(s) who committed this fraud.

(19)   (Check all that apply) I ❏ have ❏ have not reported the events described in this affidavit to the police or other law enforcement agency. The police ❏ did ❏ did not write a report. In the event you have contacted the police or other law enforcement agency, please complete the following:

(Agency #1) _____   (Officer/Agency personnel taking report)

(Date of report) _____   (Report number, if any)

(Phone number) _____   (email address, if any)

FORM 4-2 continued

(Agency #2)   (Officer/Agency personnel taking report)

(Date of report)   (Report number, if any)

(Phone number)   (email address, if any)

Documentation Checklist

Please indicate the supporting documentation you are able to provide to the companies you plan to notify. Attach copies (NOT originals) to the affidavit before sending it to the companies.

(20) ☐ A copy of a valid government-issued photo-identification card (for example, your driver's license, state-issued ID card or your passport). If you are under 16 and don't have a photo-ID, you may submit a copy of your birth certificate or a copy of your official school records showing your enrollment and place of residence.

(21) ☐ Proof of residency during the time the disputed bill occurred, the loan was made, or the other event took place (for example, a rental/lease agreement in your name, a copy of a utility bill or a copy of an insurance bill).

(22) ☐ A copy of the report you filed with the police or sheriff's department. If you are unable to obtain a report or report number from the police, please indicate that in Item 19. Some companies only need the report number, not a copy of the report. You may want to check with each company.

Signature

I certify that, to the best of my knowledge and belief, all the information on and attached to this affidavit is true, correct, and complete and made in good faith. I also understand that this affidavit or the information it contains may be made available to federal, state, and/or local law enforcement agencies for such action within their jurisdiction as they deem appropriate. I understand that knowingly making any false or fraudulent statement or representation to the government may constitute a violation of 18 U.S.C. §1001 or other federal, state, or local criminal statutes, and may result in imposition of a fine or imprisonment or both.

Signature   Date signed

(Notary Public)

My Commission expires: _____.

FORM 4-2   continued

[Check with each company. Creditors sometimes require notarization. If they do not, please have one witness (non-relative) sign below that you completed and signed this affidavit.]

Witness: _____

(Signature)

_____

(Printed name)

_____

(Date)

_____

(Telephone number)

Name _____ Phone number _____

I declare (check all that apply):

☐   As a result of the event(s) described in the ID Theft Affidavit, the following account(s) _____ was/were opened at your company in my name without my knowledge, permission or authorization using my personal information or identifying documents:

Completing this statement

- Make as many copies of this page as you need. Complete a separate page for each company you're notifying and only send it to that company. Include a copy of your signed affidavit.

- List only the account(s) you're disputing with the company receiving this form. See the example below.

- If a collection agency sent you a statement, letter or notice about the fraudulent account, attach a copy of that document (NOT the original).

Fraudulent Account Statement

Creditor Name/Address_____

_____

(company that opened the account or provided the goods or services)

Account Number _____

Type of unauthorized credit/goods/services provided by creditor (if known):

_____

Date issued or opened (if known) _____

Amount/Value provided (the amount charged or the cost of the goods/services) _____

FORM 4-2 continued

> ❏ During the time of the accounts described above, I had the following account open with your company:
>
> Billing name: _____
>
> Billing address _____
>
> Account number _____
>
> **Example**
>
> Example National Bank
>
> 22 Main Street
>
> Columbus, Ohio 22722
>
> 01234567-89 auto loan 01/05/2002 $25,500.00
>
>
> Name _____   Phone number _____

5

Residential Rental Property Forms

List of Forms and Information in This Chapter

I. Leases and Related Forms

FORM 5-1 Residential lease.

This residential lease is entered into between _____ (Landlord) and
_____ and _____, (Tenant(s)). The Landlord hereby
leases the below-described residential property to the tenant(s). The Tenant(s) hereby accepts
the lease. The terms of the lease are as follows:

1. The lease pertains to the property located at:_____.

2. The lease shall be for a period of _____, commencing on the _____ day of
_____, 20__ and ending on the _____ day of _____, 20__.

3. The Tenant shall pay Landlord the monthly rent of $ _____, payable on
the first day of every month. There will be a late fee of $ _____ if the rent is
not paid by the 5th of the month. The Tenant agrees to pay to Landlord the sum of
$ _____ as a security deposit, to be promptly returned upon the termination
of the lease and compliance with all provisions of this lease.

4. The Tenant shall be responsible for providing all utilities.

5. The Tenant agrees to return possession of the premises at the conclusion of the lease
in its present condition, except for normal wear and tear.

6. Only the following persons will reside on the premises: _____

7. The Tenant shall not assign or sublease the premises without written permission of the
Landlord.

8. No material or structural alterations of the premises will be made without the prior
written permission of the Landlord.

9. The Tenant will comply with all zoning, health, and use ordinances.

10. Pets are not allowed on the premises without prior written permission of the
Landlord.

11. This lease shall be subordinate to all present and future mortgages against the premises.

12. In the event that legal action is necessary to enforce any provisions of this contract,
attorney fees may be recovered by the prevailing party.

13. In the event of default under the terms of this lease and court action is required, the
defaulting party shall be responsible for court costs, interest, and attorney fees that are
a direct result of the default.

FORM 5-1 continued

14. Additional lease terms:_____

_____

Signed under seal this ____ day of _____, 20__.

Landlord _____   Tenant _____

Tenant _____

FORM 5-2   Amendment to residential lease.

This amendment modifies the residential lease between the parties below which was entered into on [date of original lease] between _____ (Landlord) and _____ and _____, (Tenant(s)).

The Landlord and Tenant(s) for good and valuable consideration hereby modify and amend the said lease only as to the following terms [list new terms here]:_____

_____

_____

All other terms of the original lease shall remain in force.

Signed under seal this _____ day of _____, 20__.

Landlord _____   Tenant _____

Tenant _____

FORM 5-3   Rent guaranty.

As an inducement for the Landlord to enter into a residential lease of the premises located at [location of rental property] to [name of renters] and for other good and valuable consideration, the undersigned hereby jointly and severally guaranty to the Landlord, his or her assigns, and/or successors, the prompt and full payment of all rents and other charges that may become due and owing to the Landlord under the terms of the attached lease or any renewal or extension thereof.

Signed under seal this ____ day of _____ 20__.

Landlord _____   Tenant _____

Tenant _____

FORM 5-4 Residential sublease.

This residential sublease is entered into between _____ [Tenant], _____ [Subtenant], and _____ [Tenant(s)]. The Tenant hereby subleases the below-described residential property to the Subtenant(s). The Subtenant(s) hereby accepts the lease, and the Landlord by signing this sublease agrees to the sublease. The terms of the sublease are as follows:

1. The sublease pertains to the property located at: _____ _____

2. The sublease shall be for a period of ____, commencing on ____ day of _____, 20__, and ending on ____ day of _____, 20__.

3. The Subtenant shall pay Tenant the monthly rent of $_____ payable on the first day of every month. There will be a late fee of $ _____ if the rent is not paid by the 5th of the month. The Subtenant agrees to pay to Tenant the sum of $_____ as a security deposit, to be promptly returned upon the termination of the sublease and compliance with all provisions of this sublease.

4. The Subtenant shall be responsible for providing all utilities.

5. The Subtenant agrees to return possession of the premises at the conclusion of the lease in its present condition, except for normal wear and tear.

6. Only the following persons will reside on the premises:

   _____

   _____

7. The subtenant shall not further assign or sublease the premises without written permission of the Landlord and the Tenant.

8. No material or structural alterations of the premises will be made without the prior written permission of the Landlord and Tenant.

9. The Subtenant will comply with all zoning, health, and use ordinances.

10. Pets are not allowed on the premises without prior written permission of the Landlord and Tenant.

11. This sublease shall be subordinate to all present and future mortgages against the premises.

12. In the event that legal action is necessary to enforce any provisions of this contract, attorney fees may be recovered by the prevailing party.

13. Additional sublease terms: _____ _____

Signed under seal this _____ day of _____, 20__.

Landlord _____   Tenant _____

                                              Subtenant _____

FORM 5-5   Extension of lease.

This amendment extends the lease between the below parties which was entered into on [date of original lease] _____ between _____, [Landlord], and _____ and _____, [Tenant(s)].

The Landlord and Tenant(s) for good and valuable consideration hereby extend the said lease for a period of ____ years (months) commencing on _____ and terminating on _____, 20__.

All other terms of the original lease as hereby extended shall remain in force.

Signed under seal this _____ day of _____, 20__.

Landlord _____   Tenant _____

Tenant _____

FORM 5-6   Notice to exercise option to extend lease.

Send this Certified Mail, Return Receipt Requested.

Date: _____

Re: Notice to exercise option to extend lease

To: [Landlord] _____

This is to officially notify you that we are exercising our option to extend the lease on the property located at [address of property].

Under the terms of the present lease, we have the option to extend or renew the said lease for a _____ term. Pursuant to lease options, we advise you that it is our election to so exercise the option to renew or extend the lease on the terms of the present lease.

Sincerely,

_____

Lessee (Renter)

FORM 5-7 Lessee's notice of termination of lease.

Send this Certified Mail, Return Receipt Requested.

Date: _____

Re: Notice of Termination of Lease

To: [Landlord] _____

This is to officially notify you that we are exercising our option to cancel our lease and to deliver up possession of the property located at [address of property], which we presently occupy, on [date the possession of property will be surrendered].

Sincerely,

_____

Tenant

FORM 5-8 Lessor's notice of termination of lease.

Send this Certified Mail, Return Receipt Requested.

Date: _____

Re: Notice of Termination of Lease

To: [Renter] _____

This is to officially notify you that we are exercising our option to cancel your lease and to direct you to deliver up possession of the property located at [address of property], which you presently occupy, on [date the possession of property will be surrendered].

Sincerely,

_____

Landlord

FORM 5-9   Mutual release between landlord and tenant.

Both _____ (Landlord) and _____ (Tenant) release and discharge one and the other from any and all claims arising out of the lease of the premises located at: _____

_____

_____

Landlord also acknowledges that possession of the premises have been returned to him/her and that any claims for damages to the property or past due rent are hereby waived.

Tenant acknowledges that he/she has received all monies due from the security deposit.

Signed under seal this _____ day of _____, 20__.

_____   _____
Landlord   Tenant

FORM 5-10   Residential lease provisions checklist.

1. Is there a clear provision regarding the return of the security and cleaning deposits at the termination of the lease? _____

2. What are the requirements on the landlord to maintain the property according to certain standards? _____

3. Under what circumstances or conditions may either you or the landlord cancel the lease prior to its expiration? _____

4. Does the lease provide you with an option to renew the lease in order to protect your rights to stay in the same location? __

5. Does the lease allow the landlord to enter the property at any time without any prior notice to you?_____

6. Does the landlord retain a set of keys to your business?_____

7. Does the lease obligate you to follow any rules formulated by the landlord any time after the lease is signed?_____

8. Does the lease release the landlord from responsibility for any damages to your property, even if it is his or her fault?_____

9. Under the terms of lease, are you required to maintain any fixtures, appliances, or portions of the property?_____

FORM 5-10   continued

> 10. Does the security or any other deposit that the tenant is required to post pay interest?_____
>
> 11. Do you have the right to put up signs for your business without the landlord's permission?_____
>
> 12. Do you have the right to sublease the premises for the duration of the lease if your business closes or if you can no longer use the property?_____
>
> 13. Can you use the property for any lawful purpose?_____
>
> 14. Is the landlord prohibited from renting other space in the same building or nearby to tenants who will compete with your business?__
>
> 15. What rights do you have in the use of the common property such as hallways, driveways, elevators, and parking lots?_____
>
> 16. If the amount of your rent is based on gross receipts of your business, are provisions made for deductions for returned merchandise, delivery or installation charges, refundable deposits, and sales tax?_____

II. Forms for Renters

FORM 5-11   Notice to landlord to make repairs.

> A letter similar to this may be used to give the landlord notice that repairs are needed. In most states, oral notification does not protect your rights. Get it in writing.

> (Date) _____
>
> Dear _____ [Landlord]:
>
> Re: The residential rental property located at _____ (address)
> This is to advise you that the above-referenced property is in need of repairs as follows:
> [List repairs needed] _____
> _____
>
> If the repairs are not timely made, we intend to pursue our legal remedies under state law. Legal remedies include but are not limited to making the repairs and deducting the cost of the repairs from the rent or in terminating our lease.

FORM 5-11 continued

Please advise me within __ days as to your intentions regarding the needed repairs.

Sincerely,

_____

Signature

FORM 5-12 Waiver of claim to fixtures.

For good and valuable consideration, receipt of which is acknowledged, [name], Landlord, hereby surrenders any claim to fixtures that have been attached to the real property by the Tenant under the lease dated [date of lease].

The Landlord hereby waives any claim to any personal property installed on the property leased by the Tenant, even if that property is considered as a fixture.

The Landlord acknowledges and admits that said fixtures retain their status as personal property and may be removed by the Tenant.

WITNESSED the hands of said Landlord, this____ day of _____, 20__.

ACKNOWLEDGMENT

State of   )

County of   )

On this date, [list names of person(s) who signed above] personally appeared before me and acknowledged that the above signature(s) are valid and binding.

_____

Notary Public

My Commission expires: _____

III. Forms for Landlords (If You Are Renting Out Part of Your Home, a Vacation Home, or Other Property)

FORM 5-13 Residential rental application.

If you are the renter, this form will normally be supplied by the landlord. However, if you are the landlord (for example, you are going to rent out part of your home or a second home), you may use this form with your tenants.

Name: _____ Social Sec. No. _____

Spouse: _____ Social Sec. No. _____

Present Address: _____

Previous Address: _____

Driver's Lic. No. _____ Birthdate: _____

Spouse's Driver's Lic. _____ Birthdate: _____

How long have you lived at your present address? _____

Name of landlord: _____ Telephone: _____

Employer: _____ Position: _____

Salary: _____ How long? _____

Spouse's Employer: _____ Telephone: _____

Salary: _____ How long? _____

Name of Bank: _____

Address: _____

Checking acc't no.: _____ Savings acc't no.: _____

Personal References:

Name _____ Relationship _____
Telephone _____
Credit References: _____

The above information is correct to the best of my knowledge and belief. I authorize you to check my credit and employment references in connection with processing of this application.

Date: _____ Applicant _____

FORM 5-14   Notice of additional charges.

Date: _____

To: [tenant] _____

Pursuant to the terms of your lease, you are hereby notified that an additional sum of $ _____ is due on or before [date].

The additional sum is due to the below factors:

[list reasons for additional charges] _____

_____

Payment of the additional sum should be made directly to the undersigned.

_____

Landlord

FORM 5-15   Notice of change in rent.

Date: _____

To: [tenant] _____

Pursuant to the terms of your lease, you are hereby notified that starting on the 1st day of _____, 20__, the monthly rent on your leased property will be increased to the monthly total of $ _____.

This is a change from your present rate of $ _____.

_____

Landlord

FORM 5-16   Notice of default in rent.

Send as Certified Mail, Return Receipt Requested.

(Date) _____

To: [name(s) of tenant(s)] _____

Regarding the property located at [address of property] _____, this is to notify you that you are presently in default of the terms of the rental agreement on the subject property. Presently you owe rent from [date] _____ to [date] _____ for a total past due rent of $ _____.

FORM 5-16 continued

> You are hereby directed to pay the past due rent within __ days or surrender possession of the property (quit).
>
> If payment is not received within the above period or possession of the property is not surrendered, legal proceedings may be commenced against you without any further notice.
>
> Sincerely,
>
> _____
>
> Landlord

FORM 5-17 Notice of curable default.

Send as Certified Mail, Return Receipt Requested.

> (Date) _____
>
> To: [name(s) of tenant(s)] _____
>
> Regarding the property located at [address of property], this is to notify you that you are presently in default of the terms of the rental agreement on the subject property. The default is as follows [describe the conduct that constitutes a violation of the lease]: _____
>
> _____
>
> If you do not remedy the above default within __ days, legal proceedings may be commenced against you without any further notice.
>
> Sincerely,
>
> _____
>
> Landlord

FORM 5-18 Notice of noncurable default.

Send as Certified Mail, Return Receipt Requested.

> (Date) _____
>
> To: [name(s) of tenant(s)] _____
>
> Regarding the property located at [address of property] _____, this is to notify you that you are presently in default of the terms of the rental agreement on the subject property. The default is as follows [Describe the conduct that constitutes a violation of the lease]:
>
> _____
>
> _____

FORM 5-18 continued

> The default constitutes a forfeiture of your rights under the lease. Accordingly, unless you surrender possession of the subject property within __ days, legal proceedings may be commenced against you without any further notice.
>
> Sincerely,
>
> _____
>
> Landlord

FORM 5-19 Notice of belief of abandonment of leased property.

Send as Certified Mail, Return Receipt Requested.

> [Date] _____
>
> [Tenant name(s) and address(es)] _____
>
> Re: Notice of belief of abandonment of leased property located at: _____
>
> _____
>
> To: [tenants] _____
>
> The rent on the above property is past due and owing since [date rent was due] _____.
> It also appears that you have abandoned the said property.
>
> Please be advised that unless I receive a written notice from you within the next 15 days stating both (1) that it is your intent not to abandon the property and (2) providing me with an address whereby legal process may be served on you by certified mail, I will consider the property has been abandoned and will reclaim possession of the property.
>
> Be advised also that unless I receive instructions from you regarding the disposition of the property you left on the premises, action will be taken to dispose of the property in accordance with state law.
>
> If the abandoned property has a market value of less than $ _____, the undersigned may dispose of the property after 15 days in any manner deemed reasonable. If the property value exceeds that amount, the property will be sold at a public auction. After expenses of sale, past due rent, and other allowable damages have been deducted, any excess sums will be forwarded to your last known address. [Note: Check state statutes to see if there are any different requirements.]
>
> Sincerely,
>
> _____
>
> Landlord

FORM 5-20   Demand on cotenant for payment.

Send as Certified Mail, Return Receipt Requested. This form may be sent by a landlord to a cotenant who has not paid his or her share of this rent.

Date: _____

To: [name and address of cotenant] _____

In the lease of property between you, [the Landlord], and [Tenant] entered into on [date lease was signed], you agreed to the terms of the lease.

Please be advised that the sum of $ _____ is owed to the undersigned for the following: _____

Since this debt was incurred in respect to the leased property in which you were a Cotenant, demand is hereby made upon you for the payment of $_____.

If payment or satisfactory arrangements for payment are not made within 15 days, I will take the necessary legal action to collect the sum due me, including, if applicable, court costs and attorney fees.

Sincerely,

_____

Landlord

FORM 5-21   Demand on guarantor for payment.

Send as Certified Mail, Return Receipt Requested.

Date: _____

To: [name and address of guarantor] _____

By attachment to the lease of property between [Landlord] _____ and [Tenant] _____ entered into on [date lease was signed] _____, you guaranteed the payment of rent and related charges for [Name of Tenant] _____.

Please be advised that the sum of $_____ is owed to the undersigned for the following:

Since this debt was incurred in respect to the property in which you agreed to act as the guarantor, demand is hereby made upon you for the payment of $_____.

If payment or satisfactory arrangements for payment are not made within 15 days, I will take the necessary legal action to collect the sum due me, including if applicable, court costs and attorney fees.

Sincerely,

_____

Landlord

FORM 5-22 Notice ending at-will tenancy.

Send as Certified Mail, Return Receipt Requested. This form may be sent by a landlord to a cotenant who has not paid his or her share of the rent.

Date: _____

To: [tenant] _____

You are presently occupying the property located a _____
under the terms of a lease dated [date] _____. Under that lease, your tenancy is a tenancy at will. Your tenancy shall end on [date] _____.

You must vacate the premises no later than that date.

Under the terms of the lease, you are required to leave the premises in a clean condition.

Sincerely,

_____

Landlord

6

Home Protection Forms

Forms and Information in this Chapter

I. Buying or Building a New Home

Once you have decided to buy your home, the next decision you will have to make in your home search is whether to purchase an existing home or build a new one. Each approach offers unique advantages, and your individual lifestyle, financial goals, and schedule will determine which is best for you.

Common reasons for moving in to a newly built home include:

- New homes typically require less maintenance than resale homes because they are built with new materials and appliances.
- They often must offer more safety features and fewer health hazards in order to conform to today's building codes.
- New homes are usually well insulated due to better windows, more efficient heating and cooling equipment, and greater use of insulation.
- They can be easier to customize than resale homes because you can choose many details ranging from floor plans and paint colors to faucets and light fixtures.
- New homes are more likely to be wired with new technologies in mind, such as multiple phone lines, high-speed Internet connections, and extra cable outlets.

Existing homes, on the other hand, are attractive to many buyers for the following reasons:

- Older houses and neighborhoods may have more character and charm.
- They typically have more land than newer properties due to changes in land-use patterns.
- The homes are often in older, more convenient metro areas rather than in outlying suburbs.
- They tend to be less expensive than new properties and more likely to include items that may cost extra with a new home, such as blinds, landscaping, built-ins, etc.

Selecting a Builder

If you do decide that a newly built home is best for you, keep in mind that a construction project requires detail planning. Steps to take in selecting a builder and in selecting the home plan for your new home include:

1. Check the builder's reputation. Your local Better Business Bureau, builders association, and newspaper all provide listings for builders. You can check out prospective builders by visiting their construction sites, getting references from previous clients, talking to real estate agents, or even hiring a general contractor for an assessment.
2. Decide which features you want in advance. Consider whether you want to customize the floor plan or even order particular home appliances through the builder.
3. Sign a written contract. The contract should include in detail the house model, building options, materials, payment schedules, timing for completion of construction, and how to resolve disputes.

Home Buying Checklist

Before you select your new home, ask yourself the questions below. This checklist will help you clarify what you need and value in your new home.

1. Do you want a new home or an older home?
2. If you decide on an older home, how old of a home would you accept?
3. What style of home do you want?
   a. rambler or ranch style
   b. traditional style
   c. contemporary style
   d. manufactured home
4. What level home is desired?
   a. single level
   b. two or three story
   c. split level
5. What type of construction is desired?
   a. brick
   b. stone
   c. vinyl siding
   d. stucco
   e. wood siding
   f. aluminum siding
   g. other

6. What size lot do you prefer?
   a. small
   b. medium
   c. large
   d. not important
7. How many bedrooms are needed?
   a. 1–2
   b. 2–3
   c. 4 or more
8. How many bathrooms are needed?
   a. 1
   b. 2
   c. 3 or more
9. Is a separate laundry room desired?
10. Do you want a fireplace?
11. Is a separate dining room desired?
12. What type of garage is needed?
13. Do you need central air-conditioning?
14. Do you need a fenced yard?
15. Type of heat preferred?
    a. gas
    b. oil
    c. electric
16. Do you need to be near public transportation?
17. Do you need to be in a certain school district?
18. How close is the home to your place of employment?
19. Get preapproved for financing.

Selling Your Present Home

Selling your present home takes as much planning as purchasing a new home. Take time and examine the home-selling process ahead of time. The key concepts involved in selling your present home include these factors:

- **Select an appropriate real estate agent.** One of the most critical factors in selling your home is the selection of an agent. Interview agents, ask your friends for references, and find one that you are comfortable working with.
- **Develop a plan.** Set clear goals and decide how involved you are going to be in the home selling process. Inquire regarding your agent's marketing plans. Discuss your expectations and your role with your agent. This is no time for surprise.

- **Make needed repairs.** Inspect your home as if you were a prospective buyer. The need for minor repairs may discourage many buyers or cause a lowering of the offering price.
- **Make minor improvements.** Minor improvements will increase the value of your property, especially yard work. Also remove excessive furniture from the home.
- **Settle on a realistic price for your home.**
- **Help market your home.**

Types of Mortgages

Fixed-Rate Mortgages

The interest rate remains fixed for the life of the loan.
- Offer predictable monthly payments of principal and interest throughout the life of the loan.
- Provide protection from rising rates. No matter how high market rates go, your interest rate stays the same.
- Generally well suited to borrowers who plan to stay in their homes for a long period of time, have a fixed or slowly increasing income, and have a lower tolerance for financial risk.

Adjustable-Rate Mortgages

The interest rate adjusts periodically to reflect market conditions on predetermined dates.
- The initial introductory period usually offers a lower rate relative to fixed-rate mortgages, after which the rate adjusts periodically, based on a market index.
- Borrowers are protected from steep increases in rates through annual and lifetime adjustment caps.
- The initial rate can be locked in for different periods. Many financial institutions offer introductory periods of one, three, five, seven, or ten years; typically, the rate readjusts annually after the introductory period.
- Because of the introductory period's lower rate, some borrowers may be eligible for a larger loan amount with an ARM than with a fixed-rate mortgage.
- May be more appropriate for borrowers who may want to sell or refinance early, can afford to make larger monthly payments after the rate adjusts, or are looking to buy a home when interest rates are relatively high.

Jumbo Loans

These are loans that exceed a specified size (conforming loan amounts).
- Rates are generally higher on jumbo loans than on smaller comparable loans.

FHA Loan

The Federal Housing Administration (FHA) insures a wide variety of mortgages. These loans are designed to meet the needs of homebuyers with low or moderate incomes and feature:
- Low down-payment requirements
- Loan limits based on geographic locations, generally more liberal qualifying guidelines
- Use of gift funds for down payment and/or closing costs.

VA Loans

The Department of Veterans Affairs (formerly the Veterans Administration) guarantees mortgages for qualified veterans and active-duty military personnel and their spouses who are first- or second-time homebuyers. VA loans feature:
- Low or no down-payment requirements
- A wide range of rate, term, and cost options
- Flexible qualifying guidelines
- Use of gift funds for closing costs

Alternative Financing

These programs are designed for borrowers with less-than-perfect credit histories, excessive debt, or previous bankruptcy, foreclosure, or tax delinquency.

No Documentation Loans

Designed for borrowers who are self-employed, on commission, or whose financial situation may be difficult to document. These loans allow borrowers to apply for a loan based on their credit history and stated income.

II. Forms Related to Home Protection

FORM 6-1 Encroachment quitclaim.

This form may be used when there is a question as to whether a neighbor has built a structure that encroaches upon your property, or the neighbor claims your structure encroaches upon his or her property. The form may be used to settle the dispute and allow the structure to remain on the property. If there was bank financing involved in building the structure or there is a separate mortgage on it,

FORM 6-1 continued

the lender may require that a quitclaim form be executed. If a financial institution is not involved and the structure is not the type that will last for years, you probably should use the Settlement Agreement form listed later in this chapter.

[Date] _____

The parties, _____ (Landowner) and _____ (Builder), acknowledge that an issue exists as to whether when the Builder built a recent structure, located on property owned by the owner, and located at _____ _____ (address of the property).
The Owner claims that the entire length of one wall of this structure is located on the property of the Owner.

After receiving the amount of ($ _____), the Owner hereby relinquishes to the recipient all rights and claims to the piece of land of the following dimensions and description, _____, on which the Builder's structure is built.

Only that property immediately located under the structure or that property required to support the structure is covered by this agreement. This contract will hold true for the successors of all parties involved.

Signature of Owner _____ Date _____

Signature of Builder _____ Date _____

ACKNOWLEDGMENT

State of   )

County of   )

On this date, [list names of person(s) who signed above] _____ _____

personally appeared before me and acknowledged that the above signature(s) are valid and binding.

_____

Notary Public

My Commission expires: _____

FORM 6-2   Letter to locate licensed real estate agent.

      Send as Certified Mail, Return Receipt Requested.

[Date] _____

[Name and address of state board of real estate] _____

_____

_____

Re: [Agent's name and license number] _____

Dear Madam/Sir:

I have a claim against the above-listed real estate agent in connection with the sale of our home on ____, 20__. I have been unable to locate the individual. Accordingly, please provide the most recent listed address for the above-named person.

If there is a charge for this service, please advise so that payment can be forwarded.

Sincerely,

_____

Signature

FORM 6-3   Settlement agreement landowners' encroachment.

      This agreement may be used to settle a dispute when it is alleged that one property owner has built a structure that infringes on his or her neighbor's property. This form is often used where the structure involved is not subject to a mortgage or other financing. If the latter is involved, you may wish to use the quitclaim form presented earlier in this chapter.

Date: _____

This agreement was entered into by _____ residing at _____ _____, and _____ residing at _____.

Both Parties Agree and Acknowledge as follows:

    1. That _____ (name) is the owner of property in question, described as _____ _____ (enter description of property).

    2. That the owner of the property that borders the property described above is owned by _____ and described as _____ _____.

FORM 6-3 continued

3. A building on the property described in paragraph 2 above infringes upon the property, as described in paragraph 1 above, by _____ inches.

4. _____ (property owner described in paragraph 1) relinquishes rights to the property as a result of the above-described infringement and agrees that the infringing structure owned by _____ has the right to extend beyond the property line.

5. _____, owner of the infringing building, agrees to pay the property owner _____ the sum of _____ dollars in damages and for the rights to allow the building to remain on the property.

6. This agreement will hold true for all successors of both above-described lots. Upon the elimination of the infringing structure, this agreement will terminate and all property rights revert to the property owner.

Signature _____ Date _____

Signature _____ Date _____

ACKNOWLEDGMENT

State of   )

County of   )

On this date, [list names of person(s) who signed above] personally appeared before me and acknowledged that the above signature(s) are valid and binding.

_____

Notary Public

My Commission expires: _____

FORM 6-4 Deed: grant of easement.

In a grant of easement, a property owner formally gives another person or party the right to use his or her property for a certain use. The most common easement is where an adjoining property owner gives a property owner the right to access his or her property by crossing your property; e.g., you allow the adjoining property owner to have a "shortcut" route across your property.

Recording Requested by [Name and address of person recording grant]: _____

_____

County of   )

State of   )

FORM 6-4   continued

DEED: GRANT OF EASEMENT FOR BOUNDRY FENCE

For Valuable Consideration, receipt of which is acknowledged; I, _____, grantor,

to the owners of the adjoining property, to wit [describe easement]: _____

_____

In consideration for construction of a boundary fence between the parties to this deed, grantor grants to grantee, its successors, and assigns, the right to erect, construct, or replace a boundary fence between the properties of the grantor and the grantee at the present location of boundary fence which is located on the below-described land. This Deed shall act as a grant of easement against the property located in the State of _____, County of _____, and described as follows: _____

_____

Executed on _____, 20__ at [city and state] _____.

Signature of person granting easement: _____

ACKNOWLEDGMENT

State of   )

County of   )

On this __ day of _____, 20__, before me, the undersigned, a Notary Public in and

for the State of _____, personally appeared _____, personally known to me or proved to me on the basis of satisfactory evidence to be the person whose name is subscribed to the within instrument, and acknowledged to me that he executed it.

WITNESS my hand and official Seal.

_____

Notary Public in and for said State

My Commission expires: _____

FORM 6-5   Deed: grant of easement (limited).

Recording Requested by [name and address of person recording grant]: _____

_____

State of   )

County of   )

DEED: GRANT OF EASEMENT (LIMITED)

For Valuable Consideration, receipt of which is acknowledged; I, _____, grantor, to the owners of the adjoining property, to wit [describe property]: _____

In consideration for construction of a boundary fence between the parties to this deed, grantor grants to grantee, its successors, and assigns, the right to erect, construct, or replace a boundary fence between the properties of the grantor and the grantee at the present location of boundary fence which is located on the below described land. This Deed shall act as a grant of easement

against the property located in the State of _____, County of _____, and described as follows [describe easement]: _____

_____

_____

This grant of easement shall terminate without further action on the part of the grantor _____ years from the date of the execution of this document.

Executed on _____, 20__ at [city and state] _____.

_____

[Signature of person granting easement]

ACKNOWLEDGMENT

State of   )

County of   )

On this ____ day of _____, 20 __, before me, the undersigned, a Notary Public in and for the State of _____, personally appeared _____, personally known to me or proved to me on the basis of satisfactory evidence to be the person whose name is subscribed to the within instrument, and acknowledged to me that he/she executed it.

WITNESS my hand and official Seal.

_____

Notary Public in and for Said State

FORM 6-6 Deed: grant of easement (restricted).

Recording Requested by [name address of person recording grant]: _____

_____

County of   )

State of   )

DEED: GRANT OF EASEMENT (RESTRICTED)

For Valuable Consideration, receipt of which is acknowledged; I, _____, grantor, to the owners of the adjoining property, to wit: _____.

The Grantor grants to grantee, its successors, and assigns, the right to pass through the properties of the grantor on the private road presently located on the below-described land.

This Deed shall act as a grant of easement against the property located in the State of _____ _____, County of _____, and described as follows [describe property]: _____

_____

This grant of easement shall terminate without further action on the part of the grantor _____ years from the date of the execution of this document.

This grant of easement is limited only to personal and noncommercial travel on the subject road. Vehicles exceeding the following weights (_____) or with more than two axles may not use the subject road.

Executed on _____, 20__ at [city and state] _____.

_____

[Signature of person granting easement]

ACKNOWLEDGMENT

State of   )

County of   )

On this _____ day of ____, 20 __, before me, the undersigned, a Notary Public in and for the State of _____, personally appeared _____ personally known to me or proved to me on the basis of satisfactory evidence to be the person whose name is subscribed to the within instrument, and acknowledged to me that he executed it.

WITNESS my hand and official Seal.

_____

Notary Public in and for Said State

My Commission expires: _____

FORM 6-7   Declaration of covenants and restrictions.

This form may be used to place deed restrictions on property. It is used most often in areas where there are no zoning ordinances, e.g., Houston, Texas. For example, if you own a vacant lot that adjoins your home that you want to sell, but you do not want certain activities or businesses on the lot, the recording of this form would prevent those activities.

State of   )

County of   )

DECLARATION OF COVENANTS AND RESTRICTIONS

BE IT KNOWN, that [name of person making declarations] _____,
Declarant, County of _____, State of _____, hereby declares that the
property located in the County of _____ State of _____; the following
described real property located in _____, County of _____, State of
_____, more particularly described as: [enter legal description at this point] is subject to the
following restrictions [list the restrictions]: _____

_____

The Declarant imposes on such property beneficial restrictions under a general plan of
improvement for the benefit of all future owners thereof. The parcels of property conveyed
from the original parcel described above shall be subject to the above restrictions.

SIGNED BY the hands of said Declarant(s) this _____ day of _____, 20__.

_____

Signature

ACKNOWLEDGMENT

State of   )

County of   )

On this date, [list names of person(s) who signed above] _____ personally
appeared before me and acknowledged that the above signature(s) are valid and binding.

_____

Notary Public

My Commission expires: _____

FORM 6-8 Notice of agreement regarding (disputed) boundary line.

State of   )

County of   )

AGREEMENT REGARDING (DISPUTED) BOUNDARY LINE

BE IT KNOWN, that the below-signed property holders to once and forever settle the dispute regarding the boundary lines of their property have agreed that the [describe boundary line, e.g., north/south] boundary line between their respective properties is located at [describe in detail the location of the boundary line]: _____

_____

This agreement affects and is binding on the following parcels of property [legal description of the two parcels of land affected by the boundary line agreement]: _____

_____

SIGNED BY the hands of said Declarant(s) this _____ day of _____, 20__.

_____

Signature

ACKNOWLEDGMENT

State of   )

County of   )

On this date, [list names of person(s) who signed above] _____
personally appeared before me and acknowledged that the above signature(s) are valid and binding.

_____

Notary Public

My Commission expires: _____

FORM 6-9 Notice of agreement regarding changing boundary lines.

State of   )

County of   )

AGREEMENT REGARDING BOUNDARY LINE

BE IT KNOWN, that the below-signed property holders for good and valuable consideration, receipt of which is hereby acknowledged, the boundary lines of their property have agreed to change the [describe boundary line, e.g., north/south] _____ _____ boundary line between their respective properties. The new boundary line is located at [describe in detail the location of the boundary line]: _____ _____ _____

This agreement affects and is binding on the following parcels of property [legal description of the two parcels of land affected by the boundary line agreement]: _____ _____ _____

SIGNED BY the hands of said Declarant(s) this __ day of _____, 20__.

_____

Signature

ACKNOWLEDGMENT

State of   )

County of   )

On this date, [list names of person(s) who signed above] _____ _____ personally appeared before me and acknowledged that the above signature(s) are valid and binding.

_____

Notary Public

My Commission expires: _____

III. Forms Related to Home Maintenance

FORM 6-10 Notice of termination of service.

This form may be used by the homeowner to terminate almost any type of service, e.g., lawn, pool care, dog walking.

Date: _____

To: _____

Dear Sir/Madam:

This letter is to inform you that we have decided to terminate our service with your company. Under our service agreement, your company was required to provide (indicate service, for example, weekly lawn service). The service provided was not satisfactory in that (indicate reason, for example, the lawn was not properly cut). [or] The (indicate type of service) _____ _____ has not been performed as agreed under our contract with your company. Accordingly after _____ (date), we will not be responsible for: (indicate service, for example, lawn service).

If you have any questions, please contact us at:

Sincerely,

_____

Homeowner

FORM 6-11 Notice of sale of home.

(Date) _____

To: _____

Dear Sir/Madam:

This letter is to inform you that we have sold our home located at _____ _____ (address).

Accordingly, after _____ (date), we will not be responsible for: (indicate service, e.g., lawn service or pool cleaning) _____.

We appreciate your service and will recommend your company to the new owner.

If you have any questions, please contact us at:

Sincerely,

_____

Homeowner

FORM 6-12 Agreement for maintenance of common wall.

Date: _____

This agreement is made between _____ (name and address),

and _____ (name and address).

TERMS OF AGREEMENT

1. _____ is the owner of property and a house located at _____
   _____ (address).

2. _____ is the owner of property and a house located at _____
   _____ (address).

3. The properties have a common boundary that is divided by a common wall.

4. A retaining wall extending _____ feet along the common boundary was erected for
   the purposes of protecting the property of the adjoining landowners.

5. The parties agree to pay for all the costs associated with maintaining the retaining wall as
   follows: (explain how the parties intend to pay the costs of the wall).

Signature _____   Date _____

Signature _____   Date _____

Signature of Witness _____   Date _____

FORM 6-13 Construction along common boundary.

Date _____

This agreement is made between _____, residing at _____,

and _____, residing at _____.

FACTS

1. The owner of the property located at _____ (referred to as
   the Owner) desires to do construction along the adjoining property line of the property
   owned by _____ (referred to as Neighbor).

2. The proposed building will extend __ feet into the ground along the boundary line.

3. The Owner will take all necessary precautions to prevent damage to adjoining Neighbor's
   property, if Neighbor agrees to the terms of this excavation. The Owner will be liable for
   any damages to Neighbor's property as a result of the proposed excavation.

FORM 6-13 continued

4. The Owner may continue with proposed construction along the boundary line at no cost to adjoining landowner as agreed by both parties.

5. The Owner will be held responsible for all damages to adjoining Neighbor's property.

Signature of Owner: _____ Date _____

Signature of Neighbor: _____ Date _____

Signature of Witness: _____ Date _____

FORM 6-14 Invitation for quotation.

This letter may be used to invite quotes for a home improvement project.

DATE: _____

To: _____

Re: Price quotations on [_____]

Dear Sir/Madam:

We are interested in [adding a pool to our backyard] [describe the size, etc., of the improvement] _____. We would like the construction to be completed by [date] _____.

Please provide us with a firm quote on the above-listed project. We would also need information regarding warranties involved.

Please provide information regarding the following questions:

1. Are delivery costs included in your quotes? Unless otherwise stated, we will assume the delivery costs are included in your price quotes.

2. What is the construction time from the signing of a contract until completion of the project?

3. Are your quotes inclusive or exclusive of all taxes and permit fees? Unless otherwise stated, we will assume that your quotes are inclusive of these items.

4. What are your terms of payment? Are there any discounts for early payment of invoices?

5. Please include the expiration date of all price quotes.

Any price quotes received must be firm.

Sincerely,

_____

Signature

FORM 6-15 Assignment of a mechanic's or materials' lien.

A mechanic's lien is where a property owner owes you money for work you did on his or her property. A materials' lien is a lien where materials have been supplied to a property owner. For example, you construct a new fence on your property. Your neighbor likes it and wishes to have one built on his property but currently does not have the financial resources to purchase the necessary supplies. A new fence on his property would increase your property value. If you purchase the supplies, then you, if permitted by state statute, may file a materials' lien on his property to ensure payment of the supplies.

The State of:)

The County of:)

Assignment of a Mechanic's or Materials' Lien

For good and valuable consideration, receipt of which is hereby acknowledged, on [date] _____, I, [name] _____ of the City of _____, County of _____, State of ____, assigned all my interest and benefit together with all right and interest in and to the debt there secured in the following mechanic's (or materials') lien[describe lien including property covered by lien.]: _____

_____

The affidavit and claim for which is dated [date of lien] _____ and which was executed by [name of person executing lien] _____ and which is filed in [location where lien filed] _____ and recorded on Page __, Volume __, of the Records of [describe records] _____ to: [person to whom contract was assigned, including address] _____

_____

WITNESSED this ____ day of _____, 20__.

_____

_____

ACKNOWLEDGMENT

State of   )

County of   )

On this date, [list names of person(s) who signed above] personally appeared before me and acknowledged that the above signature(s) are valid and binding.

_____

Notary Public

My Commission expires: _____

IV. Forms Related to the Homestead

A homestead is your home. It is where you live. The concept of "homestead" is an English legal tradition. The chief reason a person would want his or her home designated as a homestead is to protect the home from being taken by creditors. In addition, many states provide property tax relief for property designated as a homestead. In some states the declaration of a homestead is automatic; in others, a declaration must be filed. Many states restrict the types of loans that may be obtained when using your homestead as collateral for the loan. For example, in some states you may not obtain a second mortgage on your home unless it is for home improvement. In many states, a homestead may not be sold without the signatures of both spouses, even if the property is owned by only one of the spouses. If the restrictions hamper your plans, then you may wish to file an abandonment of your homestead.

FORM 6-16 Declaration of homestead (by unmarried person).

State of   )

County of   )

DECLARATION OF HOMESTEAD

BE IT KNOWN, that [name of person making the declaration] _____,
Declarant, County of _____, State of _____, hereby declares that the property located in the County of _____, State of _____; the following described real property located in _____, County of _____, State of _____, more particularity described as: [enter legal description at this point] _____ is our homestead.

I further declare that:

1. I am unmarried and the head of a family. My family consists of the following members:

2. The above described property is currently occupied and resided in by my family and me as our home and is therefore (our)(my) homestead.

3. I have made no former declarations of homestead [or the previous declaration of homestead made by me on (date) has been abandoned].

SIGNED BY the hands of said Declarant(s) this __ day of _____, 20__.

_____
Signature

FORM 6-16 continued

ACKNOWLEDGMENT

State of   )

County of   )

On this date, [list name(s) of person(s) who signed above] personally appeared before me and acknowledged that the above signature(s) are valid and binding.

_____

Notary Public

My Commission expires: _____

FORM 6-17 Declaration of homestead (married couple).

State of   )

County of   )

DECLARATION OF HOMESTEAD

BE IT KNOWN, that we, [names of married couple making the declaration] _____
_____, Declarants,

County of _____, State of _____, hereby declare that the property located in the County of _____, State of _____; the following described real property located in _____ County of _____, State of _____, more particularity described as: [enter legal description at this point] is our homestead _____.

We further declare that:

1. We are husband and wife and the heads of a family. Our family consists of the following members:

2. The above-described property is currently occupied and resided in by our family and us as our home and is therefore our homestead.

3. We have made no former declarations of homestead [or the previous declaration of homestead made by us on (date) _____ has been abandoned].

SIGNED BY the hands of said Declarant(s) this _____ day of _____, 20__.

_____

Signature

FORM 6-17 continued

ACKNOWLEDGMENT

State of   )

County of   )

On this date, [list name(s) of person(s) who signed above] _____

_____ personally appeared before me and acknowledged that the above signature(s) are valid and binding.

_____

Notary Public

My Commission expires: _____

FORM 6-18 Declaration of homestead (by person not head of household).

State of   )

County of   )

DECLARATION OF HOMESTEAD

BE IT KNOWN, that I, [name of person making the declaration] _____,
Declarant, County of _____, State of _____, hereby declare that the property
located in the County of _____, State of _____; the following described real
property located in _____, County of _____, State of _____,
more particularly described as: [enter legal description at this point] _____

_____

_____ is my homestead.

I further declare that:

   1. I am an unmarried person.

   2. The above-described property is currently occupied and resided in by me as my home and is therefore my homestead.

   3. I have made no former declarations of homestead [or the previous declaration of homestead made by me on (date) has been abandoned].

SIGNED BY the hands of said Declarant(s) this _____ day of _____, 20__.

_____

Signature

FORM 6-18   continued

ACKNOWLEDGMENT

State of   )

County of   )

On this date, [list name(s) of person(s) who signed above] _____
personally appeared before me and acknowledged that the above signature(s) are valid and
binding.

_____

Notary Public

My Commission expires: _____

FORM 6-19   Abandonment of homestead (by single head of household).

State of   )

County of   )

ABANDONMENT OF HOMESTEAD

BE IT KNOWN, that I, [name], Declarant, County of _____, State of _____,
hereby abandoned the homestead declared by me on [date] _____ and recorded on
[date recorded] _____ in Book __, Page ___, of the official records of _____
County, _____, state on that the property located in the County of _____,
State of _____; the following described real property located in _____,
County of ____, State of ____, more particularity described as [enter legal description at this
point]: _____

At the time that the homestead was declared, I was an unmarried head of household. My present status is unmarried, head of household.

SIGNED BY the hands of said Declarant(s) this ____ day of _____, 20__.

_____

Signature

ACKNOWLEDGMENT

State of   )

County of   )

On this date, [list name(s) of person(s) who signed above] _____
_____ personally appeared before me and acknowledged that the above signature(s) are valid and binding.

_____

Notary Public

My Commission expires: _____

FORM 6-20   Abandonment of homestead (by single person not head of household).

State of   )

County of   )

ABANDONMENT OF HOMESTEAD

BE IT KNOWN, that I, [name], Declarant, County of _____, State of _____, hereby abandoned the homestead declared by me on [date] and recorded _____ on [date recorded] in Book ____, page ____, of the official records of _____, County, _____, State, on property located in the County of _____, State of _____; the following described real property located in _____, County of _____, State of _____, more particularity described as [enter legal description at this point]:

_____

_____

SIGNED BY the hands of said Declarant(s) this ____ day of ____, 20__.

_____
Signature

ACKNOWLEDGMENT

State of   )

County of   )

On this date, [list name(s) of person(s) who signed above] personally appeared before me and acknowledged that the above signature(s) are valid and binding.

_____
Notary Public

My Commission expires: _____

FORM 6-21   Abandonment of Homestead (by married couple).

State of   )

County of   )

ABANDONMENT OF HOMESTEAD

BE IT KNOWN, that we, [names of married couple making the declaration], Declarants, County of _____, State of _____, hereby abandoned the homestead declared by us on [date] _____ and recorded on [date recorded] _____ in Book ____, page ____ of the official records of County, on the property located in the County of _____, State of _____; the following described real property located in _____, County of _____, State of _____, more particularity described as: [enter legal description at this point] _____

SIGNED BY the hands of said Declarant(s) this _____ day of _____, 20__.

_____

Signature

_____

Signature

ACKNOWLEDGMENT

State of   )

County of   )

On this date, [list name(s) of person(s) who signed above] _____
_____ personally appeared before me and acknowledged that the above signature(s) are valid and binding.

_____

Notary Public

My Commission expires: _____

7

Contractor Forms

Forms and Information in This Chapter

FORM 7-1 Sample contract with an independent contractor.

This agreement made between _____ (Homeowner) and
_____ (Contractor) whereas the Contractor intends to perform certain tasks for the Homeowner.

The Homeowner's address is _____, the work will be performed at (same address)(at the property located at) _____

The Contractor's principal place of business is located at the following address:_____
_____

The Contractor declares that he/she is engaged in an independent business and will comply
with all state and federal laws regarding taxes and licenses. In addition, Contractor declares
that he/she is engaged in the same business for other Homeowners and that the Homeowner
is not the only customer of the Contractor.

The Parties to this contract agree as follows:

    1. The Contractor will perform the following services for the Homeowner:

FORM 7-1 continued

2. The Homeowner shall pay the Contractor according to the following terms and conditions:

3. The Contractor shall furnish all equipment, tools, and supplies to accomplish the tasks except:_____

4. The Contractor maintains control over the manner in which the tasks are to be performed and the products made. The Homeowner agrees to accept and pay as set forth above all products, tasks, etc., that meet the agreed specifications.

5. Contractor understands that no payroll taxes or worker's compensation taxes will be withheld by the Homeowner and that these items are the responsibility of the Contractor.

6. The agreement will terminate on _____.

Homeowner:_____   Contractor: _____

Dated: _____   Dated: _____

FORM 7-2   Determination of worker status.

The determination of worker status is used when you are unsure as to whether the individual working for you is considered a contractor or an employee for tax and worker's compensation purposes. A homeowner needs to determine if the individual is an employee or independent contractor. If the individual is considered by the IRS to be an employee, you are required to withhold FICA (social security) taxes and income taxes. You may also be subject to state worker's compensation laws. In many cases, a homeowner has treated a worker as an independent contractor and has been assessed penalties by the IRS.

FORM 7-2 continued

Form **SS-8** (Rev. June 2003) Department of the Treasury Internal Revenue Service	**Determination of Worker Status for Purposes of Federal Employment Taxes and Income Tax Withholding**	OMB No. 1545-0004

Name of firm (or person) for whom the worker performed services	Worker's name

Firm's address (include street address, apt. or suite no., city, state, and ZIP code)	Worker's address (include street address, apt. or suite no., city, state, and ZIP code)

Trade name	Telephone number (include area code) ( )	Worker's social security number

Telephone number (include area code) ( )	Firm's employer identification number	Worker's employer identification number (if any)

If the worker is paid by a firm other than the one listed on this form for these services, enter the name, address, and employer identification number of the payer.

Important Information Needed To Process Your Request

We must have your permission to disclose your name and the information on this form and any attachments to other parties involved with this request. **Do we have your permission to disclose this information?** . . . . ☐ **Yes** ☐ **No**
If you answered "No" or did not mark a box, we will not process your request and will not issue a determination.

You must answer ALL items OR mark them "Unknown" or "Does not apply." If you need more space, attach another sheet.

A This form is being completed by: ☐ Firm ☐ Worker; for services performed _____ to _____ .
(beginning date)   (ending date)

B Explain your reason(s) for filing this form (e.g., you received a bill from the IRS, you believe you received a Form 1099 or Form W-2 erroneously, you are unable to get worker's compensation benefits, you were audited or are being audited by the IRS). ....
....
....
....
....

C Total number of workers who performed or are performing the same or similar services _____ .

D How did the worker obtain the job? ☐ Application ☐ Bid ☐ Employment Agency ☐ Other (specify) _____ .

E Attach copies of all supporting documentation (contracts, invoices, memos, Forms W-2, Forms 1099, IRS closing agreements, IRS rulings, etc.). In addition, please inform us of any current or past litigation concerning the worker's status. If no income reporting forms (Form 1099-MISC or W-2) were furnished to the worker, enter the amount of income earned for the year(s) at issue $ _____ .

F Describe the firm's business. ....
....
....
....

G Describe the work done by the worker and provide the worker's job title. ....
....
....
....
....

H Explain why you believe the worker is an employee or an independent contractor. ....
....
....
....

I Did the worker perform services for the firm before getting this position? . . . . ☐ Yes ☐ No ☐ N/A
If "Yes," what were the dates of the prior service? ....
If "Yes," explain the differences, if any, between the current and prior service. ....
....
....
....

J If the work is done under a written agreement between the firm and the worker, attach a copy (preferably signed by both parties). Describe the terms and conditions of the work arrangement. ....
....

For Privacy Act and Paperwork Reduction Act Notice, see page 5.   Cat. No. 16106T   Form **SS-8** (Rev. 6-2003)

FORM 7-2 continued

Form SS-8 (Rev. 6-2003)

Part I Behavioral Control

1 What specific training and/or instruction is the worker given by the firm? ....
....

2 How does the worker receive work assignments? ....
....

3 Who determines the methods by which the assignments are performed? ....

4 Who is the worker required to contact if problems or complaints arise and who is responsible for their resolution? ....
....

5 What types of reports are required from the worker? Attach examples. ....
....

6 Describe the worker's daily routine (i.e., schedule, hours, etc.). ....
....
....

7 At what location(s) does the worker perform services (e.g., firm's premises, own shop or office, home, customer's location, etc.)? ....
....

8 Describe any meetings the worker is required to attend and any penalties for not attending (e.g., sales meetings, monthly meetings, staff
meetings, etc.). ....

9 Is the worker required to provide the services personally? . . . . □ **Yes** □ **No**

10 If substitutes or helpers are needed, who hires them? ....

11 If the worker hires the substitutes or helpers, is approval required? . . . . □ **Yes** □ **No**
If "Yes," by whom? ....

12 Who pays the substitutes or helpers? ....

13 Is the worker reimbursed if the worker pays the substitutes or helpers? . . . . □ **Yes** □ **No**
If "Yes," by whom?

Part II Financial Control

1 List the supplies, equipment, materials, and property provided by each party:
The firm ....
The worker ....
Other party ....

2 Does the worker lease equipment? . . . . □ **Yes** □ **No**
If "Yes," what are the terms of the lease? (Attach a copy or explanatory statement.) ....
....

3 What expenses are incurred by the worker in the performance of services for the firm? ....
....

4 Specify which, if any, expenses are reimbursed by:
The firm ....
Other party ....

5 Type of pay the worker receives: □ Salary   □ Commission   □ Hourly Wage   □ Piece Work
□ Lump Sum   □ Other (specify) ....
If type of pay is commission, and the firm guarantees a minimum amount of pay, specify amount $ _____ .

6 Is the worker allowed a drawing account for advances? . . . . □ **Yes** □ **No**
If "Yes," how often? ....
Specify any restrictions. ....

7 Whom does the customer pay? . . . . □ Firm   □ Worker
If worker, does the worker pay the total amount to the firm? □ **Yes** □ **No**   If "No," explain. ....
....

8 Does the firm carry worker's compensation insurance on the worker? . . . . □ **Yes** □ **No**

9 What economic loss or financial risk, if any, can the worker incur beyond the normal loss of salary (e.g., loss or damage of equipment,
material, etc.)? ....
....

Form **SS-8** (Rev. 6-2003)

FORM 7-2 continued

Part III   **Relationship of the Worker and Firm**

1   List the benefits available to the worker (e.g., paid vacations, sick pay, pensions, bonuses). ---------------------------------------

2   Can the relationship be terminated by either party without incurring liability or penalty? . . . . ☐ **Yes** ☐ **No**
     If "No," explain your answer. --

3   Does the worker perform similar services for others? . . . . ☐ **Yes** ☐ **No**
     If "Yes," is the worker required to get approval from the firm? . . . . ☐ **Yes** ☐ **No**

4   Describe any agreements prohibiting competition between the worker and the firm while the worker is performing services or during any later
     period. Attach any available documentation. ---

5   Is the worker a member of a union? . . . . ☐ **Yes** ☐ **No**

6   What type of advertising, if any, does the worker do (e.g., a business listing in a directory, business cards, etc.)? Provide copies, if applicable.
     ----

7   If the worker assembles or processes a product at home, who provides the materials and instructions or pattern? ---------------------
     ----

8   What does the worker do with the finished product (e.g., return it to the firm, provide it to another party, or sell it)? --------------------
     ----

9   How does the firm represent the worker to its customers (e.g., employee, partner, representative, or contractor)? ---------------------
     ----

10 If the worker no longer performs services for the firm, how did the relationship end? ------------------------------
     ----

Part IV   **For Service Providers or Salespersons**—Complete this part if the worker provided a service directly to
              customers or is a salesperson.

1   What are the worker's responsibilities in soliciting new customers? --
     ----

2   Who provides the worker with leads to prospective customers? ---

3   Describe any reporting requirements pertaining to the leads. --
     ----

4   What terms and conditions of sale, if any, are required by the firm? --

5   Are orders submitted to and subject to approval by the firm? . . . . ☐ **Yes** ☐ **No**

6   Who determines the worker's territory? ---

7   Did the worker pay for the privilege of serving customers on the route or in the territory? . . . . ☐ **Yes** ☐ **No**
     If "Yes," whom did the worker pay? ---
     If "Yes," how much did the worker pay? . . . . $ _____ .

8   Where does the worker sell the product (e.g., in a home, retail establishment, etc.)? -------------------------------
     ----

9   List the product and/or services distributed by the worker (e.g., meat, vegetables, fruit, bakery products, beverages, or laundry or dry cleaning
     services). If more than one type of product and/or service is distributed, specify the principal one. ----------------------
     ----

10 Does the worker sell life insurance full time? . . . . ☐ **Yes** ☐ **No**

11 Does the worker sell other types of insurance for the firm? . . . . ☐ **Yes** ☐ **No**
     If "Yes," enter the percentage of the worker's total working time spent in selling other types of insurance. . . . _____%

12 If the worker solicits orders from wholesalers, retailers, contractors, or operators of hotels, restaurants, or other similar
     establishments, enter the percentage of the worker's time spent in the solicitation. . . . . _____%

13 Is the merchandise purchased by the customers for resale or use in their business operations? . . . . . . ☐ **Yes** ☐ **No**
     Describe the merchandise and state whether it is equipment installed on the customers' premises. -----------------------
     ----

Part V   **Signature** (see page 4)

Under penalties of perjury, I declare that I have examined this request, including accompanying documents, and to the best of my knowledge and belief, the facts
presented are true, correct, and complete.

Signature ▶ _____   Title ▶ _____   Date ▶ _____
                    (Type or print name below)

FORM 7-2 continued

General Instructions

Section references are to the Internal Revenue Code unless otherwise noted.

Purpose

Firms and workers file Form SS-8 to request a determination of the status of a worker for purposes of Federal employment taxes and income tax withholding.

A Form SS-8 determination may be requested only in order to resolve Federal tax matters. If Form SS-8 is submitted for a tax year for which the statute of limitations on the tax return has expired, a determination letter will not be issued. The statute of limitations expires 3 years from the due date of the tax return or the date filed, whichever is later.

The IRS does not issue a determination letter for proposed transactions or on hypothetical situations. We may, however, issue an information letter when it is considered appropriate.

Definition

Firm. For the purposes of this form, the term "firm" means any individual, business enterprise, organization, state, or other entity for which a worker has performed services. The firm may or may not have paid the worker directly for these services. **If the firm was not responsible for payment for services, be sure to enter the name, address, and employer identification number of the payer on the first page of Form SS-8 below the identifying information for the firm and the worker.**

The SS-8 Determination Process

The IRS will acknowledge the receipt of your Form SS-8. Because there are usually two (or more) parties who could be affected by a determination of employment status, the IRS attempts to get information from all parties involved by sending those parties blank Forms SS-8 for completion. The case will be assigned to a technician who will review the facts, apply the law, and render a decision. The technician may ask for additional information from the requestor, from other involved parties, or from third parties that could help clarify the work relationship before rendering a decision. The IRS will generally issue a formal determination to the firm or payer (if that is a different entity), and will send a copy to the worker. A determination letter applies only to a worker (or a class of workers) requesting it, and the decision is binding on the IRS. In certain cases, a formal determination will not be issued. Instead, an information letter may be issued. Although an information letter is advisory only and is not binding on the IRS, it may be used to assist the worker to fulfill his or her Federal tax obligations.

Neither the SS-8 determination process nor the review of any records in connection with the determination constitutes an examination (audit) of any Federal tax return. If the periods under consideration have previously been examined, the SS-8 determination process will not constitute a reexamination under IRS reopening procedures. Because this is not an examination of any Federal tax return, the appeal rights available in connection with an examination do not apply to an SS-8 determination. However, if you disagree with a determination and you have additional information concerning the work relationship that you believe was not previously considered, you may request that the determining office reconsider the determination.

Completing Form SS-8

Answer all questions as completely as possible. Attach additional sheets if you need more space. Provide information for all years the worker provided services for the firm. Determinations are based on the entire relationship between the firm and the worker.

Additional copies of this form may be obtained by calling 1-800-829-4933 or from the IRS website at **www.irs.gov.**

Fee

There is no fee for requesting an SS-8 determination letter.

Signature

Form SS-8 must be signed and dated by the taxpayer. A stamped signature will not be accepted.

The person who signs for a corporation must be an officer of the corporation who has personal knowledge of the facts. If the corporation is a member of an affiliated group filing a consolidated return, it must be signed by an officer of the common parent of the group.

The person signing for a trust, partnership, or limited liability company must be, respectively, a trustee, general partner, or member-manager who has personal knowledge of the facts.

Where To File

Send the completed Form SS-8 to the address listed below for the firm's location. However, for cases involving Federal agencies, send Form SS-8 to the Internal Revenue Service, Attn: CC:CORP:T:C, Ben Franklin Station, P.O. Box 7604, Washington, DC 20044.

Firm's location:	Send to:
Alaska, Arizona, Arkansas, California, Colorado, Hawaii, Idaho, Illinois, Iowa, Kansas, Minnesota, Missouri, Montana, Nebraska, Nevada, New Mexico, North Dakota, Oklahoma, Oregon, South Dakota, Texas, Utah, Washington, Wisconsin, Wyoming, American Samoa, Guam, Puerto Rico, U.S. Virgin Islands	Internal Revenue Service SS-8 Determinations P.O. Box 630 Stop 631 Holtsville, NY 11742-0630
Alabama, Connecticut, Delaware, District of Columbia, Florida, Georgia, Indiana, Kentucky, Louisiana, Maine, Maryland, Massachusetts, Michigan, Mississippi, New Hampshire, New Jersey, New York, North Carolina, Ohio, Pennsylvania, Rhode Island, South Carolina, Tennessee, Vermont, Virginia, West Virginia, all other locations not listed	Internal Revenue Service SS-8 Determinations 40 Lakemont Road Newport, VT 05855-1555

Instructions for Workers

If you are requesting a determination for more than one firm, complete a separate Form SS-8 for each firm.

 Form SS-8 is not a claim for refund of social security and Medicare taxes or Federal income tax withholding.

If the IRS determines that you are an employee, you are responsible for filing an amended return for any corrections related to this decision. A determination that a worker is an employee does not necessarily reduce any current or prior tax liability. For more information, call 1-800-829-1040.

FORM 7-2 continued

Time for filing a claim for refund. Generally, you must file your claim for a credit or refund within 3 years from the date your original return was filed or within 2 years from the date the tax was paid, whichever is later.

Filing Form SS-8 does not prevent the expiration of the time in which a claim for a refund must be filed. If you are concerned about a refund, and the statute of limitations for filing a claim for refund for the year(s) at issue has not yet expired, you should file **Form 1040X,** Amended U.S. Individual Income Tax Return, to protect your statute of limitations. File a separate Form 1040X for each year.

On the Form 1040X you file, do not complete lines 1 through 24 on the form. Write "Protective Claim" at the top of the form, sign and date it. In addition, you should enter the following statement in Part II, Explanation of Changes to Income, Deductions, and Credits: "Filed Form SS-8 with the Internal Revenue Service Office in (Holtsville, NY; Newport, VT; or Washington, DC; as appropriate). By filing this protective claim, I reserve the right to file a claim for any refund that may be due after a determination of my employment tax status has been completed."

Filing Form SS-8 does not alter the requirement to timely file an income tax return. Do not delay filing your tax return in anticipation of an answer to your SS-8 request. In addition, if applicable, do not delay in responding to a request for payment while waiting for a determination of your worker status.

Instructions for Firms

If a **worker** has requested a determination of his or her status while working for you, you will receive a request from the IRS to complete a Form SS-8. In cases of this type, the IRS usually gives each party an opportunity to present a statement of the facts because any decision will affect the employment tax status of the parties. Failure to respond to this request will not prevent the IRS from issuing a determination letter based on the information he or she has made available so that the worker may fulfill his or her Federal tax obligations. However, the information that you provide is extremely valuable in determining the status of the worker.

If **you** are requesting a determination for a particular class of worker, complete the form for **one** individual who is representative of the class of workers whose status is in question. If you want a written determination for more than one class of workers, complete a separate Form SS-8 for one worker from each class whose status is typical of that class. A written determination for any worker will apply to other workers of the same class if the facts are not materially different for these workers. Please provide a list of names and addresses of all workers potentially affected by this determination.

If you have a reasonable basis for not treating a worker as an employee, you may be relieved from having to pay employment taxes for that worker under section 530 of the 1978 Revenue Act. However, this relief provision cannot be

considered in conjunction with a Form SS-8 determination because the determination does not constitute an examination of any tax return. For more information regarding section 530 of the 1978 Revenue Act and to determine if you qualify for relief under this section, you may visit the IRS website at **www.irs.gov**.

Privacy Act and Paperwork Reduction Act Notice. We ask for the information on this form to carry out the Internal Revenue laws of the United States. This information will be used to determine the employment status of the worker(s) described on the form. Subtitle C, Employment Taxes, of the Internal Revenue Code imposes employment taxes on wages. Sections 3121(d), 3306(a), and 3401(c) and (d) and the related regulations define employee and employer for purposes of employment taxes imposed under Subtitle C. Section 6001 authorizes the IRS to request information needed to determine if a worker(s) or firm is subject to these taxes. Section 6109 requires you to provide your taxpayer identification number. Neither workers nor firms are required to request a status determination, but if you choose to do so, you must provide the information requested on this form. Failure to provide the requested information may prevent us from making a status determination. If any worker or the firm has requested a status determination and you are being asked to provide information for use in that determination, you are not required to provide the requested information. However, failure to provide such information will prevent the IRS from considering it in making the status determination. Providing false or fraudulent information may subject you to penalties. Routine uses of this information include providing it to the Department of Justice for use in civil and criminal litigation, to the Social Security Administration for the administration of social security programs, and to cities, states, and the District of Columbia for the administration of their tax laws. We may also disclose this information to Federal and state agencies to enforce Federal nontax criminal laws and to combat terrorism. We may provide this information to the affected worker(s) or the firm as part of the status determination process.

You are not required to provide the information requested on a form that is subject to the Paperwork Reduction Act unless the form displays a valid OMB control number. Books or records relating to a form or its instructions must be retained as long as their contents may become material in the administration of any Internal Revenue law. Generally, tax returns and return information are confidential, as required by section 6103.

The time needed to complete and file this form will vary depending on individual circumstances. The estimated average time is: **Recordkeeping,** 22 hrs.; **Learning about the law or the form,** 47 min.; and **Preparing and sending the form to the IRS,** 1 hr., 11 min. If you have comments concerning the accuracy of these time estimates or suggestions for making this form simpler, we would be happy to hear from you. You can write to the Tax Products Coordinating Committee, Western Area Distribution Center, Rancho Cordova, CA 95743-0001. **Do not** send the tax form to this address. Instead, see **Where To File** on page 4.

FORM 7-3 Release of lien.

This form may be used to clear a lien that has been filed against your property. Note that you will be required to have the lienholder sign the release.

Date:_____

Notice is hereby given that the below described lienholder has released the lien filed on the real property known as: [street address, including city and state]: _____

_____

Said real estate is more particularly described in Book or Volume _____, page __ of the County Registry of Deeds.

_____ is listed as the owner of the said property.

The notice of lien was duly recorded in Book, __, page __ of the Lien Records of _____ _____ County.

The Lienholder releases the above described property and owner from all liability arising from the labor performed or the materials furnished by the unsigned lienholder. The Lien is hereby discharged.

Dated: _____

Signed: _____

ACKNOWLEDGMENT

State of   )

County of   )

On this date, [list names of person(s) who signed above] _____
_____ personally appeared before me and acknowledged the foregoing.

_____   _____
Notary Public   Date expired

My Commission expires: _____

FORM 7-4 Agreement to extend performance date.

This form is used to extend the performance date of a contract. For example, if you hire a contractor to install a pool or build a garage on your property and the contractor is having problems completing the project by the original performance date, you may agree to extend the date.

For good and valuable consideration, [individual having work accomplished, generally the homeowner] _____, First Party and [name of independent contractor] _____, Contractor in and to a certain agreement to: [indicate service to be performed] _____

dated _____ [date of original agreement] do hereby agree:

1. That the original performance date was on or before [date]. _____

2. That the parties agree that the said performance cannot reasonably be completed by that date.

3. The parties hereby mutually agree to extend the date of performance to [new date]. Time being of the essence, and there are no other changes in terms or additional time allowed.

This agreement shall be binding on and inure to the benefit of the parties, their assigns and successors.

Signed this ____ day of _____, 20__.

_____

Signed

ACKNOWLEDGMENT

State of   )

County of   )

On this date, [list names of person(s) who signed above] _____ _____ personally appeared before me and acknowledged that the above signatures are valid and binding.

_____   _____

Notary Public   Date signed

My Commission expires: _____

FORM 7-5 Arbitration agreement with contractor (binding).

Arbitration is used where there is a conflict. Rather than pursue legal action, both parties agree to refer the matter to an independent third party (arbitrator) and be bound by the findings of the arbitrator. If the agreement is for nonbinding arbitration, the parties are not forced to accept the arbitrator's decision. For information on arbitration, visit www.abanet.org/dispute or www.adr.com.

The undersigned parties hereby acknowledge that there is a conflict, dispute, or controversy between _____(name), Homeowner, and _____ (name), the Contractor, as follows [briefly describe dispute] _____

_____

The parties hereby agree to resolve this conflict, dispute, or controversy and any future disputes, conflicts, or controversies between them by binding arbitration.

The arbitration will be conducted according to the rules of the American Arbitration Association for the City of _____, which rules and procedures for arbitration are incorporated herein by reference and the decision or award made by the arbitrator shall be final, binding, and conclusive upon each of the parties and enforceable in a court of law.

SIGNED this _____ day of _____, 20 __.

_____

Signature

ACKNOWLEDGMENT

State of _____   )

County of _____   )

On this date, [list names of person(s) who signed above] _____

_____ personally appeared before me and acknowledged that the above signature(s) are valid and binding.

_____   _____

Notary Public   Date signed

My Commission expires: _____

FORM 7-6 Arbitration agreement with contractor (nonbinding).

The undersigned parties hereby acknowledge that there is a conflict, dispute, or controversy between the Homeowner and the Contractor as follows [briefly describe dispute]: _____

_____

The parties hereby agree to attempt to resolve this conflict, dispute, or controversy and any future disputes, conflicts, or controversies between them by nonbinding arbitration.

The arbitration will be conducted according to the rules of the American Arbitration Association for the City of _____, which rules and procedures for arbitration are incorporated herein by reference and the decision or award made by the arbitrator shall be advisory only and not binding or conclusive upon each of the parties.

SIGNED this____ day of _____, 20__.

_____

Signature

ACKNOWLEDGMENT

State of   )

County of   )

On this date, [list names of person(s) who signed above] _____

_____ personally appeared before me and acknowledged that the above signature(s) are valid and binding.

_____   _____

Notary Public   Date signed

My Commission expires: _____

8

Pet Forms

Forms and Information in This Chapter

FORM 8-1   Pet care agreement.

Date: _____

This agreement is made between _____ (Owner), who is the pet owner

of the pet known as _____ (name and description of pet),

and _____ (Care Giver), who has agreed to care for _____

(pet's name).

   1. The parties agree that Care Giver shall care for Owner's pet from _____ until _____.

   2. The pet shall be cared for at _____ (Owner's house
      or other location).

   3. The pet shall be fed and given fresh water at least __ times each day.

FORM 8-1 continued

> 4. Care Giver shall be paid the sum of $ _____ per _____ for said services.
>
> 5. If Owner cannot be reached, Care Giver is authorized to consent to any emergency medical care that may be necessary.
>
> Owner: _____
>
> Care Giver: _____

FORM 8-2 Contract for the sale of a dog (or other animal).

This form may be used as a contract for the sale of a dog or other animal. Describe the animal as specifically as possible to prevent later identification problems. Use a contract for the sale prior to the completion of the sale. If the sale has been completed and the new owner has taken possession of the animal, you should then use the bill of sale form provided later in this chapter.

[Date] _____

For the payment of the sum of $ _____, _____ (name of present Dog Owner), referred to as the Seller agrees, to sell to _____ (name of the buyer), referred to as the Buyer, the following described Dog: (describe the dog at this point) _____
_____
____

Payment terms are as follows: (Describe payment terms.) _____

The Dog was:

____ bred by the Seller.

____ bred by _____ and acquired from the breeder by the Seller.

____ acquired by the Seller from _____.

The Seller warrants that the Dog:

____ Is purebred.

____ Is not purebred.

____ Is registered with _____.

____ Is not registered with _____, but is eligible for registration, and the Seller will provide the Buyer with the necessary documents for registration.

____ Is not eligible for registration.

FORM 8-2 continued

> ____ Is believed to be healthy.
>
> ____ Has received the following vaccinations: _____
>
> (The Seller will provide the Buyer with the necessary shot records.)
>
> ____ Has received the special training listed below: (List training of the Dog.) _____
> _____
>
> Except as noted below, the Dog is sold in "as is" condition.
>
> [List any exception; otherwise state NONE] _____
>
> The Dog is located at _____ (address), and
> the Buyer will take possession and responsibility of the Dog on _____ (date), pro-
> vided that the Buyer has complied with the payment terms listed above.
>
> The parties agree that if any controversy or claim or dispute arises out of this contract of sale,
> the issue shall be submitted to arbitration. Each party will select one arbitrator, and the two
> selected arbitrators will select a third arbitrator. If any legal action is required, the prevailing
> party shall be entitled to reasonable cost and attorney's fees.
>
> Signed under seal and accepted this __ day of _____, 20__.
>
> Seller:_____   Address:_____
>
> Witness:_____

FORM 8-3 Bill of sale for dog.

> This form may be used as a Bill of Sale for a Dog or other animal. Describe the animal as specifically as possible to prevent later identification problems.

> [Date] _____
>
> For good and valuable consideration and the payment of the sum of $ _____,
> receipt of which is hereby acknowledged, the Seller, _____
> (name of seller) hereby sells and transfers to the Buyer _____
> (name of buyer) the following described Dog: (describe the dog at this point) _____
> _____

FORM 8-3   continued

The Seller warrants to Buyer and its assigns and successors that Seller has good and marketable title to said Dog and the full authority to sell the Dog free of all liens, encumbrances, liabilities, and adverse claims of every nature and description whatsoever. The above-described Dog is sold and transferred free of all liens, encumbrances, liabilities, and adverse claims of every nature and description whatsoever.

Seller further warrants to Buyer that Seller will fully defend, protect, indemnify, and hold harmless the Buyer and Buyer's lawful successors and assigns from any adverse claim as to ownership of the Dog.

The Dog was

_____ bred by the Seller

_____ bred by _____ and acquired from the breeder by the Seller.

_____ acquired by the Seller from _____.

The Seller warrants that the Dog:

_____ Is purebred.

_____ Is not purebred.

_____ Is registered with _____.

_____ Is not registered with _____, but is eligible for registration, and the Seller will provide the Buyer with the necessary documents for registration.

_____ Is not eligible for registration.

_____ Is believed to be healthy.

_____ Has received the following vaccinations: _____
_____

(The Seller will provide the Buyer with the necessary shot records.)

_____ Has received the special training listed below: (List training of the Dog.) _____
_____

Except as noted below, the Dog is sold in "as is" condition.

[List any exception; otherwise state NONE.]

The Dog is located at _____ (address), and immediately upon the execution of this Bill of Sale, the Buyer will, at his/her expense, take possession of the Dog.

Signed under seal and accepted this __ day of _____, 20__.

Seller _____   Address _____

Witness _____

Legal Issues Involving Pets

Generally, there are four general areas where pets are involved in legal issues. The areas are as follows:

1. When a landlord attempts to evict a tenant because the tenant has an animal in violation of the provisions of a lease.
2. When the dog or other pet injures another person.
3. When the pet owner discovers that the pet had a physical problem when the pet was purchased.
4. When there is the issue of cruelty to a pet.

For more information on these issues, please refer to the accompanying CD.

FORM 8–4   Dog walking agreement.

This form may be used to establish an agreement with an individual to walk your dog.

This Dog Walking Agreement is made by and between _____
_____ (Name and address of Walker) hereinafter referred to as "Walker"
and _____ (Name and address of dog owner)
hereinafter referred to as "Owner" on _____ (date).

The parties agree for valuable consideration that the Walker will provide exercise (by walking) and provide safe and humane care for the following dog: _____
_____ (name and description of dog),
hereinafter referred to as the "Dog".

Terms of Contract

1. The dog walking under this greement will commence on _____ (date) and will continue until _____ (date) unless the contract is terminated upon ten days' written notice by either party.

2. The Walker's duties shall include: (list all important duties)

    a. keeping the Dog in a safe and humane environment.

    b. walking the Dog for approximately __ minutes each day and the distance the Dog is walked should be approximately __ yards.

    c. keeping the Dog under a safe leash during the exercise.

    d. obtaining any emergency medical care.

    e. the Dog shall be walked in the following area [describe area]: _____

    f. such other duties as agreed on.

3. The Walker is hereby given permission to consent on behalf of the Owner to any necessary medical treatment of the Dog, and any costs associated with the medical treatment shall be reimbursed by the Owner.

4. The Walker's fee will be __ per (hour, day, or week) paid (each week or semi-monthly). Paid on __ day of each (week)(month).

5. This contract supersedes all prior agreements and understandings between the parties and may only be modified in writing signed by both parties.

6. This contract may not be assigned without the prior consent of both parties.

7. This contract shall be governed by the laws of the State of _____ (name of local state) and the City of _____ (name of local city).

8. This contract is in force when signed by both parties.

Date signed: _____

Signed:

_____   _____
Walker   Owner

FORM 8–5 Pet care contract.

> The below form may be used to contract with a pet care provider who will take care of your pet.

This Contract for Pet Care is made by and between _____
(Name and address of Caretaker) hereinafter referred to as "Caretaker" and _____
_____ (Name and address of pet owner)
hereinafter referred to as "Owner" on _____ (date).

The parties agree for valuable consideration that the Caretaker will provide safe and humane pet care for the following pet: _____ (name and description of pet), hereinafter referred to as the "Pet."

Terms of Contract

1. The pet care will commence on _____ (date) and will continue until _____ (date) unless the contract is terminated upon ten days' written notice by either party.

2. The Caretaker's duties shall include: (list all important duties of the Caretaker)

   a. keeping the pet in a safe and humane environment

   b. feeding the pet

   c. grooming and exercising the pet

   d. obtaining needed medical care

   e. such other duties as agreed on

3. The Caretaker is hereby given permission to consent to any necessary medical treatment of the Pet, and any costs associated with the medical treatment shall be reimbursed by the Owner.

4. The Caretaker's fee will be __ per (hour, day, or week) paid (each week or twice monthly). Paid on __ day of each (week) (month).

5. This contract supersedes all prior agreements and understandings between the parties and may only be modified in writing signed by both parties.

6. This contract may not be assigned without the prior consent of both parties.

7. This contract shall be governed by the laws of the State of _____ (name of local state) and the City of _____ (name of local city).

8. This contract is in force when signed by both parties.

Date signed: _____

Signed:

_____   _____
Caretaker   Owner

9

Common Legal Forms

Forms and Information in This Chapter

Forms marked with an asterisk (*) only appear on the accompanying CD. Portions of forms marked with a dagger (†) only appear on the CD.

III. Forms Related to Real Property

IV. Forms Related to Employment

V. Forms Related to Copyrights and Patents

VI. Other Legal Forms

I. Forms and Information Related to Contracts

Checklist for Contracts

This checklist may be used to ensure that all necessary items are included in any proposed contracts.

1. Who are the parties involved?
2. Date of agreement and list of all documents to be attached to contract.
3. Define goods to be delivered or work to be accomplished.
4. What are the prices to be paid for the goods or work?
5. In the case of goods, who pays freight?
6. Date that goods are to be delivered to company or work to be completed.
7. Define any special inspection requirements.
8. Describe specifications for goods or work.
9. Provide directions for packaging, shipping, and delivery.
10. Describe warranties furnished.
11. At what point does title of the goods transfer to buyer?
12. Who is authorized to agree to modifications in the contract?
13. Describe how disputes will be resolved.
14. When are payments due under the contract?
15. How will be payments be accepted?
16. Any financing agreed to under the contract?
17. Penalties for late performance?

FORM 9-1 Modification of a contract.

This letter may be used to modify a contract. Certified Mail, Return Receipt Requested.

Date : _____

To: _____

Address: _____

Re: _____

Dear Madam or Sir:

This letter will serve as a written modification of the contract dated _____, between your company and us. [This modification is in accordance with the modification clause of the basic contract.][This modification is in accordance with our telephone conversation of _____.]

FORM 9-1 continued

The contract is revised as follows:

[State the revision.]_____

If you agree with the modifications and they comport with your understanding of our oral agreement to modify the contract, please sign below and return the signed letter to us at the above address. If there is any problem, please contact us within _____ days of the date of this letter.

Sincerely,

_____

_____   _____
[Signature of other party]   [Date accepted by other party]

FORM 9-2   Terminating a contract.

This agreement may be used to terminate an existing contract.

Date _____

FOR GOOD AND VALUABLE CONSIDERATION mutually exchanged between the parties, _____ and _____, and whereas the parties have previously entered into an agreement dated _____, the parties hereby agree to terminate that agreement.

Both parties agree to terminate the contract [immediately] [effective as of _____].

Both parties agree to release each other of liability.

In witness thereof, both parties have executed this agreement on the day and year first above written.

_____   _____
Signatures

FORM 9-3 Arbitration clause.

This clause may be inserted in a contract so that if there are any disputes between the parties, the matter will be referred to arbitration rather than other legal action being pursued. For information on arbitration, visit www.abanet.org/dispute or www.adr.com.

This arbitration clause is added to the contract signed between the parties on _____ day of _____ 20__. The parties to the agreement are _____ (name and address) and _____ (name and address). If there is a dispute or disagreement between the parties concerning the terms and conditions or any other matter associated with the contract, to avoid legal proceedings, the parties hereby agree to submit the matter to binding arbitration.

If the parties cannot agree on a single arbitrator, then each party will select one arbitrator, and the two selected arbitrators will select a third arbitrator.

The arbitrator or arbitrators will decide all issues of law and fact related to the dispute. Judgment upon an award may be entered in any court having jurisdiction.

If the award is required to be enforced in legal proceedings, the prevailing party is entitled to reasonable attorney fees and costs.

Signed under seal this ____ day of _____, 20 __.

_____ (Signature)

_____ (Signature)

ACKNOWLEDGMENT

State of   )

County of   )

On this date, [list names of person(s) who signed above] _____
_____ personally appeared before me and acknowledged that the above signature(s) is valid and binding.

_____

Notary Public

My Commission expires: _____

FORM 9-4 Mediation agreement clause.

> This clause may be included in a contract to require the mediation of any disputes that arise. In arbitration, a third person (the arbitrator) listens to each of the parties and then issues a decision. In mediation, a professional mediator attempts to get the parties to agree to a compromise. For information on mediation, visit www.abanet.org/dispute or www.adr.com. This clause is included in contracts to require parties to go through the mediation process before a party may file a legal action.

The parties to this contract (or the contract previously entered into between the parties on _____ [date]) agree that any controversy, claim or dispute arising out of or related to this contract shall be submitted to mediation. The parties agree to use _____ _____ [for a local mediator, check the Web site at www.nasd.com/ArbitrationMediation] as the mediator. If the named mediator is not available and the parties cannot agree on a substitute mediator, the parties will request the appointment of a mediator from the _____ _____ [use a local mediation center]. The parties agree that the expenses of mediation shall be divided equally by the parties.

_____   _____

Signatures

FORM 9-5 Extending a contract.

> This agreement may be used to extend an existing contract.

Date _____

FOR GOOD AND VALUABLE CONSIDERATION mutually exchanged between the parties, _____ and _____, and whereas the parties have previously entered into an agreement dated _____, the parties hereby agree to extend the above-mentioned agreement. Accordingly, both parties will be bound under the terms of the above-mentioned agreement as modified by this agreement.

The modifications of the previously entered agreement are as follows [list changes] _____
_____
_____

Except as modified above, the original terms of the earlier agreement shall be binding on both parties.

In witness thereof, both parties have executed this agreement on the day and year first above written.

_____   _____

[Signed by both parties.]

FORM 9-6   Extending time for performance of contract.

> This agreement may be used to extend time for the performance of an existing contract.

Date _____

FOR GOOD AND VALUABLE CONSIDERATION mutually exchanged between the parties, _____ and _____, and whereas the parties have previously entered into an agreement dated _____, the parties hereby agree to extend the above-mentioned agreement. Accordingly, both parties will be bound under the terms of the above-mentioned agreement as modified by this agreement.

The modification of the previously entered agreement is as follows: [List changes.] _____

The due date of performance is changed to _____ [date].

Except as modified above, the original terms of the earlier agreement shall be binding on both parties.

In witness thereof, both parties have executed this agreement on the day and year first above written.

_____   _____

[Signed by both parties to the contract.]

FORM 9-7   General release.

> This agreement may be used to release a person from a contract.

Date _____

In consideration for one dollar and other valuable consideration received, _____ [Obligee] hereby relieves and releases _____ [Obligor], his or her heirs and assigns from all claims and liabilities owed to me, my heirs, and assigns, by the Obligor as of the date of the execution of this release.

_____

Signed by obligee

FORM 9-8   Guaranty, limited.

> The guaranty documents are designed to be used by a buyer who needs another party or person to guarantee payment for the goods. The guaranty document should be used in conjunction with one of the installment notes. The document may be used, for example, where you wish to sell your old vehicle to a college student who cannot pay cash for the vehicle. If you are concerned about whether he or she will pay for the vehicle, you could request that the student get his or her parents to sign a guaranty note.

FORM 9-8   continued

For good and valuable consideration, and as an inducement for [name of creditor] _____, Creditor, to extend credit from time to time to [name of borrower] _____, Borrower, the undersigned jointly and severally and unconditionally guarantees to the Creditor the prompt and full payment of all sums due from Borrower to Creditor. This limited guaranty is limited to the sum of $ _____.

The undersigned agrees to remain fully bound to this guaranty notwithstanding any extension, modification, waiver, release, discharge, or substitution of any collateral or security for the debt. In addition, the undersigned consents to and waives all notice of the same. In the event of default, the Creditor may seek payment directly from the undersigned without need to proceed first against the Borrower. All suretyship defenses are waived by the undersigned.

In the event of default, the undersigned shall be responsible to pay attorney fees, collection costs, and other fees associated with collection of the note.

The guaranty is limited as to amount and may also be terminated as to future credit by delivery of notice of termination to Creditor by certified mail, return receipt requested. Termination does not discharge guarantor's obligations as to debts incurred prior to delivery of notice of termination.

This guaranty is binding upon and inures to the benefit of the parties, their successors, assigns, and personal representatives.

Signed under seal this _____ day of _____, 20__.

_____   _____
Guarantor   Seller or Creditor

FORM 9-9   Assignment of contract.

This agreement may be used to assign a contract to purchase goods from a seller. Note: The contract must be one that is assignable. For example, you have a contract to purchase all the heating oil you need for your home at a discounted rate. You decide to sell your home and move to one of the southern states. If the contract is assignable, as part of the agreement to sell your home, you agree to assign the heating oil contract to the new home owner.

For good and valuable consideration, the undersigned hereby unconditionally and irrevocably assigns and transfers over to [Assignee] _____ and his or her successors and assigns all rights, title, and interest in and to the following described contract with _____ _____, dated _____, 20__.

[Describe contract here.] _____
_____

The undersigned Assignor warrants that the said contract is in full force and effect in the form and terms annexed and that the contract is fully assignable. The Assignee assumes and agrees to perform all the remaining and executory obligations of the Assignor under the contract, if

FORM 9-9 continued

any, and to indemnify and hold Assignor harmless from any claim or demand resulting from nonperformance therein by the Assignee. The Assignee is entitled to all monies and other benefits accrued or remaining to be paid under the contract, which rights are also assigned hereunder. Assignor warrants that he or she has all rights and full authority to make this assignment and transfer. The undersigned also warrants that the rights and benefits assigned hereunder are free and clear of any liens, encumbrances, adverse claims, or interest. In addition, the Assignor also warrants that he or she has no knowledge of any disputes or defenses thereon.

This assignment shall be binding upon and inure to the benefit of the parties, their successors, assigns, and personal representatives.

Signed under seal this _____ day of _____, 20__.

_____
Assignor [person assigning contract]

_____
Assignee [person receiving contract]

FORM 9-10   Assignment of contract benefits.

This agreement may be used to assign the benefits of a contract. For example, the homeowner may have a contract that allows an association to use the lake on his or her property for a set annual fee. The homeowner needing additional money now agrees to assign the benefits, that is, annual fee, to someone else in order to receive a lesser sum immediately.

For good and valuable consideration, to wit: _____ [state consideration or value received] the undersigned hereby unconditionally and irrevocably assigns and transfers over to [Assignee] _____ and his or her successors and assigns all benefits to be received from the following described contract with _____, dated _____, 20__.
[Describe contract here.] _____
_____

The undersigned Assignor warrants that the said contract is in full force and effect in the form and terms annexed and that the contract is fully assignable.

The Assignee is entitled to all monies and other benefits accrued or remaining to be paid under the contract, which rights are also assigned hereunder. Assignor warrants that he or she has full rights and full authority to make this assignment and transfer. The undersigned also warrants that the rights and benefits assigned hereunder are free and clear of any liens, encumbrances, adverse claims, or interest. In addition, the Assignor also warrants that he or she has no knowledge of any disputes or defenses thereon.

This assignment shall be binding upon and inure to the benefit of the parties, their successors, assigns, and personal representatives.

Signed under seal this _____ day of _____, ____.

_____
Assignor [person assigning benefits]

FORM 9-11   Notice of assignment of contract.

> This form is used to notify parties to the contract that an assignment of the contract has been made. For instance, in the example noted in the previous form, this form would be used to notify the association that payment of the annual fee should be made to a different party. Certified Mail, Return Receipt Requested.

Date: _____

To: [party to original contract] _____

On [date] _____, I assigned all my interest and benefit in the following contract:

[Describe contract] _____

_____

To: [Person to whom contract was assigned, including address] _____

_____

Accordingly, any payments to be made under the contract should be addressed to the above named Assignee.

Assignor _____

II. Forms Related to Personal Property

FORM 9-12   Contract for purchase of personal property.

This contract is for the purchase of personal property made by and between _____ _____ (Seller) and _____ (Buyer).

For good and valuable consideration the parties agree as follows:

1. Seller agrees to sell and Buyer agrees to buy the below described property:_____

_____

2. The mutually agreed purchase price is $ _____; payable as follows: $ _____ as a deposit due no later than _____, 20__. The balance of $ _____ will be payable on delivery by cash or certified check.

3. Seller warrants it has good and legal title to the said property and has full authority to sell it. The said property is to be sold by warranty bill of sale free and clear of all liens, encumbrances, liabilities, and adverse claims of any kind.

4. Said property is sold as is. There is no warranty of merchantability, fitness, or working order or condition of the property except that it is sold in its present condition.

5. The parties agree that title to the property will transfer to the Buyer when said property is delivered to the Buyer's address.

FORM 9-12   continued

6. This agreement shall be binding upon and inure to the benefit of the parties, their assigns, successors, and personal representatives.

IN WITNESS WHEREOF the undersigned have hereunto set their hands this __ day of _____, 20__.

Buyer _____   Seller _____

FORM 9-13   Conditional sales contract.

Unlike the previous form, a conditional sale agreement is one in which the seller agrees to sell if a certain condition occurs. For example, you agree to sell your automobile to a young person if he or she can get the parents' permission, or if the individual can give you a cash payment of a certain amount. Another use would be where an individual agrees to purchase the apples from the trees in your backyard provided that there are at least 10 bushels. Another typical conditional sale is one in which the buyer agrees to purchase the automobile with the right to return it within five days if a certain mechanic finds that there are major mechanical problems with the vehicle.

For good and valuable consideration, this conditional sales contract is entered into between _____ (Seller) and _____ (Buyer). Seller agrees to sell and the Buyer agrees to buy the following goods on a conditional sale:

[List goods, merchandise, or supplies] _____

_____

[Also list the conditions of the sale, e.g., the buyer reserves the right to return the merchandise (goods or supplies) if the buyer is not completely satisfied with them.] _____

_____

Sale price	$ _____
Sales tax	$ _____
Other charges	$ _____
Finance charges	$ _____
Total purchase price	$ _____

Deductions

Down payment	$ _____
Other credits	$ _____

FORM 9-13 continued

Total deductions $ _____

Amount financed $ _____

ANNUAL INTEREST RATE   _____%

The amount financed is payable in _____ monthly payments of $ _____ each, starting on the __ day of the month of _____, 20__, and continuing on the same day each succeeding month until paid in full.

The title to the goods remain with the Seller until payment of the full purchase price, subject to allocation of payments and release of security interest as required by law. The Buyer agrees to keep the goods free from other liens and encumbrances and not to remove the goods from the below address without the written consent of the Seller.

Buyer agrees to execute all financing statements as may be required of Seller to perfect this conditional sales contract.

The entire balance shall become immediately due upon default on any installment due or other breach of this agreement.

In the event of a default, Seller may enter upon the premises of the Buyer and reclaim said goods. If the Seller retakes the goods, he/she has the right to resell them for credit to the balance purchased, and Seller may reacquire same all as further defined and set forth under state law.

On the demand of the Seller, the Buyer shall keep the goods adequately insured with the Seller named as the loss payee. On request, the Buyer shall provide Seller with proof of insurance.

In the event of default, the defaulting party shall be responsible to pay attorney fees, collection costs, and other fees associated with enforcement of this agreement. This agreement is binding upon and inures to the benefit of the parties, their successors, assigns, and personal representatives.

The full balance shall become due on default. Upon default, Seller will have the further right to retake the goods, hold and dispose of same and collect expenses, together with any deficiency due from the Buyer, but subject to the Buyer's right to redeem pursuant to law and the Uniform Commercial Code.

This agreement shall also be in default upon the death, insolvency, or bankruptcy of Buyer.

Signed under seal and accepted this __ day of _____, 20__.

Buyer _____   Seller _____

_____

Notary public

My commission expires: _____

FORM 9-14 Modification of conditional sale agreement.

The modification agreement below may be used to modify a conditional sale agreement. For example, you purchase a used riding lawn mower for your yard with the right to return the mower within five days if a mechanic determines that it has mechanical problems. You then discover that your mechanic is on vacation and will not return for a week. You should then see if the seller will modify the conditional sale agreement.

A conditional sale agreement was executed on the ___ day of _____, 20__, by and between ___ _____ [Seller] and _____ [Buyer]. The parties agreed to modify the agreement as follows: _____

_____

The terms of the purchase are modified as follows:

Price:	_____
Sales tax:	_____
Finance charges:	_____
Shipping charges:	_____
Total price:	_____

The payment schedule is modified as follows: A down payment of _____ dollars ($) and the remaining amount in equal installments of _____ dollars ($) payable on the _____ day of each month, starting on _____, 20__.

This is a modification to a conditional sales agreement and therefore title to the goods will still remain with the Seller until payment in full has been received by the Seller.

The Seller still retains the right to repossess the items sold, subject to any apportionment for payments made, should the Buyer fail or refuse to make all the required payments.

Agreed to:

_____   _____
Buyer   Seller

FORM 9-15 Sample conditional sale agreement.

This form only appears on the accompanying CD.

FORM 9-16   Receipt for delivery of goods.

Date: _____

To: [seller] _____

The undersigned hereby acknowledges receipt of the goods described on the attached invoice. They have been inspected and found to be without defect and conforming to the purchase order.

_____

Buyer

FORM 9-17   Request for return authorization.

This letter may be used to request authorization to return goods.

Date: _____

To: _____

Re: Our order no. _____, your invoice no. _____

Dear Madam/Sir:

This letter is to request your authorization to return the above-referenced goods. We are not satisfied with the goods for the reasons set forth below. According to your guarantee, we request a full credit or a refund when you have received the goods.

The reason(s) that the goods were not acceptable to us:

[State reason(s).] _____

_____

Sincerely,

_____

Signature

FORM 9-18   Sale on approval.

This letter may be used to request goods on a "sale on approval" basis.

Date: _____

To: _____

Dear Madam/Sir:

We request that the goods on the attached order form be delivered on a "sale on approval" basis. We request __ days after receipt of the goods to return them in good condition and receive full credit or refund, including cost of return. If the goods are not returned within that time period, they will be deemed accepted without right of return.

Upon acceptance by us, the balance of the purchase price shall be paid within the terms stated on your invoice. Until the goods are accepted by us, you retain title to them.

Sincerely,

_____

Signature

FORM 9-19   Order confirmation.

This letter may be used to confirm an order placed over the telephone. Certified Mail, Return Receipt Requested.

Date: _____

To: _____

Dear Madam/Sir:

This letter is to confirm our order of [date] _____, which we placed with your company by telephone. A purchase order authorizing the order on the terms that we discussed is attached to this letter.

If any of the products listed or terms set forth in the purchase order are not available or acceptable, please advise us within _____ days of the date of this letter. Otherwise, we shall consider that the order is accepted in this form, and we will anticipate prompt delivery.

Sincerely,

_____
Buyer

FORM 9-20   Overcharge claim.

This form may be used to state a claim for an overcharge.

Date: _____

Vendor Name: _____

Address: _____

Order No: _____

Instructions: Please check your invoices regarding the above order number. It appears that we have been overcharged on the listed items. Please refer to your (quotes) (catalog) regarding the list price [or contract price] of the items.

Quantity	Unit	Name and Description	Listed price	Invoice price

FORM 9-21   Acceptance of damaged goods.

This letter may be used for situations in which you have agreed to accept damaged goods at an adjusted price.

Date: _____

To: _____

Re: Our purchase order no. _____ Dated _____

Dear Madam/Sir:
This is to advise you that we are in receipt of certain goods that were shipped pursuant to the above order.

[Describe damage or defect of the goods.] _____

_____

Pursuant to our telephone conservation of [date] _____, we agreed to accept the damaged [or defective] items subject to an adjustment of _____ dollars ($ _____).
Please issue a new invoice showing the adjustment and correct our account accordingly.

Sincerely,

_____
Signature

FORM 9-22   Acceptance of nonconforming goods.

This letter should be used to notify a seller that the goods received didn't meet the specifications requested; however, you are willing to keep the goods at a discounted price.

Date: _____

To: _____

Re: Acceptance of nonconforming goods

Dear Madam/Sir:

This letter is to advise you that the goods you shipped pursuant to our purchase order no. _____ of [date] _____ do not conform to the specifications set forth in the purchase order. The goods do not meet the specifications in that they [State how goods do not conform.] _____

_____

However, we are accepting the goods that you shipped. Because of the nonconformance, we request that you discount the purchase price by __ percent or $__. In addition, please be advised that we expect all future orders to conform to our specifications.

Sincerely,

_____
Signature

FORM 9-23 Cancellation: failure of timely delivery.

This letter may be used to cancel goods because the goods were not delivered in a timely manner. Certified Mail, Return Receipt Requested.

Date: _____

To: _____

Re: Our purchase order no. _____ dated _____

Dear Madam/Sir:

You have failed to deliver in a timely manner the items that we ordered shown on the above-referenced purchase order. Accordingly, this letter is to advise you that pursuant to the terms of the purchase order, we hereby cancel the order in its entirety.

Sincerely,

_____

Signature

FORM 9-24 Cancellation of back-ordered goods.

This letter may be used to cancel back-ordered goods.

Date: _____

To: _____

Dear Madam/Sir:

You notified us that certain goods listed on our purchase order no. _____ dated _____ are not in stock and have been back-ordered.

This letter will serve as written notice to cancel the back-ordered goods and ship the remainder of the order immediately. The timely receipt of the goods is a necessity for us. Therefore, they will be ordered elsewhere. Please ensure that the invoice you send us correctly reflects only the goods shipped by your company.

Sincerely,

_____

Signature

FORM 9-25 Cancellation of purchase order (late delivery).

> This letter may be used to notify the vendor that you are canceling your order because of late delivery.

Date: _____

To: _____

Re: purchase order no. _____ of [date]_____; cancellation

Dear Madam/Sir:

We ordered the following goods: [List goods ordered.] _____
_____

Payment in the amount of $__ was forwarded to your company on [date] _____ as payment in full for the order. The goods were to be delivered not later than [date] _____.

As of this date, we have not received the ordered goods. Therefore, please cancel the order and return our money. If we have not received a refund within __ days of the above date, we will take the necessary legal action to obtain the refund.

Sincerely,

_____

Signature

FORM 9-26 Conditional acceptance of nonconforming goods.

> This letter may be used to indicate conditional acceptance of nonconforming goods. Nonconforming goods are goods that are not the same goods or the same quality as ordered.

Date: _____

To: _____

Re: Our order no. _____; your invoice no. _____

Dear Madam/Sir:

We have received your shipment in response to our above order. The goods received do not conform to the specifications set forth in our order as noted below:

[State the nonconformance.] _____
_____

We are prepared to accept the nonconforming goods if you will allow us a credit of $ _____, making the total purchase price of the order $ _____. Please let us know immediately whether this arrangement is satisfactory.

If we do not receive notice of your agreement within the next _____ days, we will reject the nonconforming goods.

Sincerely,

_____

Signature

FORM 9-27   Demand for the delivery of goods.

This letter may be used in an attempt to obtain delivery of late goods.

Date: _____

To: _____

Re: Demand for the delivery of goods

On [date] _____, we ordered the following goods [list goods]: _____
_____

Although the delivery date has passed, we have not received the goods.

Unless we receive the goods by date _____, we will cancel the order and seek the return of our payment. If necessary, we will take legal action.

Sincerely,

_____

Signature

FORM 9-28   Demand for shipping date.

This letter may be used to demand a shipping date for merchandise that you have ordered. Certified Mail, Return Receipt Requested.

Date: _____

To: _____

Re: Our order no. _____ dated _____

Dear Madam/Sir:

Pursuant to the terms of the above-referenced order, we demand that you provide notice of the shipping arrangements for the goods that we have ordered. We also demand that you provide us with adequate assurance that you will conform to those arrangements.

Should you be unable or unwilling to provide the above information and assurance, you will be in violation of the terms of the order and we may choose to cancel it.

Sincerely,

_____

Signature

FORM 9-29 Rejection of goods (nonconforming).

Date: _____

To: _____

Re: Rejection of nonconforming goods

Dear Sir/Madam:

I ordered the following goods: [Include purchase order, description of goods and other iden-tification data.] _____

_____

Payment in the amount of $_____ was forwarded to your company on [date] _____ as pay-ment in full for the order. The goods received did not conform to my purchase order as noted below: [State reason for rejection of goods.] _____

Accordingly, I reject the goods and demand return of my money. If I have not received a refund within ten days of the above date, I will take the necessary legal action to obtain the refund. Please advise us as to the disposition of the goods. I do not accept any responsibility for their safekeeping if I do not receive disposal instructions from you within the next ____ days.

Sincerely,

_____

Signature

FORM 9-30 Partial rejection of goods [nonconforming].

Date: _____

To: _____

Re: Rejection of nonconforming goods

Dear Sir/Madam:

I ordered the following goods [list goods ordered]: _____

_____

Payment in the amount of $ _____ was forwarded to your company on [date] _____ as payment in full for the order. Part of the goods received did not conform to my purchase order as noted below [state reason for rejection of goods.]: _____

I reject those goods that do not conform to those listed in the purchase order and demand return of the money that was paid for the goods that have been rejected. If I have not received a refund within __ days of the above date, I will take the necessary legal action to obtain the refund.

Please advise me as to the disposition of the rejected goods. I do not accept any responsibility for their safekeeping if I do not receive disposal instructions from you within the next ____ days.

Sincerely,

_____

Signature

FORM 9-31 Return of rejected goods.

Date: _____

To: _____

Re: Return of rejected goods

Dear Sir/Madam:

On [date] _____ we notified you that the goods you sent us have been rejected, and we provided the reasons for the rejection. At that time, we requested instructions regarding the return or other disposition of the goods.

Since we have not received any instructions regarding them, we no longer accept any responsibility for them. Please advise us within the next 10 days as to their disposition.

Sincerely,

_____

Signature

FORM 9-32 Consignment agreement.

This agreement may be used for consignments. A consignment is when you assign goods, supplies, or property to someone else or a company for resale. For example, you decide to refurnish your home, and therefore you assign to a used furniture store all of your old furniture. The furniture store will then attempt to sell the old furniture for you.

Date: _____

Consignor's name:_____ Address: _____

_____

Consignee's name:_____ Address:_____

_____

This document is a Consignment Agreement between _____ (Consignor) and _____ (Consignee) for the property listed in Attachment A and hereinafter referred as inventory.

1. The inventory shall be picked up by the Consignee and delivered to his or her premises: where it shall be inventoried, sorted, identified, and cataloged by both vendor and consignee numbers.

2. Consignee shall take the necessary steps to offer the merchandise (or goods) for sale to the best-qualified buyers and to obtain the greatest amount of revenue.

3. All expenses of sale shall be the responsibility of the Consignee. The Consignee shall also insure the inventory for at least $ _____, and, in the event of loss, Consignee will pay the Consignor the full benefits guaranteed under Paragraph 5 below and pursuant to the requirements set forth in this agreement.

4. The inventory shall be processed immediately for sale.

FORM 9-32 continued

5. In full consideration of this consignment, the Consignor is guaranteed a minimum of $ _____. The Consignee shall pay Consignor $ _____ on receipt of the inventory by Consignee; __ percent of all sales in excess of $ _____ shall be paid to Consignor on a monthly basis.

6. A statement of all units sold shall be submitted by Consignee to Consignor on a monthly basis.

7. The entire inventory remains the property of Consignor until it is sold.

8. The period of consignment shall be for __ months beginning _____.

9. At the end of the consignment, the Consignee will return the remaining inventory to Consignor. The only cost for the return of any inventory shall be the transportation costs.

10. The Consignee may purchase any unsold inventory at a price equivalent to the acquisition cost plus __ percent.

11. The acknowledgment copy of this Consignment Agreement shall be executed on behalf of the Consignee and returned to the Consignor as approval of the terms and conditions set forth above.

By: _____   By: _____
    Title   Title

FORM 9-33 Bill of sale (with warranty).

For good and valuable consideration, and the payment of the sum of $_____, receipt of which is hereby acknowledged, the Seller _____ hereby sells and transfers to the Buyer _____ the following described personal property:_____
_____

The Seller warrants to Buyer and its assigns and successors that Seller has good and marketable title to said property and the full authority to sell and transfer the property free of all liens, encumbrances, liabilities, and adverse claims of every nature and description whatsoever. The said property is sold and transferred free of all liens, encumbrances, liabilities, and adverse claims of every nature and description whatsoever.

Seller further warrants to Buyer that Seller will fully defend, protect, indemnify, and hold harmless the Buyer and Buyer's lawful successors and assigns from any adverse claim thereto.

Except as noted above, the goods are sold in "as is" condition and where presently located.

Signed under seal and accepted this __ day of _____, 20__.

Seller: _____ Address: _____

Buyer: _____ Address: _____

FORM 9-34   Bill of sale (with encumbrances).

This form could be used in a situation in which the individual is selling property that he or she still owes money on. For example the lawn tractor has not been paid for when it is sold to another homeowner. Under this agreement, the new owner agrees to accept the debt associated with the property and to pay it.

For good and valuable consideration, and the payment of the sum of \$_____, receipt of which is hereby acknowledged, the Seller _____ hereby sells and transfers to the Buyer _____ the following described personal property [describe property]: _____

_____

_____

The Seller warrants to Buyer and its assigns and successors that Seller, except as noted below, has good and marketable title to said property and the full authority to sell and transfer the property free of all liens, encumbrances, liabilities, and adverse claims of every nature and description whatsoever. Except as noted below, the said property is sold and transferred free of all liens, encumbrances, liabilities, and adverse claims of every nature and description whatsoever.

The said property is sold subject to a certain security interest, lien, or encumbrance on said property in the favor of _____ (lien holder) with a balance owed thereon of \$____. Buyer agrees to assume and promptly pay said secured debt and indemnify and hold Seller harmless from any claim arising thereon.

Seller further warrants to Buyer that, except for claims arising out of above encumbrance, Seller will fully defend, protect, indemnify, and hold harmless the Buyer and Buyer's lawful successors and assigns from any other adverse claim thereto.

Except as noted above, the goods are sold in "as is" condition and where presently located.

Signed under seal and accepted this __ day of _____, 20__.

Seller: _____ Address: _____

Buyer: _____ Address: _____

FORM 9-35   Bill of sale (quitclaim).

For good and valuable consideration, and the payment of the sum of \$____, receipt of which is hereby acknowledged, the Seller _____ hereby sells and transfers with quitclaim covenants to the Buyer _____ the following described personal property:

The Seller hereby sells and transfers only such rights, title, and interest as Seller may hold. The said property is sold subject to such prior liens, encumbrances, and adverse claims, if any, that may exist, and Seller hereby disclaims any and all warranties thereto.

Except as noted above, the goods are sold in "as is" condition and where presently located.

Signed under seal and accepted this __ day of _____, 20__.

Seller: _____ Address: _____

Buyer: _____ Address: _____

FORM 9-36 Bill of sale for motor vehicle.

For good and valuable consideration, and the payment of the sum of $_____, receipt of which is hereby acknowledged, the Seller _____ hereby sells and transfers to Buyer _____ and his/her successors and assigns the below-described motor vehicle:

Make: _____

Model: _____

Year: _____

License number: _____

Vehicle serial number: _____

Color: _____

Seller warrants that he/she is the legal owner of the above described vehicle and that the vehicle is being sold free and clear of all adverse liens, claims, and encumbrances and that Seller has full right and authority to sell and transfer the said vehicle. Seller will protect, defend, save harmless, and indemnify Buyer from any adverse claims thereto.

The odometer reading on the vehicle is _____. To the best of the Seller's knowledge, the reading is (correct)(not correct).

The said vehicle is sold "as is" without any expressed or implied warranty as to condition or working order.

Signed under seal and accepted this___ day of____, 20__.

Seller: _____ Address: _____

Buyer: _____ Address: _____

FORM 9-37 Return of goods received on approval.

This letter may be used when returning goods that were received on approval.

Date: _____

To: _____

Re: Our order no. _____, your invoice no. _____

Dear Madam/Sir:

The above order included our right to return the goods if we did not approve them. Accordingly, we are electing to return the goods that we received on approval.

[Optional.] The reasons we are returning the goods are as follows:_____
_____

Sincerely,

_____

Signature

FORM 9-38   Notice of defective goods.

> This letter may be used to notify the seller that the goods received are defective. Certified Mail, Return Receipt Requested.

Date: _____

To: _____

Re: Our purchase order no. _____

Dear Madam/Sir:

We are in receipt of the goods shipped by you on [date] _____ in response to our purchase order referenced above. Please be advised that the goods received are defective as noted below [list the defects.]: _____

_____

Please advise as to the action you intend to take to remedy this problem. Unless we receive a satisfactory response within __ days, we will take the necessary action, to include possible legal action to protect our rights.

Sincerely,

_____

Signature

FORM 9-39   Notice of disputed account balance.

> This letter puts the seller on notice that there is a dispute regarding the balance due on an account. Note: In many states the failure to notify the creditor that there may be an error in the statement submitted to you creates a presumption that the amount billed is correct. Certified Mail, Return Receipt Requested.

Date: _____

To: _____

Dear _____:

Notice is hereby given that your invoice or statement of [date] _____ is incorrect for the following reasons:

❑ Payment of [date] _____ not reflected on statement.

❑ The goods have been returned.

❑ The price listed for the goods is incorrect.

❑ The goods listed on the statement have not been received.

❑ Goods were not ordered and are being held for your instructions regarding return.

❑ Other: _____

The correct balance on the statement should be: $ _____.

Sincerely,

_____

Signature

FORM 9-40 Conditional payment for goods.

> This letter may be used to accompany conditional payment for goods. By sending this letter, the buyer is reserving his or her right to reject the goods if they do not conform to the specifications.

Date: _____

To: _____

Re: Conditional payment for goods received in accordance with our order no. _____

Dear Madam/Sir:

We have received goods from you in response to our order. Payment is enclosed pursuant to your request. We have not, however, had the opportunity to inspect the goods to determine if they meet our requirements and specifications. Therefore, we reserve the right to reject any nonconforming goods discovered after a full and proper inspection. We also expect proper credit for any goods discovered to be nonconforming.

Sincerely,

_____
Signature

FORM 9-41 Receipt of goods.

> This letter may be used to acknowledge delivery of goods.

Date: _____

To: _____

Dear Madam/Sir:

This is to acknowledge that we have received the items listed on the attached invoice, we have inspected them, and we accept them as in good form without apparent defect. If any latent defects are discovered, we expect that those defective items will be replaced as per our agreement.

Sincerely,

_____
Buyer

Checklist for Express Warranty Requirements

There are two types of warranties involved when personal property is sold. The first type is an implied warranty. An *implied warranty* is one that is implied or established by law between the parties. For example, when you sell property, there is an implied warranty that you have the right to sell the property. An *express warranty* is one that is spelled out by the seller. A statement that a lawn tractor has no major mechanical problems is considered as an express warranty.

The Magnuson-Moss Act

The Magnuson-Moss Act requires that express warranties contain in clear and understandable language the following terms:

- The identity of the persons to whom the warranties are extended.
- A description of the products or goods covered by the warranties.
- A description of the products or goods excluded by the warranties.
- Remedial action to be provided by the warrantor (person issuing the warranties) if defects, malfunctions, or failures occur.
- The period covered by the warranties.
- The steps or procedures that the consumer should follow to obtain relief under the warranties.
- Information on any informal procedures for dispute resolution that will be used in case of disputes under the warranties.
- All limitations or exclusions of coverage of the warranties.
- Information regarding the consumer's legal rights. For example, a statement such as: "This warranty is a valid contract and provides you with specific legal rights and other rights, which may vary from state to state."
- Any limitations on the duration and coverage of implied warranties. Note: Some states restrict limitations on implied warranties.

FORM 9-42   Bailment or storage contract.

Frequently, goods need to be stored. This bailment or storage contract may be used for that purpose. For example, an individual lives in a northern state and he or she contracts with a neighbor to allow him or her to store a boat and fishing equipment in the neighbor's garage during the winter.

This storage contract is entered into by [owner of property] _____, Bailor, and [person receiving the property] _____, Bailee, for the storage of the listed items of property:

Article: _____   Value: _____   Condition: _____

Article: _____   Value: _____   Condition: _____

Article: _____   Value: _____   Condition: _____

Storage Charges: _____

In consideration of the payment of storage charges as listed above, Bailee agrees to store the listed articles of personal property for __ months. Thereafter, monthly storage charges in the amount of $__ will be due in advance on the first day of each month. This is a month-to-month contract and may be canceled by either party on one month's notice.

_____   _____

Bailor   Bailee

FORM 9-43 Bailee's notice to recover property.

> This form may be used when a homeowner has agreed to store property in his or her garage or on his or her property and the homeowner wants the property owner to remove the property. Certified Mail, Return Receipt Requested.

NOTICE TO REMOVE PERSONAL PROPERTY

To: [Owner of property] _____

[Address of owner] _____

You are hereby notified that the [description of property] _____ _____, now on the premises of the undersigned at [address and location of property, including city and state] _____ _____, must be removed on or before [include date and time, including year] _____.

This notice is given to inform you that the Bailee's duties cease with respect to the bailed property on your failure to remove the property, after being given notice to remove it.

Dated: _____

Signature of Bailee _____

FORM 9-44 Bailee's notice of intent to sell property.

> This form may be used, for example, when someone has left property at your home and, after notification, has failed to remove the property. Certified Mail, Return Receipt Requested.

NOTICE OF INTENT TO SELL PROPERTY

To: [Owner of property] _____

[Address of owner] _____

You are hereby notified that the [description of property] _____ _____, now on the premises of the undersigned at [address and location of property, including city and state] _____ _____, will be sold at a public auction if the property is not claimed by you prior to [date and time, including year] _____. You were notified on [date] _____ to remove the subject property. You have not taken any action. If the property is sold at public auction, the proceeds will first be used to cover the cost of the sale, and then storage charges. If any proceeds are remaining, they will be forwarded to you at your last known address.

This notice is given to inform you that the Bailee's duties cease with respect to the bailed property on your failure to remove the property after being given notice to remove it.

Dated: _____

Signature of bailee: _____

FORM 9-45   Bailee's notice of loss of property.

> This form could be used if you are keeping someone's property for him or her and the property is destroyed. Certified Mail, Return Receipt Requested.

To: [Owner of property.] _____

[Address of owner] _____

You are hereby notified that the [description of property], _____

_____, now on the premises of the undersigned at [address and location of property, including city and state] _____

_____, was on [date] _____ [lost, damaged, destroyed, etc.] _____ as the result of: _____.

This notice is given to inform you of the loss so that you may file any claims with your insurance company and the like.

Dated: _____   Signature of Bailee: _____

FORM 9-46   Bailor's demand for information.

> Certified Mail, Return Receipt Requested.

To: [Bailee of property] _____

[Address] _____

You notified me on [date] _____ that my property that was under your care had been [destroyed, lost, damaged, etc.] _____. Demand is hereby made for further information as to the circumstance of the [loss or damage] _____

_____.

This demand is given to inform you of the Bailor's duty to explain any damage or loss to the bailed property. Accordingly, unless the information is provided within __ days, steps will be taken to enforce my legal rights regarding this property.

Dated: _____   Signature of Bailor: _____

FORM 9-47   Bailor's demand for delivery of property.

Certified Mail, Return Receipt Requested.

To: [Bailee of property] _____

[Address] _____

You are hereby requested to deliver the [description of property] _____
_____, to [address and location, including city and state]
_____.

This demand is given to inform you of the Bailor's duty to return the bailed property. Accordingly, unless the property is returned within __ days, steps will be taken to enforce my legal rights to recover my property.

Dated: _____   Signature of Bailor: _____

III. Forms Related to Real Property

Most of the forms related to real property are generally completed by a broker, title firm, and/or attorney, and therefore they are included on the CD only. The forms that are commonly used by a homeowner are included both in this chapter and on the CD.

The following forms, 9-48 through 9-54, only appear on the accompanying CD.

- Form 9-48 Grant Deed with Reservations of Mineral Rights
- Form 9-49 Grant Deed with the Assumption of Encumbrances (Note)
- Form 9-50 Grant Deed with the Assumption of Encumbrances (Lease)
- Form 9-51 Grant Deed Creating a Joint Tenancy
- Form 9-52 Grant Deed by Joint Tenants to a Third Person
- Form 9-53 Grant Deed of Life Estate
- Form 9-54 Grant Deed Reserving Life Estate

FORM 9-55 Discharge and satisfaction of mortgage.

This form would be used to record the release of a mortgage.

BE IT KNOWN, we, the holders of a real estate mortgage from [name of persons holders of mortgage] _____, for value received, hereby acknowledge full satisfaction and discharge of the below-listed mortgage [enter a complete mortgage description at this point] _____, the said mortgage was recorded in Book or Volume __, page __, of the _____ County Registry of Deeds.

Signed under seal this ____ day of _____, 20__.

_____   _____ [Signatures]

ACKNOWLEDGMENT

State of   )

County of   )

On this date, [list names of person(s) who signed above] _____ personally appeared before me and acknowledged that the above signature(s) are valid and binding.

_____

Notary Public

My Commission expires: _____

FORM 9-56 Notice of exercise option to purchase.

This form may be used to notify the seller that you wish to exercise your option to purchase certain real estate that you are currently leasing if the lease contains an option to purchase.

Certified Mail, Return Receipt Requested

[Date] _____

[Company or person's name and address] _____

_____

Re: Notice to exercise option to purchase property

To: [Lessor] _____

This is to officially notify you that we are exercising our option to purchase the leased property located at [address of property] _____.

Under the terms of the present lease, we have the option to purchase the said property. Pursuant to lease, we hereby exercise the option to purchase the property at the option price of $ _____. Enclosed is our required down payment in the amount of $ _____.

Sincerely,

_____   _____

[Signatures] Lessee(s)

FORM 9-57   Notice of cancellation of option to purchase real estate.

This form may be used by a homeowner to cancel an option to purchase his or her home. For example, you are considering selling your home, and an individual has an option to purchase it. The individual has failed to comply with the terms of the agreement, and you want to look for a new buyer. Before agreeing with a new buyer, you will need to cancel the option to purchase with the person who currently has the option. Certified Mail, Return Receipt Requested.

BE IT KNOWN that the below described option to purchase real estate located at [description of real estate in question] _____

_____

has been canceled in that the holder of the option has failed to comply with the terms of the option agreement.

Description of option [enter a complete option description at this point]: _____

_____

Description of terms of option that were not complied with [describe the acts on which the cancellation is based, e.g., failed to pay a prescribed amount by a certain date.]: _____

_____

The said option was recorded in Book or Volume __, page __, of the _____ County Registry of Deeds.

Signed under seal this ____ day of _____, 20 __.

_____
Signature

ACKNOWLEDGMENT

State of   )

County of   )

On this date, [list names of person(s) who signed above] _____

_____ personally appeared before me and acknowledged that the above signature(s) are valid and binding.

_____
Notary Public

My Commission expires: _____

FORM 9-58 Assignment of a real estate contract.

This form would be used to assign a contract that you have to purchase real property. For example, you signed a contract to purchase a vacant lot next to your home. Later you decide that you cannot afford the lot. Since the contract was for a good price, you can take advantage of the good price and sell your right to purchase the property. Note: The original contract must be assignable.

For good and valuable consideration, receipt of which is hereby acknowledged, on [date] _____, I assigned all my interest and benefit in the following contract for the sale and purchase of [legal description of real estate]: _____

to: [person to whom contract was assigned, including address] _____
_____

WITNESSED this ____ day of _____, 20__.

Assignor _____   Assignee _____

ACKNOWLEDGMENT

State of   )

County of   )

On this date, [list names of person(s) who signed above] _____
_____ personally appeared before me and acknowledged that the above signature(s) are valid and binding.

_____
Notary Public

My Commission expires: _____

IV. Forms Related to Employment

FORM 9-59 Employment resignation.

Date: _____

To: [employer] _____

Re: Letter of resignation

Please accept this letter as my resignation from the company, effective on [date] _____. It is my intention to terminate my employment in all capacities with the company.

I will return all company property prior to the above termination date. I am also aware that I am under an obligation to protect and keep confidential all company trade secrets.

FORM 9-59 continued

> Please send all money due me to the address below.
>
> This is a voluntary resignation.
>
> Sincerely,
>
> [Signature of employee] _____ [print name] _____
>
> [Street address] _____

FORM 9-60 Assignment of wages.

> The assignment of wages is prohibited in some states. Generally an assignment of wages is used as a means of obtaining a loan.

> For good and valuable consideration, the undersigned hereby unconditionally and irrevocably assigns and transfers and orders paid to [Assignee] _____ the sum of $__ per pay period of wages or salary earned or to be earned and payable to me by [employer] _____.
>
> This assignment is given to satisfy a debt of [debtor] _____.
>
> I authorize and direct my employer to pay Assignee named above until the full amount of the debt has been paid.
>
> The undersigned Assignor warrants that there are no conflicting assignments of wages. The undersigned also warrants that the rights and benefits assigned hereunder are free and clear of any liens, encumbrances, adverse claims, or interest. In addition, the Assignor also warrants that he/she has no knowledge of any disputes or defenses thereon.
>
> This assignment shall be binding upon and inure to the benefit of the parties, their successors, assigns, and personal representatives.
>
> Signed under seal this__ day of _____, 20__.
>
> Assignor _____

FORM 9-61 Employment eligibility verification Form I-9.

Department of Homeland Security
U.S. Citizenship and Immigration Services

OMB No. 1615-0047; Expires 03/31/07
Employment Eligibility Verification

Please read instructions carefully before completing this form. The instructions must be available during completion of this form. ANTI-DISCRIMINATION NOTICE: It is illegal to discriminate against work eligible individuals. Employers CANNOT specify which document(s) they will accept from an employee. The refusal to hire an individual because of a future expiration date may also constitute illegal discrimination.

Section 1. Employee Information and Verification. To be completed and signed by employee at the time employment begins.

Print Name: Last	First	Middle Initial	Maiden Name

Address (Street Name and Number)		Apt. #	Date of Birth (month/day/year)

City	State	Zip Code	Social Security #

I am aware that federal law provides for imprisonment and/or fines for false statements or use of false documents in connection with the completion of this form.

I attest, under penalty of perjury, that I am (check one of the following):
- [ ] A citizen or national of the United States
- [ ] A Lawful Permanent Resident (Alien #) A _____
- [ ] An alien authorized to work until _____
(Alien # or Admission #)

Employee's Signature	Date (month/day/year)

Preparer and/or Translator Certification. (To be completed and signed if Section 1 is prepared by a person other than the employee.) I attest, under penalty of perjury, that I have assisted in the completion of this form and that to the best of my knowledge the information is true and correct.

Preparer's/Translator's Signature	Print Name

Address (Street Name and Number, City, State, Zip Code)	Date (month/day/year)

Section 2. Employer Review and Verification. To be completed and signed by employer. Examine one document from List A OR examine one document from List B and one from List C, as listed on the reverse of this form, and record the title, number and expiration date, if any, of the document(s).

List A	OR	List B	AND	List C
Document title: _____		_____		_____
Issuing authority: _____		_____		_____
Document #: _____		_____		_____
Expiration Date (if any): _____		_____		_____
Document #: _____		_____		
Expiration Date (if any): _____				

CERTIFICATION - I attest, under penalty of perjury, that I have examined the document(s) presented by the above-named employee, that the above-listed document(s) appear to be genuine and to relate to the employee named, that the employee began employment on (month/day/year) _____ **and that to the best of my knowledge the employee is eligible to work in the United States. (State employment agencies may omit the date the employee began employment.)**

Signature of Employer or Authorized Representative	Print Name	Title

Business or Organization Name	Address (Street Name and Number, City, State, Zip Code)	Date (month/day/year)

Section 3. Updating and Reverification. To be completed and signed by employer.

A. New Name (if applicable)	B. Date of rehire (month/day/year) (if applicable)

C. If employee's previous grant of work authorization has expired, provide the information below for the document that establishes current employment eligibility.

Document Title: _____	Document #: _____	Expiration Date (if any): _____

I attest, under penalty of perjury, that to the best of my knowledge, this employee is eligible to work in the United States, and if the employee presented document(s), the document(s) I have examined appear to be genuine and to relate to the individual.

Signature of Employer or Authorized Representative	Date (month/day/year)

NOTE: This is the 1991 edition of the Form I-9 that has been rebranded with a current printing date to reflect the recent transition from the INS to DHS and its components.

Form I-9 (Rev. 05/31/05)Y Page 2

V. Forms Related to Copyrights and Patents

How to Obtain a Copyright

Obtaining a copyright involves a lengthy but not complicated process. If you want to obtain a copyright or have specific questions regarding the process, visit the Web site at http://www.copyright.gov/. You may also obtain forms for filing a copyright at the Web site. A similar Web site is available for patents: http://www.uspto.gov/.

FORM 9-62 Assignment of copyright.

If you have obtained or own a copyright, it is considered a form of property and can be assigned, that is, sold to someone else. For example, you have written a book and had it copyrighted. But you lack resources to publish it. You may assign (sell) the copyright to someone with resources to publish it.

For good and valuable consideration, receipt of which is hereby acknowledged, [name of Assignor] _____, Assignor hereby assigns all copyright in [name of work being assigned] _____ the Work, to [person receiving the assignment] _____, Assignee.

Both Assignee and Assignor agree that the Assignee can register and dispose of the copyright of the Work in the Assignee's own name.

Assignor warrants:

1. That he/she is the owner of the copyright of the Work and has the right to assign the copyright.

2. The Work has been copyrighted.

3. There is no dispute or pending dispute over the existence, ownership, or right to assign the Work.

WITNESSED this __ day of _____, 20__.

Assignor _____   Assignee _____

ACKNOWLEDGMENT

State of   )
County of   )

On this date, [list names of person(s) who signed above] _____
_____ personally appeared before me and acknowledged that the above signature(s) are valid and binding.

_____
Notary Public
My Commission expires: _____

FORM 9-63   Permission for one-time use of copyright or patent.

For good and valuable consideration, receipt of which is hereby acknowledged, [name of assignor] _____, Grantor hereby grants permission for the one-time use of the below-described Work that is copyrighted [patented][name of work] _____ _____, to [person receiving the permission] _____ Grantee.

Grantee agrees to use the Work for the below stated purpose only [state purpose]: _____ _____

Grantor warrants:

1. That he/she is the owner of the copyright [patent] of the Work and has the right to grant permission to use the copyright.

2. The Work item has been copyrighted [patented].

3. There is no dispute or pending dispute over the existence, ownership, or right to use the Work [item].

WITNESSED this __ day of _____, 20__.

Grantor _____   Grantee _____

ACKNOWLEDGMENT

State of   )

County of   )

On this date, [names of person(s) who signed above] _____ _____ personally appeared before me and acknowledged that the above signature(s)are valid and binding.

_____
Notary Public
My Commission expires: _____

FORM 9-64 License to use trademark.

A trademark is a distinct sign or mark that the public will recognize as belonging to one company or person. For example you publish an electronic newsletter by the name of *Rent for Profit* and have registered the name as your trademark. If anyone else uses the trademark in a manner that will represent to the public that it is your newsletter, you may bring legal action to prevent its use. The following form allows others with your permission to use your trademark.

For good and valuable consideration, receipt of which is hereby acknowledged, [Assignor] _____, Licensor hereby allows, permits, licenses [person receiving the right to use the license] _____, Licensee, the rights to use the below-described trademark [describe trademark]: _____
_____

This license to use the described trademark is subject to the below limitations [list limitations here]: _____
_____

This license to use the above trademark will expire on [date] _____ or on use of the trademark in violation of the above-listed limitations.

Licensor warrants:

    1. That he/she is the owner of the trademark and has the right to license the use of it.

    2. The trademark has been registered as permitted by state and federal law.

    3. There is no dispute or pending dispute over the existence, ownership, or right to the trademark.

WITNESSED this __ day of ____, 20__.

Licensor _____   Licensee _____

ACKNOWLEDGMENT

State of   )
County of   )
On this date, [names of person(s) who signed above] _____
_____ personally appeared before me and acknowledged that the above signature(s) are valid and binding.

_____
Notary Public
My Commission expires: _____

FORM 9-65   Assignment of patent.

See the discussion under assignment of copyright. A patent is issued for a new item or process. A patent works similarly to a copyright.

For good and valuable consideration, receipt of which is hereby acknowledged, [Assignor] _____, Assignor hereby assigns all patent rights in patent number _____ namely: [describe patent being assigned] _____ the Patent, to [person receiving the assignment] _____, Assignee.

Both Assignee and Assignor agree that the Assignee can register and dispose of the Patent in the Assignee's own name.

Assignor warrants:

1. That he/she is the owner of the said patent and has the right to assign it.

2. The patent is a valid patent.

3. There is no dispute or pending dispute over the existence, ownership, or right to assign the patent.

WITNESSED this __ day of _____, 20__.

Assignor _____   Assignee _____

ACKNOWLEDGMENT

State of   )

County of   )

On this date, [names of person(s) who signed above] _____ _____ personally appeared before me and acknowledged that the above signature(s)are valid and binding.

_____

Notary Public

My Commission expires: _____

FORM 9-66   Assignment of pending patent application.

For good and valuable consideration, receipt of which is hereby acknowledged, [Assignor] _____, Assignor hereby assigns all patent rights in pending patent described in and identified by an application for United States Letters Patent, filed [date filed] _____ namely: [describe patent being assigned] _____, the Pending Patent, to [person receiving the assignment] _____, Assignee.

Both Assignee and Assignor agree that the Assignee can register and dispose of the pending patent in the Assignee's own name.

FORM 9-66 continued

Assignor warrants:

1. That he/she is the owner of the said item or process involved in the pending patent and has the right to assign it.

2. That pending patent is covered by a valid patent application.

3. That is no dispute or pending dispute over the existence, ownership, or right to assign the matter covered in the patent application.

WITNESSED this __ day of _____, 20__.

Assignor _____   Assignee _____

ACKNOWLEDGMENT

State of   )

County of   )

On this date, [names of person(s) who signed above] _____ _____ personally appeared before me and acknowledged that the above signature(s) are valid and binding.

_____

Notary Public

My Commission expires: _____

FORM 9-67 License to use patent right.

Unlike an assignment of a patent, the right to use a patent merely gives an individual the right to use the item or process as stated in the license. The ownership of the patent does not change and still belongs to the person who obtained it.

For good and valuable consideration, receipt of which is hereby acknowledged, [Assignor] _____, Licensor [person who owns the patent] hereby allows, permits, licenses [person receiving the right to use the patent] _____, Licensee [person wanting to use the patent] _____ the rights to use the below described patent [describe patent]: _____ _____ _____

This license to use the described patent is subject to the below limitations [list limitations here]: _____ _____

This license to use the above patent will expire on [date] _____ or on use of the patent rights in violation of the above-listed limitations.

FORM 9-67   continued

Licensor warrants:

    1. That he/she is the owner of the patent and has the right to license the use of its rights.

    2. That is no dispute or pending dispute over the existence, ownership, or right to the patent.

WITNESSED this __ day of _____, 20__.

Assignor _____   Assignee _____

ACKNOWLEDGMENT

State of   )

County of   )

On this date, [names of person(s) who signed above] _____
_____ personally appeared before me and acknowledged
that the above signature(s)are valid and binding.

_____

Notary Public

My Commission expires: _____

VI. Other Legal Forms

FORM 9-68   Specific release.

    This agreement may be used to release a person from a contract.

Date: _____

In consideration for one dollar and other valuable consideration received, [Obligee] _____
_____ hereby relieves and releases [Obligor] _____, and his or her
heirs, and assigns from any claims and liabilities arising out of the following: [Describe the obligation or contract.] _____
_____

This release does not act as a release of any other claims or debts that may be owed to me, my
heirs, and assigns, by the Obligor.

_____

[Signature of Obligee]

FORM 9-69   Satisfaction of judgment.

> This form may be used to indicate that a court judgment has been satisfied and is released.

Date: _____

The undersigned Plaintiff, [Name] _____ hereby certifies that he/she has received full payment and satisfaction of the judgment rendered by [Name of the court] _____ on [date of judgment] _____ in case number _____ [case number] in the case entitled _____ v. _____.

The Plaintiff hereby affirms that Defendant(s) do not owe any more monies under the terms of the judgment.

_____

[Signed by Plaintiff]

ACKNOWLEDGMENT

State of   )

County of   )

On this date, [names of person(s) who signed above] _____ _____ personally appeared before me and acknowledged that the above signature(s) are valid and binding.

_____

Notary Public

My Commission expires: _____

FORM 9-70   Consent to release confidential information.

Date: _____

To: [Employee] _____

A request for release of confidential information has been received from [name of requesting person, agency, or company] _____.

Please initial each of the items below for which you consent to the release of information regarding those data:

Salary: _____

Dates of employment: _____ to _____

Whether you worked under any other names: _____

Reasons for separation: _____

Position and duties: _____

_____

FORM 9-70   continued

Part-time or full-time employment: _____

Name of your supervisor: _____

Other information: _____

_____

Please return to the human resources department.

Date: _____   Employee: _____

FORM 9-71   Request for information under Freedom of Information Act.

Date: _____

To: [Government agency with records] _____

Pursuant to the Freedom of Information Act, I request disclosure of any information on me that may be maintained in your files, and to the extent the disclosure is required by law.

Please forward the information to the address below:

[Complete mailing address at this point] _____

_____

Sincerely,

[Signature] _____

[Printed name] _____

[Date of birth] _____

[Social Security number] _____

Signature witnessed by:

[Signature] _____

[Printed name] _____

FORM 9-72   General assignment.

A general assignment may be used to assign any rights, title, or interest that you have in some form of property. For example, you have an assignable right to use the lot next to your home to store one boat during the winter months. You no longer use the area to store your boat and therefore assign to your neighbor the right to use the storage slot.

FORM 9-72 continued

> For good and valuable consideration, the undersigned hereby unconditionally and irrevocably assigns and transfers unto [Assignee] _____ all rights, title, and interest in and to the following [List assignments]: _____
>
> _____
>
> The undersigned warrants that she/he has full rights and full authority to make this assignment and transfer. The undersigned also warrants that the rights and benefits assigned hereunder are free and clear of any liens, encumbrances, adverse claims, or interest.
>
> This assignment shall be binding upon and inure to the benefit of the parties, their successors, assigns, and personal representatives.
>
> Signed under seal this __ day of _____, 20__.
>
> Assignor _____   Address _____

FORM 9-73 Assignment of accounts receivable.

> The assignment of accounts receivable is used to assign any sums of money owed to you by others.

> For good and valuable consideration, the undersigned hereby unconditionally and irrevocably assigns and transfers all rights, title, and interest in and to the accounts receivable as annexed to [Assignee] _____ and his/her successors and assigns.
>
> The undersigned Assignor warrants that the said accounts are just and due in the amounts stated and that he/she has not received payment for the same or any part thereof and that he/she has full rights and full authority to make this assignment and transfer. The undersigned also warrants that the rights and benefits assigned hereunder are free and clear of any liens, encumbrances, adverse claims, or interest. In addition, the Assignor also warrants that he/she has no knowledge of any disputes or defenses thereon. The accounts are sold without warranty or guaranty of collection and without recourse to the undersigned Assignor in the event of nonpayment. Assignee may prosecute collection of any receivable in his/her own name.
>
> This assignment shall be binding upon and inure to the benefit of the parties, their successors, assigns, and personal representatives.
>
> Signed under seal this __ day of _____, 20__.
>
> Assignor _____   Address _____

FORM 9-74   Assignment of a partner's interest in partnership.

For good and valuable consideration, receipt of which is hereby acknowledged, on [date] _____, I assigned all my interest in the partnership of [name of partnership] _____ located at [address of partnership] _____ to [person to whom the interest is being assigned, including address] _____.

The Assignor warrants that he/she is a general [or limited] partner in the above-listed partnership and has the right to assign his/her interest in the partnership.

WITNESSED the hands of said Assignor this __ day of_____, 20__.

Assignor _____   Assignee _____

ACKNOWLEDGMENT

State of   )

County of   )

On this date, [names of person(s) who signed above] _____ _____ personally appeared before me and acknowledged that the above signature(s)are valid and binding.

_____

Notary Public

My Commission expires: _____

FORM 9-75   Assignment of interest in joint venture.

For good and valuable consideration, receipt of which is hereby acknowledged, on [date] _____, I assigned all my interest in the joint venture of [description of joint venture] _____ located at [business address of venture] _____ _____ to [person to whom the interest is being assigned, including address] _____ _____.

The Assignor warrants that he/she has the right to assign his/her interest in the above described joint venture. The Assignor also warrants that his/her interest in the joint venture is as follows: _____

WITNESSED the hands of said Assignor this __ day of_____, 20__.

Assignor _____   Assignee _____

ACKNOWLEDGMENT

State of   )

County of   )

On this date, [names of person(s) who signed above] _____ _____ personally appeared before me and acknowledged that the above signature(s)are valid and binding.

_____

Notary Public

My Commission expires: _____

FORM 9-76 Assignment of income from a trust.

For good and valuable consideration, receipt of which is hereby acknowledged, on [date] ____,
I assign $_____ of my share in the income from a trust fund established by the Will
of _____, deceased, which trust fund is in the custody of [trustee's
name and address] _____ to:
[person to whom account is being assigned, including address] _____
_____

I direct the trustee to the above-described trust fund to pay to the Assignee the amount named
above from the income that is due or may become due until the amount stated above is paid
in full.

The Assignor warrants that he/she has the right to assign his/her interest in trust fund.

WITNESSED this __ day of _____, 20__.

Assignor _____   Assignee _____

ACKNOWLEDGMENT

State of   )

County of   )

On this date, [names of person(s) who signed above] _____
_____ personally appeared before me and acknowledged
that the above signature(s) are valid and binding.

_____

Notary Public

My Commission expires: _____

FORM 9-77 Assignment of claim for damages.

For good and valuable consideration, receipt of which is hereby acknowledged, on [date]
_____, I assign and transfer to _____[person to whom account is
being assigned, including address] Assignee any and all sums of money due or owing to me,
and all claims, demands, and cause or causes of action of whatsoever kind and nature that I
have had, now have, or may have against _____ of [address] _____
_____ or any other person or persons, whether jointly or
severally, arising out of, or for, any loss, injury, or damage sustained by me in connection with:
[describe incident or basis of claim] _____
_____

This assignment is without recourse, and Assignor does not guarantee payment of the assigned
claim.

The Assignor warrants that he/she has the right to assign his/her claim and appoints the
Assignee as his or her attorney with power to demand and received satisfaction of the assigned
claim and, in the name of the Assignor, but at Assignee's expense, to sue or any other legal
process necessary for the collection of this claim.

WITNESSED this __ day of _____, 20__.

Assignor _____   Assignee _____

FORM 9-77   continued

ACKNOWLEDGMENT

State of   )

County of   )

On this date, [names of person(s) who signed above] _____
_____ personally appeared before me and acknowledged
that the above signature(s)are valid and binding.

_____   My Commission expires: _____

Notary Public

FORM 9-78   Assignment of a judgment.

> This form may be used to assign a judgment to someone else. For example, you
> take a neighbor to small claims court because the neighbor damaged your fence,
> and the neighbor refuses to pay the court judgment. You could assign the judgment
> to a debt collector for a lesser sum or for a percentage of the judgment collected.

For good and valuable consideration, receipt of which is hereby acknowledged, on [date]
_____, I assign and transfer to [person to whom account is being assigned, including address]
_____
Assignee, any and all sums of money due or owing to me, and all claims, demands, and cause
or causes of action of whatsoever kind and nature that I have had, now have, or may have from
that certain judgment against _____ of [Address] _____
_____ to wit; [List court number and court in which judgment was
granted.] _____.

This assignment is without recourse, and Assignor does not guarantee payment of the assigned
claim.

The Assignor warrants that he/she has the right to assign his/her judgment and appoints the
Assignee as his or her attorney with power to demand and receive satisfaction of the assigned
judgment and, in the name of the Assignor, but at Assignee's expense, to sue or pursue any
other legal process necessary for the collection of this judgment.

WITNESSED this __ day of _____, 20__.

Assignor _____   Assignee _____

ACKNOWLEDGMENT

State of   )

County of   )

On this date, [names of person(s) who signed above] _____
_____ personally appeared before me and acknowledged
that the above signature(s)are valid and binding.

_____

Notary Public

My Commission expires: _____

FORM 9-79   Notice of assignment (by assignee).

> This form would be used by a person who receives an assignment of a contract benefit to notify the original parties to the contract that the benefits, probably money, now belong to them. Certified Mail, Return Receipt Requested.

Date: _____

To: [party to original contract] _____ on [date] _____,
[name of Assignor] _____ assigned all his/her interest and benefit in the following: [describe what was assigned] to [person to whom contract was assigned, including address] _____

_____

Accordingly, any payments, rights, benefits to be paid or distributed as the results of the assigned property should be addressed to the above named Assignee.

Attached to this notice is a copy of the assignment.

Assignee: _____

FORM 9-80   Notice of assignment (by assignor).

> This form is similar to the prior notice of assignment, but in this case the notice is sent by the person who assigned the contract, that is, the original party to the contract who assigned his or her benefits to someone else. Certified Mail, Return Receipt Requested.

Date: _____

To: [party to original contract] _____

On [date] _____, [name of Assignor] _____
assigned all his/her interest and benefit in the following [describe what was assigned] _____
_____ to [person to whom contract was assigned, including address] _____

Accordingly, any payments, rights, benefits to be paid or distributed as the results of the assigned property should be addressed to the above-named Assignee. Attached to this notice is a copy of the assignment.

Assignor: _____

FORM 9-81   Notice of cancellation of assignment.

Certified Mail, Return Receipt Requested.

Date: _____

To: [party to original contract] _____

On [date] _____, you were notified that [name of Assignor] _____
___ assigned all his/her interest and benefit in the following: [describe what was assigned]
_____ to [person to whom contract was assigned, including
address]: _____

Notice is hereby given that the above-stated assignment has been canceled by agreement
between the parties. A copy of the cancellation agreement is attached.

Accordingly, the undersigned is now the owner of any benefits, income, and the like of the
subject of the previous assignment. All payments and so forth should be forwarded to the below
person at the below address [name and address of person to whom payments should now be
made]: _____

_____

Signed: _____

FORM 9-82   Demand for proof of assignment.

This form is used when a person receives notice that a contract that he or she is a
party to has been assigned. For example, you have a contract to pay your neighbor
a monthly fee to park your RV on her property. You receive a letter from a third
person informing you to pay the monthly fee to him. You may wish to demand
proof that he has the right to receive payment before you pay him the monthly fee.
Certified Mail, Return Receipt Requested.

Date: _____

To: [party to giving notice of assignment] _____

On [date] _____, I was notified that [name of Assignor] _____
assigned all his/her interest and benefit in the following: [describe what was assigned] _____
_____ to [person to whom contract was assigned, including address] _____
_____

Demand is hereby given for reasonable proof that the [account, debt, stock certificate, and so
forth] was assigned.

Signed: _____

FORM 9-83   Notice of rescission.

This letter may be used when you are rescinding a contract with a seller. Certified Mail, Return Receipt Requested.

Date: _____

To: _____

Dear _____:

Re: Rescission of contract with your company dated [date] _____

You are hereby notified that I am exercising my right to rescind the contract entered into with your company on [date] _____. Accordingly, please cancel said contract and return my deposit of $_____. Please note that under the provisions of the Federal Truth in Lending Act, I have three days to cancel said contract and this rescission is pursuant to that right.

In addition, you are requested to cancel any lien against our property within ten days as required by law.

Sincerely,

_____   _____

Signature   Address

FORM 9-84   Objection to assignment of account balance.

This letter may be used to object to the assignment of an account balance. Before objecting, however, check the terms of the contract to ensure that the vendor does not have the right to assign the account. For example, you borrowed money from a friend. Under the terms of the written contract, the contract is not assignable. When you receive notice to make the monthly payments to a finance company, which is a violation of the contract, you may want to object to the assignment. Certified Mail, Return Receipt Requested.

Date: _____

To: _____

Dear Madam/Sir:

We have been notified that you have assigned the account balance on our account to [Assignee] _____. Please be advised that this assignment is without our approval and in violation of our agreement with your company. To ensure that we receive proper credit, all future payments will be placed in escrow with [trust company] until we receive valid instructions from your company.

According to our records, the outstanding balance is $_____, and the next payment in the amount of $_____ is due on _____. If this is not correct, please notify us as soon as possible.

Sincerely,

_____

Signature

10

Handling the Death of a Relative and Life Insurance

Forms and Information in This Chapter

Information marked with an asterisk (*) is available only on the accompanying CD.

*Federal Estate Tax and Life Insurance
*Your Small Business and Life Insurance
*Family-Owned Businesses
*Specific Situations
*Buyout Agreements

I. Death of a Relative or Friend

FORM 10-1   Obtaining a death certificate.

In many cases, you may obtain a death certificate from the funeral home shortly after the death. If it is not available from the funeral home, check with the local county records office. To get the address of the local department that handles death certificates, call the National Center for Health Statistics, Division of Data Services, telephone number (301) 458-4636, or online at www.cdc.gov/nchs/howto/w2w/welcome.htm. The below form letter may be used to request the certificate. Note: You will need a certified death certificate for many purposes.

Date: _____
To: Clerk; Office of Vital Statistics [their local address]

_____

_____

Re: Request for death certificate of [insert full name] _____

Date of death: _____   Decedent's social security number: _____

Place of death: [Give name and full address of hospital or elsewhere including city and state.]:
_____
_____

A certified certificate is needed for [reason certificate is needed] _____.

My relationship to the decedent is _____.

Enclosed is a [certified check] [money order] for [check for amount of fee] $_____

Please forward certificate to the undersigned at [address] _____
_____

Sincerely,

_____
Signature

FORM 10-2 Notice of death of social security recipient.

This form may be used to notify the Social Security Administration of the death of a person receiving social security benefits

---

[Date]: _____

To: Social Security Administration Office

[Address] _____

Re: [Decedent] _____   SSN: _____

This notice is to inform you that the above-named person who is currently receiving social security benefits died on [date] _____. On the date of his/her death he/she resided at _____
_____ .

Enclosed in this letter are any payments received after his/her death. Any additional payments received will be returned.

If you need any additional information, you may contact me at [address] _____
_____, [daytime telephone number] _____.

Sincerely,

_____
Signature

FORM 10-3 Notice of death of debtor.

Use this form to notify the creditors of the death of a debtor.

Date: _____

To: [Creditor] _____

Re: _____, SSN _____,

Account No. _____

This letter is to inform you that the above-referenced individual died on [date of death] _____.

[Include one of the following statements.]

No probate proceedings are planned.

[or]

Probate proceedings are have been filed in _____ Court.

[or]

Probate proceedings are planned. For more information contact _____.

Sincerely

_____

Address: _____

FORM 10-4   Notice of death to decedent's home mortgage company.

Use this form to notify the mortgage company of the death of the mortgagee.

Date:_____

To: [home mortgage company] _____

Re: _____, SSN: _____,

Account No.: _____

This letter is to inform you that the above-referenced individual died on [date of death] _____. Attached is a certified copy of the death certificate. I am the executor of the estate. Please contact me regarding the mortgage.

Sincerely,

_____

Address: _____

FORM 10-5   Notice of death to decedent's home insurance company.

Use this form to notify the home insurance company of the death of the home-owner.

Date:_____

To: [home mortgage insurance company] _____

_____

Re: _____, SSN: _____,

Policy No.: _____

This letter is to inform you that the above-referenced individual died on [date of death] ____. Attached is a certified copy of the death certificate. I am the executor of the estate and would like to be added to the policy as a named payee to this insurance policy. Please contact me regarding the home insurance policy.

Sincerely,

_____

Address: _____

FORM 10-6 General notice of death.

Use this form to notify individuals and organizations of the death of a person.

Date: _____

To: [person or organization] _____

Re: _____, SSN _____,

I regret to inform you that the above-referenced individual died on [date] _____.
Please advise me if you need additional information regarding this matter.

Sincerely,

_____ (Signature)

Address: _____

FORM 10-7 Obituary fact sheet.

Decedent: _____ (full name)

Date of death: _____

Age at death: _____

Location of death: _____ (city and state)

Address of decedent on date of death: _____

Place of birth: _____

Religious affiliation: _____

Organization affiliations: _____

Education: _____

Military service: _____

Occupation or profession: _____

Honors, awards, etc.: _____

Survived by: _____

_____

Predeceased by: _____

Funeral services planned: _____

Contact person: _____

FORM 10-8   Inventory worksheet.

This worksheet can serve three purposes. First, it can be used to help organize information for an elderly relative; second, it can be used as a worksheet in your own estate planning process; and third, it can be used as a personal affairs record of certain vital and necessary information for the administrator of your estate. It should be updated at least annually.

Family Information

Complete name: _____

Date of birth: _____   Place of birth: _____

Social security number: _____

Spouse's name: _____

Spouse's date of birth: _____ Spouse's place of birth: _____

Spouse's social security number: _____

Home address: _____

Business address: _____
_____

Place and date of present marriage: _____

Place and date of any divorce proceedings: _____

Name of former spouse: _____

Children

Name	Date of birth	Marital status
_____	_____	_____
_____	_____	_____
_____	_____	_____
_____	_____	_____

Advisers

Attorney: _____

Financial adviser: _____

Insurance agent: _____

Banker: _____

Accountant: _____

Trustee of trusts: _____

Alternate trustee: _____

FORM 10-8 continued

Records

[Indicate the location of the following records.]

Family records: _____

Military records: _____

Will: _____

Trust documents: _____

Retirement and pension records: _____

Safe deposit box: _____

Insurance policies, etc.: _____

Property deeds and titles: _____

Powers of attorney: _____

Prior federal tax returns: _____

Gift tax records: _____

Medical records: _____

Cemetery deeds: _____

Promissory notes: _____

Postnuptial/antenuptial agreements: _____

Banking

Bank Accounts

Institution	Account type	Account number
_____	_____	_____
_____	_____	_____
_____	_____	_____
_____	_____	_____

Insurance

[List all insurance coverage.]

Type of policy	Policy number
_____	_____
_____	_____
_____	_____
_____	_____

FORM 10-8 continued

Business interests and agreements

List all business interests you are currently involved with and any business agreements that you are a party to.

_____

_____

_____

_____

Stocks, Bonds, etc.

Description	Location	Date acquired	Original cost
_____	_____	_____	_____
_____	_____	_____	_____
_____	_____	_____	_____
_____	_____	_____	_____

Real Property

[List all interests in any real properties.]

Type of property	Location	Interest owned
_____	_____	_____
_____	_____	_____
_____	_____	_____
_____	_____	_____

Automobiles

[List all interests in automobiles.]

Type	License number	Insured by
_____	_____	_____
_____	_____	_____
_____	_____	_____
_____	_____	_____

Other Personal Property

[List major items of person property owned.]

Description of item	Location
_____	_____
_____	_____
_____	_____
_____	_____

II. Life Insurance

Life insurance is a popular method used by many persons to build a sizable estate for the loved ones they leave behind. By using a life insurance trust, you can ensure that there is a sum of money left to those selected by you and without the possibility that this money will be attached by your creditors if your estate is not otherwise adequate to cover your debts.

Life insurance is a contract between the owner of the policy and the insurance company. The owner of the policy agrees to pay premiums to the company. In return, the company will pay a stated amount on the death of the insured. When you're buying life insurance, consider the questions below:

1. Why do I need life insurance?
2. How much do I need?
3. What type of insurance do I need?
4. How should the proceeds of the policy be paid?

Recent Developments in Life Insurance

In recent years, there have been some major changes in the life insurance industry. Therefore, we need to reexamine our beliefs and the rules regarding the use of life insurance in estate planning. The major changes include:

1. Insurance policies are now more complex and offer more flexibility than they did in prior years. In some cases it now takes a computer program to determine premiums.
2. Insurance agents are more professional and better informed than they were in prior years.
3. Recent consumer legislation and Federal Trade Commission rules have resulted in better insurance buys for the individual.
4. Improved health care and heightened health consciousness have led to lower mortality rates. Accordingly, with people living longer, the actual cost of life insurance should be lower.
5. Flexible interest rates on insurance investments have required insurance companies to be more flexible in their treatment of policy cash reserves.

Note: Because of the increased flexibility in the market, a larger number of insurance companies are going bankrupt. Deal only with established companies.

Types of Life Insurance Policies

Term

Term insurance is simply a contract to provide money in the event of death in return for regular premium payments. As you get older, the premiums become higher. Eventually, the premiums become too expensive to afford. Some term policies are renewable for one or more terms. The advantage of term insurance is that it provides the largest immediate death protection for your money. Some term policies are "convertible." This normally means that they can be converted into whole life or endowment insurance policies even when the insured parties are not in good health.

Whole Life Insurance

Whole life insurance is designed to provide coverage for the insured person's entire life. It is also called *straight life*. One of the key features of most whole life insurance policies is that the premiums remain constant over the duration of the policy. Some whole life policies are designed so that the premiums are paid up at age 65 or after 20 years.

Single Premium Whole Life

Single premium whole life insurance is more a form of investment than life insurance. In most cases, the policies are in multiples of $100,000. Typically, included in the policy is the right to borrow against it. The big advantage of the single premium whole life policy is that you can borrow against the face value of the policy (normally about 10 percent of the face amount) and obtain a tax advantage from the interest that the cash value earns. For example, a taxpayer buys a single premium whole life policy. The insurance company invests the premium and receives interest on the investment. Most of the interest is credited to the policy. Since the interest income is credited to the policy and not paid to the taxpayer, the taxpayer is not required to pay income tax on the interest in most cases. The taxpayer then borrows on the policy. By doing this, the taxpayer receives money from the investment without paying income tax on it.

Annuities

There are four basic types of annuities. They are as follows:

1. *Straight life.* This type of policy provides for annuity payments for the life of the insured (the person covered by the policy). There are no guaranteed number of payments, and on the death of the insured no further payments are made.

2. *Life with a term contract:* Under this contract, annuity payments are made for the life of the insured. If the insured dies prior to the expiration of a fixed term, then payments will be made to a designated person until the expiration of the fixed term.
3. *Refund annuity:* Under this policy, annuity payments are made for the life of the insured. If the insured dies prior to a fixed term, then a refund for the unused portion of the annuity is made to a designated person.
4. *Joint and survivor annuity:* This is an annuity payable for the life of two persons (normally husband and wife). On the death of one of the insured parties, the payments continue being made to the survivor.

Additional information on life insurance can be found on the CD that accompanies this book.

11

Estate Planning Forms

Forms and Information in This Chapter

Items marked with an asterisk (*) only appear on the accompanying CD.

I.   Introduction

II.   Trusts

I. Introduction

The most often used formal estate planning instrument is the individual will. If the deceased has a valid will, it controls the disposition of all property subject to probate. It, however, does not control property that is not a part of the probate estate.

Estate planning is more than planning for the transfer of property when we die; it is also planning our estate to ensure effective enjoyment of the property in the estate during our lifetime. This chapter is intended to help you understand estate planning techniques, make rational decisions regarding your estate, and judge the competency of any estate planning advisers you use. Included are discussions on probate, wills, trusts, and other estate planning devices.

The chapter is not designed to present definitive advice on all aspects of estate planning. Each individual's situation is different. Understanding estate planning's general concepts, however, should help you to make intelligent decisions as to whether you are capable of doing your own estate planning, when you need professional help, and the type of professional help needed. Estate planning is one of the most jargon-ridden areas of law. For this reason, please refer to the glossary for those terms you do not understand.

Estate planning includes, to a great extent, the planning for our deaths. Not a very popular subject. We would like to think that we will live forever. For this reason, most Americans delay estate planning until "next week." Not only is this practice costly, but it also increases the burdens of our death on the ones we love. The business of estate planning is too important to be left to chance. If you don't take care of it yourself, the government, in its bureaucratic ways, will do your planning for you. The pain and grief of your death on your loved ones will be increased greatly by your failure to plan for the financial and practical problems that are associated with death.

Americans in general are concerned with saving on their taxes. Often, major decisions affecting our lives are made on the basis of least tax liability. In estate planning, however, the nontax considerations may be of greater concern than the tax considerations. The general rules and requirements for a valid will are discussed along with an overview of the law of wills.

II. Trusts

The Advantages of Using Living Trusts

The advantages of living trusts when compared to wills are considerable. Under a will, an estate must be settled in probate court. Lawyers' fees and court costs often are substantial; there may be exasperating delays; and the proceedings are a matter of public record. In contrast, a living trust is settled without a court proceeding; a successor trustee simply distributes assets according to the trust's instructions, with an accountant, notary public, or lawyer certifying any transfer of titles. The process is much quicker, cheaper, and more private than settling a will, and it may save on estate taxes.

Common Misconceptions Regarding Trusts

The two most common misconceptions regarding trusts are:

1. You lose control of your property.
2. Trusts are for only wealthy people with large estates.

For a detailed discussion on trusts, see the article "Additional Information on Trusts" included on the CD that accompanies this book, pages 258A–258S.

An Example of a Living Trust for a Married Couple With a Modest Estate

Joe and Mary Smith have been married for 21 years. They have five children ranging in age from 20 years to 5 years. Their total estate is valued at less than $600,000. They create a living trust, which includes the following terms (Note: The terms are summarized):

1. The trust is a revocable living trust with both Joe and Mary as trustees and primary beneficiaries.
2. The terms of the trust can be amended or revoked by either trustee.
3. If one of the trustees becomes unable to act, then the other trustee assumes complete control of the trust.
4. On the death of one of the trustees, the surviving trustee acts as sole trustee with complete control of the trust.
5. On the death of the surviving spouse Joe Friend assumes the position of trustee of the trust.
6. If on the death of the surviving spouse there are children under the age of 18, the funds of the trust are to be used to provide the necessary support for the minor children until they reach the age of 18. When the youngest child reaches 18, any remaining assets of the trust are to be divided equally among the children.

Under the terms of this trust, Joe and Mary have complete control of the assets of the trust during their lifetime. On the death of one spouse, the other spouse has complete control of the assets without the need to probate the estate. No federal estate tax is due because of the marital deduction. If one spouse becomes incompetent and thus unable to manage assets, the other spouse can continue to manage the assets of the trust.

On the death of the surviving spouse, if any children are under the age of 18, the trustee provides for their support out of the trust income and if necessary the trust assets. When the last child reaches the age of 18, the trustee divides the property equally among the children. No probate is required. On the death of the surviving spouse, if the value of the estate is above a certain amount, there may be federal estate taxes to pay.

Additional Information on Trusts

Additional information on trusts, including an example of a living trust for a married couple with a large estate and an example of a living trust for a single person, is contained on the accompanying CD.

Checklist of Trust Considerations

The items listed below should be considered when you're making decisions regarding the terms of a possible trust:

1. Size of your estate.
2. Future growth of your estate.
3. Needs of spouse and children.
4. Special needs of any beneficiary.
5. Successor trustees.
6. Is a trustee bond needed?
7. Residence of trust.
8. Trust income disposition.
9. Special powers of trustee.
10. Pour-over will.
11. If more than one trustee, is unanimity of cotrustees required?
12. Accounting requirement for the trust.
13. Will any beneficiary be under the age of 18?
14. Provisions if beneficiaries are deceased.
15. When may trustee invade the assets of the trust?
16. Provisions for payment of estate taxes.
17. Authority of trustee to hire assistance.

Trustee's Checklist

When a person assumes the duties of trustee, the following items should be considered:

1. Questions regarding the trust instrument:
   a. Is the instrument signed and notarized?
   b. Who has copies of the instrument?
   c. Do the copies conform with respect to the date signed?
   d. How will the original copy of the trust instrument be safeguarded?

2. Questions regarding the trust property:
   a. Have the real property titles been transferred to the trustee's name? (Note: Titles should be transferred to the trustee with the designation of trustee, for example, Joe Smith, Trustee.)
   b. Have the securities been registered in the trustee's name?
   c. Have deeds been recorded?
   d. Are property taxes paid, including any transfer and recording taxes or fees?

    e. Have payors, tenants, and so forth, been instructed to send future payments to the trustee?

    f. Has insurance protection been obtained for the trust property?

    g. Have bank accounts and the like been transferred to the trust?

3. Questions regarding accounting and records:

    a. Is there an opening inventory of assets?

    b. Have account books been established?

    c. Who is responsible for keeping the account books?

    d. To whom will accounting be made?

    e. What periodic financial statement will be prepared, and who will prepare them? Who will be given the statements?

    f. Who is responsible for obtaining tax numbers and preparing tax returns?

    g. Are gift tax returns required? If so, who will prepare them?

    h. What types of audits will be conducted, and who will conduct them?

    i. What distributions of income will be made and to whom?

    j. Will there be investment reviews of the trust assets, and, if so, who will conduct the reviews?

    k. How will records and receipts that pertain to the trust be safeguarded?

FORM 11-1   Declaration of trust (married couple with children).

This form may be used by a married couple with children, where the property being left is to children.

We, *John Robinson* (Husband) and *Joan Robinson* (Wife), Trustees (also referred to as the Trustee), declare that *John Robinson* and *Joan Robinson,* the Settlors, have transferred and delivered to the Trustees without any consideration the property listed and described in Exhibit A attached to this document and incorporated by reference herein.

I

The property listed in Exhibit A is subject to this instrument and is hereafter referred to as the Trust Estate. The Trust Estate shall be held, administered, and distributed in accordance with the provisions of this instrument.

II

Either Settlor may during his or her lifetime or by testamentary Wills make additions to the Trust Estate.

III

During the lifetime of each Settlor, the Trustee shall pay to the Settlors or surviving Settlor, or shall apply for the Settlors or the surviving Settlor's benefit, the net income of the Trust Estate in monthly installments.

FORM 11-1 continued

IV

If the Trustee considers that the net income is insufficient, the Trustee may pay to the Settlors or surviving Settlor or apply for either's benefit as much of the principal as is necessary in the Trustee's discretion for either or both Settlors' adequate health, maintenance, and support.

V

The Trustee shall have liberal power to invade the principal, and the rights of the remainder persons in the trust shall be considered of secondary importance.

VI

If at any time, either of the Settlors is certified in writing by two licensed physicians as being physically or mentally incapacitated, whether or not a court of competent jurisdiction has declared him or her incompetent, mentally ill, or in need of a conservator, Trustee shall pay the amount of net income and principal necessary for the proper health, support, and maintenance of him or her, until he or she, as certified by two licensed physicians, is competent to manage his or her own affairs or until his or her earlier death. Any income received by the Trust Estate in excess of the amount applied to for the benefit of the Settlor or Settlors shall be accumulated and added to the Trust Estate.

VII

If a guardian or conservator of either Settlor or of the estate is appointed, the Trustees or Trustee shall take into account any payments made for any Settlor's benefit by the guardian or conservator.

VIII

The Settlors or surviving Settlor may at any time direct the Trustee in writing to pay sums or make periodic payments to other persons or organizations.

IX

On the death of the surviving Settlor, the Trustee shall divide the trust estate into as many shares as there are children of the Settlors then living, and as there are deceased children of the Settlors leaving issue then living. The Trustee shall:

   a. Allocate one such equal share to each then living child of the Settlor, and one such equal share to each group of then living issue of a deceased child of the Settlors.

   b. Distribute each share allocated to a living child of the Settlors, free of the trust.

   c. Distribute each share allocated to a group of living issue of a deceased child of the Settlors to such issue, by right of representation, free of trust.

X

On death of the surviving Settlor, the Trustee, in his or her discretion, may pay out of the Trust Estate debts of either Settlor any estate and inheritance taxes, including interest and penalties, arising from the either Settlor's death, last illness and funeral expenses, attorney's fees, and other costs in administering the Settlors' Probate Estates. Any payments made under this paragraph shall be charged against the Trust Estate.

FORM 11-1   continued

XI

During the lifetime of either Settlor, this trust may be revoked in whole or in part by an instrument in writing signed by either Settlor and delivered to the Trustee. On revocation, the Trustee shall promptly deliver to the Settlors or the surviving Settlor all of the remaining trust assets. The Settlors or the surviving Settlor may at any time during his or her lifetime amend any of the terms of this instrument by an instrument in writing signed by the Settlors or surviving Settlor and delivered by mail or in person to the Trustee. The powers of the Settlors or surviving Settlor to amend or revoke this agreement are personal to the Settlors and the surviving Settlor and may not be exercisable on either's behalf by any guardian, conservator, or other person except that revocation or amendment may be authorized after notice to the Trustee by the Court that appointed the guardian or conservator.

XII

On the death of the surviving Settlor, the trust may not be amended, revoked, or terminated, except as provided within this instrument.

XIII

To carry out the purposes and provisions of the Trust created by this instrument, the Trustee shall have these powers and discretion in addition to those now or hereafter conferred by law, and except as elsewhere herein specifically restricted:

a. Power to retain and to continue to hold any property that becomes a part of the Trust Estate.

b. Power to sell, dispose of, exchange, partition, convey, divide, repair, manage, control, and grant options and rights of refusal of property that becomes a part of the Trust Estate for cash, credit, deferred payments, or exchange.

c. Power to lease or rent any property belonging to the Trust Estate for a reasonable term of years, months, or days and for any purpose including exploration and removal of gas, oil, and other minerals, to include community leases and pooling agreements.

d. Power to acquire, at the expense of the Trust Estate, insurance of any kind and in amounts as the Trustee deems advisable.

e. Power to invest all or any part of the Trust Estate in every kind of property, whether real or personal, and every kind of investment.

f. Power to litigate and compromise claims with respect to the Trust Estate as the Trustee deems advisable.

g. Power to manage securities, to include all the rights, powers, and privileges of an owner.

h. Power to allocate to principal or income all monies and properties received on behalf of the Trust Estate.

i. Power to make distributions of the Trust property as required, pursuant to the provisions of this Trust.

j. Power to employ and pay any custodian, investment adviser, attorney, accountant, or other consultant deemed necessary.

k. Power to hold and operate any business interest that may be or become a part of the Trust Estate.

l. Power to pay with funds from the Trust Estate any tax, charge, or assessment against the Trust Estate which the Trustee shall be required to pay.

m. Power to deposit funds in commercial, savings, or savings and loan accounts, subject to the usual restrictions upon withdrawal in effect at the that time.

XIV

Other property acceptable to the Trustee may be added to the Trust Estate by any person.

XV

Unless sooner terminated in accordance with other provisions of this instrument, the Trust created by this instrument shall terminate 21 years after the death of the surviving Settlor.

XVI

No interest in the principal or income of any trust created under this instrument shall be anticipated, assigned, encumbered, or subject to creditor's claim or legal process before being received by a beneficiary.

XVII

The validity of this trust and the construction of its beneficial provisions shall be governed by the laws of the State of _____.

XVIII

Any Trustee shall have the right to resign at any time. The term "Trustee" as used in this instrument includes also "Trustees," "Cotrustees," "Sole Trustee," and "Successor Trustee or Trustees."

XIX

In the event that the Trustee dies, becomes physically or mentally incapacitated (as defined in this instrument), or shall, for any reason, be unable or fail to qualify or cease to act as Trustee, the other Trustee shall act as Sole Trustee. In the event that both Trustees are unable or fail to qualify or cease to act as Trustee, then Jim Robinson and Jane Robinson shall act as Cotrustees. In the event that either one of them, for any reason, fails to qualify or ceases to act as Trustee, then the other of them shall act as Sole Trustee.

XX

No bond shall be required of any Trustee or Cotrustee named in this instrument.

FORM 11-1   continued

XXI

The Trustee may receive reasonable compensation of his or her services on behalf of the Trust.

XXII

The Trust created under/in/by this instrument may be referred to as the JOHN AND JOAN ROBINSON REVOCABLE TRUST of 20____.

Executed in Houston, Texas, on _____ 20____.

_____   _____

Joan Robinson, Settlor   John Robinson, Settlor

_____   _____

Joan Robinson, Trustee   John Robinson, Trustee

State of Texas)

City of Houston)

On _____, 20____, before me, the undersigned, a Notary Public in and for the State, personally appeared John Robinson and Joan Robinson known to me to be the Trustees and the Settlors of the JOHN AND JOAN ROBINSON REVOCABLE TRUST of 20____, and acknowledged to me that he executed the same.

Witness my hand and official seal

_____

Notary public

My Commission expires _____.

Schedule A for JOHN AND JOAN ROBINSON REVOCABLE TRUST of 20__

[List all property on this schedule.]

_____

_____

_____

_____

_____

_____

The following forms are only contained on the accompanying CD.

- Form 11-2: Declaration or Trust (Single Person with Children)
- Form 11-3: Declaration or Trust (Single Person with No Children)

FORM 11-4   Sample letter to insurance company to designate trust as beneficiary of revocable living trust.

Date: _____

John and Joan Robinson
2428 Any Street
Columbia, MO 56749

Re: Change of Beneficiary and Ownership of Life Insurance Policy

No._____, on the life of John Robinson

Dear Sir/Madam:

Enclosed is an original and one copy of a change of beneficiary and ownership form and a copy of the declaration of trust.

Please change the beneficiary designation to "Joan Robinson as Trustee of the JOHN AND JOAN REVOCABLE LIVING TRUST of 20__."

Please record the change and send me acknowledgment of the change. If you have any questions, please contact me.

Sincerely,

_____
John Robinson

Form 11-5: Registration of Motor Vehicles for Trust only appears on the accompanying CD.

FORM 11-6 Bill of sale for trust (for a married couple).

To be used in transferring tangible personal property to a trust.

BILL OF SALE

This Bill of Sale dated _____ (1), by and between _____ (2) and

_____ (2), hereinafter called Settlors, and _____

(3) and _____ (4), hereinafter called Trustees, under the Declaration

of Trust dated _____ (5) and referred to as the Living Trust of _____

_____ (6).

For good and valuable consideration, the Settlors assign, transfer, and convey to the Trustees all their rights, title, and interest in and to all the below-listed tangible property, to hold in trust according to the terms of the Living Trust of _____

_____ (6). The tangible personal property assigned, transferred, and conveyed pursuant to this Bill of Sale is as followed: (7)

_____

_____

_____

_____

_____

_____

_____

_____

Settlors: _____ (8)
                          (9)

         _____ (8)
                          (9)

Trustees: _____ (10)
                          (11)

         _____ (10)
                          (11)

Instructions for Completing Bill of Sale (Married Couple)

1. Insert date on which this bill of sale is signed.
2. Insert the names of the Settlors (persons who are transferring the property to the trust) on these lines.
3. Insert the name of the first-listed Trustee in the original trust document.
4. If there are two trustees, insert the name of the second trustee in this blank. If there is only one trustee, then leave this line blank.

FORM 11-6 continued

---

5. Insert the date indicated on the original trust document.
6. On these lines, provide the name of the living trust as indicated in the original trust document.
7. List items of property on these blanks. Note: Describe the items in detail to clearly indicate the property being transferred.
8. One Settlor should sign on the first line, and the other on the second line.
9. Type in name of the appropriate Settlor in this blank.
10. The trustees should sign in this blank. If there is only one trustee, leave the second line blank. (Note: Trustees should sign their names as listed in the original trust document.)
11. Type names of Trustees in this blank space.

Form 11-7: Bill of Sale for Trust (for an Individual Person) only appears on the accomparying CD.

FORM 11-8   Revocation of living trust (revocable trust, married couple).

WHEREAS, we have previously created a Living Revocable Trust by a Declaration of Trust dated _____ (1) and referred to as the _____ (2) REVOCABLE LIVING TRUST OF 20 _____.

WHEREAS, pursuant to the terms of the Declaration of Trust, we reserved the right to amend or revoke the trust created thereunder without the consent of any beneficiary.

NOW THEREFORE, we do hereby revoke in its entirety the trust of all terms and provisions contained in the aforesaid Declaration of Trust. The trustee or trustees are hereby directed to transfer, assign, and/or convey back to the settlors all property belonging to the trust.

WITNESSED WHEREOF, We have hereunto set our hand and seal this __ day of _____ 20__.(3)

Signed: _____ (4)
              (5)

Signed: _____ (6)
              (7)

ACKNOWLEDGMENT

State of   )(8)

County of   )(8)

I, _____, a Notary Public, within and for the State and County aforesaid do hereby certify that the foregoing instrument entitled "REVOCATION OF LIVING TRUST (REVOCABLE TRUST)" was signed and executed in said County and State by _____ _____ (9) and _____ (9) in my presence and acknowledged to by said parties to be their free act and voluntary deed.

WITNESSED THIS _____ day of _____, 20__.

_____
Notary Public

My Commission expires: _____

Instructions for Completing Revocation of Trust

1. Insert the date the original trust document was signed.
2. Insert title by which the trust is referred in the original trust document.
3. Insert the date that this document is executed.
4. Signature of one spouse on this line.
5. Typed name of the above spouse on this blank.
6. Signature of the other spouse on this line.
7. Typed name of other spouse on this blank.
8. County and state in which this document is being signed.
9. Names of spouses signing this document.

Form 11-9: Revocation of Living Trust (Revocable Trust, Individual Person) only appears on the accompanying CD.

FORM 11-10 Example of an irrevocable trust for a child.

IRREVOCABLE TRUST FOR LISA CARR

JOHN CARR (husband) and JOAN CARR (wife), hereinafter referred to as Trustors, and JOE SMITH, hereinafter referred to as Trustee, hereby enter into the following agreement:

I

At the time that this agreement is executed, Trustors convey and transfer without any consideration running from the Trustee the properties and assets listed in Schedule A attached to this document.

II

The Trustee acknowledges the receipt of the aforesaid property and agrees to hold the same and any other property that may be added to this Trust and to perform the duties of a trustee, subject to the terms and conditions stated in this instrument.

III

As used in this instrument, "Husband" shall refer to JOHN CARR, and "Wife" shall refer to JOAN CARR. "Trustors" shall refer to both JOHN and JOAN CARR.

IV

JOE SMITH is hereby designated and appointed as Trustee of all trusts created by or to be created pursuant to this instrument (Trust Agreement). Should JOE SMITH become unable or unwilling to act as trustee for any reason, before the natural termination of all trusts created pursuant to this instrument, JERRY SMITH shall serve as Trustee of all trusts provided for in this instrument. The term "trustee" shall include any alternate trustees named under the terms and conditions of this instrument. No bond shall be required of any trustee appointed under the terms and conditions of this instrument.

V

The Trustors, jointly, or either of them or any person may at any time, with the consent of the Trustee, add in any manner other property to the Trust Estate.

VI

The trusts created by this document are irrevocable and not subject to amendment by any person and may not be terminated except through distributions of all trust assets as permitted by this trust agreement.

VII

The Trustee shall pay to or apply for the benefit of the minor child, Lisa Carr, such sums out of the principal and income of the Trust as, in the Trustee's discretion, shall be necessary for the proper health, support, and maintenance of Lisa Carr. In determining the sums necessary for Lisa Carr's support, the Trustee may consider any of the child's income or other resources available to the child.

FORM 11-10   continued

VIII

No payments shall be made under this document which would discharge, in whole or in part, any of the Trustors' legal obligations to support and educate the child or any other person.

IX

No power enumerated herein or accorded the Trustee shall be construed to permit any person to purchase, exchange, or otherwise deal with or dispose of the Trust Estate or income of the trust for less than fair and adequate consideration. Notwithstanding any provisions herein to the contrary, the Trustee shall have no powers over this Trust which would have the result of treating either Trustor as the owner within the meaning of section 675 of the Internal Revenue Code or any statute which would result in any portion of trust proceeds being included in the estate of either Trustor for federal estate tax purposes. It is the intent of the Trustors that this trust shall be other than a "grantor trust" as described in Subpart E, of Subchapter J, Part I of the Internal Revenue Code.

X

At the time that Lisa Carr attains age twenty-five (25), the Trustee shall distribute to her free of the Trust, the trust estate, as then constituted. If Lisa Carr dies before attaining age twenty-five (25), she shall have a testamentary general power of appointment over the trust estate. If she dies prior to reaching age twenty-five and on her death she has no valid Will, then the trust estate shall be distributed to her heirs under the principles of intestate succession then in effect in the State of _____.

XI

Any Trustee shall be entitled to reasonable compensation for his or her services in accordance with the compensation being paid for similar services to other trustees with similar duties.

XII

To carry out the purposes and provisions of the Trust created by this instrument, the Trustee shall have these powers and discretion in addition to those now or hereafter conferred by law, and except as elsewhere herein specifically restricted:

a. Power to retain and to continue to hold any property that becomes a part of the Trust Estate.

b. Power to sell, dispose of, exchange, partition, convey, divide, repair, manage, control, and grant options and rights of refusal of property that becomes a part of the Trust Estate for cash, credit, deferred payments, or exchange.

c. Power to lease or rent any property belonging to the Trust Estate for a reasonable term of years, months, or days and for any purpose including exploration and removal of gas, oil, and other minerals, to include community leases and pooling agreements.

d. Power to insure, at the expense of the Trust Estate, insurance of any kind and in amounts as the Trustee deems advisable.

FORM 11-10   continued

e. Power to invest all or any part of the Trust Estate in every kind of property, whether real or personal, and every kind of investment.

f. Power to litigate and compromise claims with respect to the Trust Estate as the Trustee deems advisable.

g. Power to manage securities, to include all the rights, powers, and privileges of an owner.

h. Power to allocate to principal or income all monies and properties received on behalf of the Trust Estate.

i. Power to make distributions of the Trust property as required, pursuant to the provisions of this Trust.

j. Power to employ and pay any custodian, investment adviser, attorney, accountant, or other consultant deemed necessary.

k. Power to hold and operate any business interest that may be or become a part of the Trust Estate.

l. Power to pay with funds from the Trust Estate any tax, charge, or assessment against the Trust Estate which the Trustee shall be required to pay.

m. Power to deposit funds in commercial, savings, or savings and loan accounts, subject to the usual restrictions upon withdrawal in effect at the that time.

XIII

Other property acceptable to the Trustee may be added to the Trust Estate by any person.

XIV

Unless sooner terminated in accordance with other provisions of this instrument, the Trust created by this instrument shall terminate 21 years after the death of the surviving Settlor.

XV

No interest in the principal or income of any trust created under this instrument shall be anticipated, assigned, encumbered, or subject to creditor's claim or legal process before being received by a beneficiary.

XVI

The validity of this trust and the construction of its beneficial provisions shall be governed by the laws of the State of _____.

XVII

Any Trustee shall have the right to resign at any time. The term "Trustee" as used in this instrument includes also "Trustees," "Cotrustees," "Sole Trustee," and "Successor Trustee or Trustees."

FORM 11-10   continued

XVIII

The Trust created under/in/by this instrument may be referred to as the JOHN AND JOAN CARR IRREVOCABLE TRUST of 20__.

Executed at Los Angeles, California, on January 31, 20__.

_____
Joan Carr, Settlor/Trustor

_____
John Carr, Settlor/Trustor

_____
Jim Smith, Trustee

State of California)

City of Los Angeles)

On January 31, 20_____, before me, the undersigned, a Notary Public in and for the State, personally appeared Joan Carr and John Carr known to me to be the Trustees and the Settlors of the JOHN AND JOAN CARR IRREVOCABLE TRUST of 20__, and acknowledged to me that they executed the same.

Witness my hand and official seal

_____
Notary Public

My Commission expires: _____

Schedule A to JOHN AND JOAN CARR IRREVOCABLE TRUST of 20__

[List all property on this schedule.]

_____

_____

_____

_____

_____

_____

III. JOINT TENANCY AND TENANCY IN COMMON

Using Joint Tenancy in Estate Planning

Joint tenancy is a form of co-ownership of property in which two or more people own the property in question in equal, undivided interests. The right of survivorship is the chief feature of this form of ownership and is what makes it attractive as an estate planning device. On the death of a joint tenant, the property goes without probate to the remaining property owners. The deceased's interest is not subject to disposition by will or trust.

For a detailed discussion of joint tenancy and tenancy in common, please refer to the CD that accompanies this book.

IV. PUTTING A VALUE ON YOUR ESTATE
General Rules of Evaluation

In evaluating the value of property, three major approaches are commonly used: fair market value, alternate valuation, and special use evaluation. The general rule is that all assets are evaluated at their fair market value (FMV). FMV is defined as the price at which the property would change hands between a willing buyer and a willing seller, neither being under any pressure to buy or sell the property in question and both having reasonable knowledge of all the basic facts regarding the property.

For more detailed information on putting a value on your estate, refer to the accompanying CD.

V. WILLS

For a detailed discussion of the general rules regarding wills, please refer to the CD that accompanies this book.

FORM 11-11   Will to use with living trust (married person with children).

LAST WILL AND TESTAMENT

OF

_____ [1]

Article I

I, _____ [2], also known by the name of _____ [3], hereby declare that this is my Last Will and Testament. I hereby revoke any prior wills and codicils.

I am currently married to_____[Name of spouse]. I have the below-named children: _____
_____[4]

Article II

Personal and Household Items

I make the following gifts, bequests, and devices of personal property to the persons listed below:

Item: _____   To:_____

Item: _____   To:_____

Item: _____   To:_____

Item: _____   To:_____[5]

I give, devise, and bequest all my furniture, furnishings, household items, personal automobiles, and personal items not otherwise provided for in this Will to _____
_____ [6] if _____ [7] survives me by 60 days. If _____ [7] does not survive me by 60 days, then and only then I give the above-listed personal and household items to _____ [8].

Article III

I make the following cash gifts to:

Name: _____   Amount:_____

Name: _____   Amount: _____

Name: _____   Amount: _____[9]

FORM 11-11 continued

I make the following cash gifts, bequests, and devises to the below-listed charities.

Name of Charity _____ Amount: _____

Name of Charity _____ Amount: _____ [10]

If any person named in Article III does not survive me or any charity named in Article III does not accept the gift, then the attempted gift to that person or that charity is withdrawn. The withdrawal of one or more gifts under Article III does not affect the other gifts listed under this Article.

Article IV

Residuary Estate

I give, devise, and bequeath all the residue of my estate to _____ the then serving trustee of the Revocable Living Trust created by me on the __ day of _____, 20__, and created prior to the execution of this Will, as that trust may be amended from time to time, to be added to the principal of that trust and held, administered, and distributed in accordance with the terms, limitations, and conditions of the instrument creating the Revocable Living Trust. If this gift to that trust is ineffective for any reason, then and only then I give the residue of my estate to my personal representative, to hold in trust, subject to the same terms, conditions, and limitations set forth in the document creating the Revocable Living Trust, the terms of which are specifically incorporated by reference into this document.

Article V

If any person, devisee, legatee, beneficiary under this Will, or any legal heir of mine, or any person claiming to be a legal heir of mine, shall in any manner either directly or indirectly attack the distribution of my estate or oppose, contest, or attempt to set aside any part of this Will, then and in such event, any gifts to that person or persons provided for in this Will are revoked, and that person or persons shall take only the sum of one dollar ($1.00).

Article VI

I nominate _____ [11] to serve as the executor of this Will. If _____ _____[11] is unable or unwilling to serve or after accepting the duties resigns as executor, then I nominate _____ [12] as executor of this Will. No bond shall be required of any executor of this Will.

Article VII

If it becomes necessary at any time to appoint a representative of my estate in any state other than the state in which I reside on the date of my death, I nominate and appoint such person or persons as may be selected by my executor to serve as such representative.

Article VIII

I direct that my body be buried or disposed of as follows: _____ _____[13]

FORM 11-11   continued

Article IX
Guardian

If a guardian is needed for any child of mine, then I nominate _____
_____ [14] to serve as guardian of that child. If that person is unwilling or unable to serve as guardian, then I nominate _____ [15] to serve as guardian of that child. No bond shall be required of any guardian appointed by this Will.

IN WITNESS WHEREOF, I have hereunto signed my name to this my Last Will and Testament on ____ day of_____, 20__, at the City of _____ in the State of_____.

_____
Testator [16]

ATTESTATION CLAUSE

Each of us declares under the penalty of perjury under the laws of the State of _____ [17] that the testator signed this Will in our presence, all of us being present at the same time, and we now, at the testator's request, in the testator's presence, and in the presence of each other, sign below as witnesses, declaring that the testator appears to be of sound mind and under no duress, fraud, or undue influence.

EXECUTED on _____, 20__, at the City of _____ State of _____ [18]

Witness's Name and Address   Witness's Signature

_____   _____ [19]

_____   _____

_____

Instructions for Completing the Blanks in the Above Will

1. Enter your full legal name in this blank.
2. Repeat your name in this blank.
3. Enter any other names or nicknames that you are known by in this blank.
4. Enter the names and addresses of your children in these blanks.
5. Enter any special items of property that you wish to give to certain persons in these blanks. For example, "Item: *my gold wristwatch* To: *my sister, Marilyn Ashe.*"
6. List the name of the person to receive the remaining personal and household items in this blank.
7. Insert the pronoun "he" or "she."
8. List the person to receive those items if the primary beneficiary predeceases you or fails to survive you by 60 days.
9. List persons' names and amounts. If no cash gifts are intended, then insert "none" in the first blank.
10. List any charities that you wish to give gifts to. If none, then insert "none" in the first blank.
11. Enter the name of the person you wish to appoint as the executor of your estate.
12. Enter the name of the alternate executor.
13. List your burial or cremation instructions at this point in your Will.
14. Insert the name of the person who you wish to be appointed as guardian of your minor children.

FORM 11-11 continued

15. Enter the name of an alternate guardian in case the first choice is unable or unwilling to serve as guardian.
16. The person who is making the will (you) should sign at this point in front of the witnesses.
17. Insert the name of the state in which the will is being signed in this blank.
18. The date and place that the will is signed and witnessed should be entered on this line.
19. Have witnesses sign and list their addresses at this point. If possible, use three witnesses. Do not use relatives or persons who will receive property under the terms of the will.

The following forms, 11-12 through 11-15, only appear on the accompanying CD:

- Form 11-12: Will to Use with Living Trust (Single Person with Children)
- Form 11-13: Will to Use with Living Trust (Single Person with no Children)
- Form 11-14: Standard Will for Single Person with Children
- Form 11-15: Standard Will for Single Person with No Children

FORM 11-16 Standard will for married person (no trust involved, with majority of estate to surviving spouse).

LAST WILL AND TESTAMENT

OF

_____ [1]

Article I

I, _____ [2], also known by the name of _____ [3], hereby declare that this is my Last Will and Testament. I hereby revoke any prior wills and codicils.

I am married to_____. Any reference to "my spouse" in this Will shall refer to my present spouse. We have the below-named children: _____
_____[4]

I have the below-named children by a former marriage: _____
_____[5]

Any reference to "my children" shall refer to all of my children living or deceased.

Article II

Personal and Household Items

I make the following gifts, bequests, and devices of personal property to the persons listed below:

Item: _____   To:_____

Item: _____   To:_____

Item: _____   To:_____

Item: _____   To:_____[6]

I give, devise, and bequest all my furniture, furnishings, household items, personal automobiles, and personal items not otherwise provided for in this will to my spouse _____ _____ if my spouse survives me by 60 days. If spouse does not survive me by 60 days, then and only then I give the above listed personal and household items to my children who survive me. These items shall be divided equally among my children.

Article III

I make the following cash gifts to:

Name: _____   Amount:_____

Name: _____   Amount: _____

Name: _____   Amount: _____[7]

FORM 11-16   continued

I make the following cash gifts, bequests, and devises to the below-listed charities.

Name of Charity _____   Amount: _____

Name of Charity _____   Amount: _____ [8]

If any person named in Article III does not survive me or any charity named in Article III does not accept the gift, then the attempted gift to that person or that charity is withdrawn. The withdrawal of one or more gifts under Article III does not affect the other gifts listed under this Article.

Article IV

Real Property

If my spouse, _____ [9], survives me by sixty days, I hereby give, devise, and bequeath that real property located at _____ [address] to my spouse. If my spouse _____ [9] does not survive me by sixty days, then I hereby give, devise, and bequeath the above-described real property to my children to be divided in equal shares and distributed as follows: one share to each living child and one share to each group composed of the living issue of any deceased child of mine, to be shared equally among them.

Article V

Residuary Estate

I give, devise, and bequeath all the residue of my estate to my spouse, _____, provided that my spouse survives me by sixty days. If my spouse fails to survive me by sixty days, then and only then I give the residue of my estate to my children to be divided in equal shares and distributed as follows: one share to each living child and one share to each group composed of the living issue of any deceased child of mine.

Article VI

If any person, devisee, legatee, beneficiary under this Will, or any legal heir of mine, or any person claiming to be a legal heir of mine, shall in any manner either directly or indirectly attack the distribution of my estate or oppose, contest, or attempt to set aside any part of this Will, then and in such event, any gifts to that person or persons provided for in this Will are revoked and that person or persons shall take only the sum of one dollar ($1.00).

Article VII

I nominate _____ [11] to serve as the executor of this Will. If _____ _____ [12] is unable or unwilling to serve or after accepting the duties resigns as executor, then I nominate _____ [13] as executor of this Will. No bond shall be required of any executor of this Will.

Article VIII

If it becomes necessary at any time to appoint a representative of my estate in any state other than the state in which I reside on the date of my death, I nominate and appoint such person or persons as may be selected by my executor to serve as such representative.

FORM 11-16   continued

Article IX

I direct that my body be buried or disposed of as follows: _____

_____[14]

Article X

Guardian

If a guardian is needed for any child of mine, then I nominate _____[15] to serve as guardian of that child. If that person is unwilling or unable to serve as guardian, then I nominate _____ [16] to serve as guardian of that child. No bond shall be required of any guardian appointed by this Will.

IN WITNESS WHEREOF, I have hereunto signed my name to this my Last Will and Testament on the __ day of _____, 20__, at the City of _____ in the State of _____.

_____

Testator [17]

ATTESTATION CLAUSE

Each of us declares under the penalty of perjury under the laws of the State of _____ _____ [18] that the testator signed this Will in our presence, all of us being present at the same time, and we now, at the testator's request, in the testator's presence, and in the presence of each other, sign below as witnesses, declaring that the testator appears to be of sound mind and under no duress, fraud, or undue influence.

EXECUTED on_____, 20__, at the City of _____ State of _____ [19]

Witness's Name and Address   Witness's Signature

_____   _____ [20]

_____

_____   _____

_____   _____

Instructions for Completing the Blanks in the Above Will

1. Enter your full legal name in this blank.
2. Repeat your name in this blank.
3. Enter any other names or nicknames that you are known by in this blank.
4. Enter the names and addresses of any children that you may have in these blanks. If you have no children, insert "none."
5. If there are no children by a former marriage, insert "none."
6. Enter any special items of property that you wish to give a certain persons in these blanks. For example, "Item: *my gold wristwatch* To: *my sister, Marilyn Ashe.*"
7. List persons' names and amounts. If no cash gifts are intended, then insert "none" in the first blank.

FORM 11-16 continued

8. List any charities that you wish to give gifts to. If none, then insert "none" in the first blank.
9. List the person or institution to receive your real property. If the person is not your spouse, delete the word "spouse." Also include a description of the real property. If you have no real property, insert "none."
10. Same name as for item 9.
11. Enter the name of the person you wish to appoint as the executor of your estate.
12. Same as item 11.
13. Enter the name of the alternate executor, if the first-named person is unable or unwilling to serve as executor.
14. List your burial or cremation instructions at this point in your Will.
15. Name the person you want appointed as guardian of any minor children if a guardian is needed.
16. Enter the name of the alternate guardian in case the first-named guardian is unable or unwilling to serve.
17. The person who is making the will [you] should sign at this point in front of the witnesses.
18. Insert the name of the state in which the will is being signed in this blank.
19. Date and place that the will is signed and witnessed should be entered on this line.
20. Have witnesses sign and list their addresses at this point. Use two or (preferably) three witnesses. Do not use relatives or persons who will receive property under the terms of the will.

FORM 11-17   Will with trust (married person).

[Testamentary trust]

LAST WILL AND TESTAMENT

OF

_____ [1]

Article I

I, _____ [2], also known by the name of _____ [3], hereby declare that this is my Last Will and Testament. I hereby revoke any prior wills and codicils.

I am married to_____. Any reference to "my spouse" in this Will shall refer to my present spouse. We have the below-named children: _____
_____[4]

I have the below-named children by a former marriage: _____
_____[5]

Any reference to "my children" shall refer to all of my children living or deceased.

Article II

Personal and Household Items

I make the following gifts, bequests, and devices of personal property to the persons listed below:

FORM 11-17   continued

Item: _____   To:_____

Item: _____   To:_____

Item: _____   To:_____

Item: _____   To:_____[6]

Article III

I make the following cash gifts to:

Name: _____   Amount:_____

Name: _____   Amount: _____

Name: _____   Amount: _____[7]

I make the following cash gifts, bequests, and devises to the below-listed charities.

Name of Charity _____   Amount: _____

Name of Charity _____   Amount: _____ [8]

If any person named in Article III does not survive me or any charity named in Article III does not accept the gift, then the attempted gift to that person or that charity is withdrawn. The withdrawal of one or more gifts under Article III does not affect the other gifts listed under this Article.

Article IV

Residuary Estate

If my spouse survives my by sixty days, I give, devise, and bequeath all my residuary estate to my spouse, _____. If my spouse fails to survive me by sixty days and any child of mine under 21 years of age survives me, then I give all my residuary estate to the trustee, in trust, on the following terms:

(a) As long as any child of mine under 21 years of age is living, the trustee shall distribute from time to time to or for the benefit of any one or more of my children and the descendants of any deceased child (the beneficiaries) of any age as much, or all, of the (i) principal or (ii) net income of the trust, or (iii) both, as the trustee deems necessary for their health, support, maintenance, and education. Any undistributed income shall be accumulated and added to the principal. "Education" includes, but is not limited to, college, graduate, postgraduate, and vocational studies, and reasonably related living expenses. Consistent with the trustee's fiduciary duties, the trustee may distribute trust income or principal in equal or unequal shares and to any one or more of the beneficiaries to the exclusion of other beneficiaries. In deciding on distributions, the trustee may take into account, so far as known to the trustee, the beneficiaries' other income, outside resources, or sources of support, including the capacity for gainful employment of a beneficiary who has completed his or her education.

FORM 11-17 continued

(b) In addition to any powers now or hereafter conferred upon trustees by law, the trustee shall have the additional powers listed below:

(i) To hire and pay from the trust fees of investments advisers, accountants, tax advisers, agents, attorneys, and other assistants for the administration of the trust and for the management of any trust asset and for any litigation affecting the trust.

(ii) On any distribution of assets from the trust, the trustee shall have the discretion to partition, allot, and distribute the assets, in kind, including undivided interests in an asset or in any part of it; or partly in cash and partly in kind; or entirely in cash. If a distribution is being made to more than one beneficiary, the trustee shall have the discretion to distribute assets among them on a pro rata or non-pro rata basis, with the assets valued as of the date of distribution.

(c) The Trust shall terminate when there is no living child of mine under 21 years of age. The trustee shall distribute any remaining principal and accumulated net income of the trust to my descendants who are then living.

If my spouse does not survive me by sixty days and if no child of mine is under 21 years of age, then I give all my residuary estate to my children in equal shares.

Article V

If any person, devisee, legatee, beneficiary under this Will, or any legal heir of mine, or any person claiming to be a legal heir of mine, shall in any manner either directly or indirectly attack the distribution of my estate or oppose, contest, or attempt to set aside any part of this Will, then and in such event, any gifts to that person or persons provided for in this Will are revoked, and that person or persons shall take only the sum of one dollar ($1.00).

If a trustee is needed under this Will, I hereby appoint _____ [9] to serve as trustee of any trust created by this Will. If this person is unable or unwilling to act, then I appoint _____ [10] to serve as trustee. No bond shall be required of any trustee appointed under the provisions of this Will.

Article VI

I nominate _____ [11] to serve as the executor of this Will. If _____ _____ [12] is unable or unwilling to serve or after accepting the duties resigns as executor, then I nominate _____ [13] as executor of this Will. No bond shall be required of any executor of this Will.

Article VII

If it becomes necessary at any time to appoint a representative of my estate in any state other than the state in which I reside on the date of my death, I nominate and appoint such person or persons as may be selected by my executor to serve as such representative.

Article VIII

I direct that my body be buried or disposed of as follows: _____ _____[14]

FORM 11-17 continued

Article IX

Guardian

If a guardian is needed for any child of mine, then I nominate _____ [15] to serve as guardian of that child. If that person is unwilling or unable to serve as guardian, then I nominate _____ [16] to serve as guardian of the person of that child. No bond shall be required of any guardian appointed by this Will.

IN WITNESS WHEREOF, I have hereunto signed my name to this my Last Will and Testament on the __ day of_____ 20__, at the City of _____ in the State of _____.

_____

Testator [17]

ATTESTATION CLAUSE

Each of us declares under the penalty of perjury under the laws of the State of _____ [18] that the testator signed this Will in our presence, all of us being present at the same time, and we now, at the testator's request, in the testator's presence, and in the presence of each other, sign below as witnesses, declaring that the testator appears to be of sound mind and under no duress, fraud, or undue influence.

EXECUTED on_____, 20__, at the City of _____ State of _____ [19]

Witness's Name and Address   Witness's Signature

_____   _____ [20]

_____

_____   _____

_____

_____   _____

_____

_____

Instructions for Completing the Blanks in the Above Will

1. Enter your full legal name in this blank.
2. Repeat your name in this blank.
3. Enter any other names or nicknames that you are known by in this blank.
4. Enter the names and addresses of any children that you may have in these blanks. If you have no children, insert "none."
5. If there are no children by a former marriage, insert "none. "
6. Enter any special items of property that you wish to give a certain persons in these blanks. For example, "Item: *my gold wristwatch* To: *my sister, Marilyn Ashe.*"
7. List persons' names and amounts. If no cash gifts are intended, then insert "none" in the first blank.
8. List any charities that you wish to give gifts to. If none, then insert "none" in the first blank.
9. List the person or institution who will act as trustee if one is needed under the provisions of this Will. This should be someone or an institution whose judgment you are willing to rely on.

FORM 11-17   continued

10. Enter the name of the alternate trustee in case the first-named person or institution is unwilling or unable to act as trustee.
11. Enter the name of the person you wish to appoint as the executor of your estate.
12. Same as item 11.
13. Enter the name of the alternate executor, if the first-named person is unable or unwilling to serve as executor.
14. List your burial or cremation instructions at this point in your Will.
15. Name the person you want appointed as guardian of any minor children if a guardian is needed.
16. Enter the name of the alternate guardian in case the first named guardian is unable or unwilling to serve.
17. The person who is making the will [you] should sign at this point in front of the witnesses.
18. Insert the name of the state in which the will is being signed in this blank.
19. The date and place that the will is signed and witnessed should be entered on this line.
20. Have witnesses sign and list their addresses at this point. If possible use three witnesses. Do not use relatives or persons who will receive property under the terms of the will.

Appendix A

Sources of Assistance: Federal Agencies

National Offices

U.S. Equal Employment Opportunity Commission
Washington, DC 20507
(See also the list of field offices below.)

Civil Rights Division
U.S. Department of Health and Human Services
Washington, DC 20201

Social Security Administration
U.S. Department of Health and Human Services
Baltimore, MD 21235

Internal Revenue Service
U.S. Department of the Treasury
Washington, DC 20224

Office of Revenue Sharing
U.S. Department of the Treasury
Washington, DC 20226

Federal Trade Commission
Washington, DC 20580

Pension Benefit Guaranty Corporation
2020 K Street, NW
Washington, DC 20006

Office of Labor Management Standards
U.S. Department of Labor
Washington, DC 20210

Office of Pension and Welfare Benefit Programs
U.S. Department of Labor
Washington, DC 20210

Occupational Safety and Health Administration
U.S. Department of Labor
Washington, DC 20210

Office of Federal Contract Compliance Programs
Employment Standards Administration
U.S. Department of Labor
Washington, DC 20210
(See also the list of regional offices below.)

Office of Workers' Compensation Programs
Employment Standards Administration
U.S. Department of Labor
Washington, DC 20210

Women's Bureau
Office of the Secretary
U.S. Department of Labor
Washington, DC 20210

Wage and Hour Division
Employment Standards Administration
U.S. Department of Labor
Washington, DC 20210
(See also the list of field offices below.)

Office of Federal Contract Compliance Programs (OFCCP)
Regional, Area, and Field Offices

Addresses and telephone numbers for area or field offices are listed in the telephone directory under "United States Department of Labor."

Boston: U.S. Department of Labor, JFK Building, Room 1612-C, Government Center, MA 02203.

New York: U.S. Department of Labor, 1515 Broadway, Room 3308, NY 10036.

Philadelphia: U.S. Department of Labor, Gateway Building, Room 1310, 3535 Market Street, PA 19104.

Atlanta: U.S. Department of Labor, 1371 Peachtree Street, NE, Room 111, GA 30367.

Chicago: U.S. Department of Labor, New Federal Building, Room 570B, 230 South Dearborn Street, IL 60604.

Dallas: U.S. Department of Labor, 525 Griffin Street, Federal Building, Room 840, TX 75202.

Kansas City: U.S. Department of Labor, Federal Office Building, Room 2011, 911 Walnut Street, MO 64106.

Denver: U.S. Department of Labor, 1412 Federal Office Building, 1961 Stout Street, CO. 80294.

San Francisco: U.S. Department of Labor, 450 Golden Gate Avenue, Room 9418, CA 94102.

Seattle: U.S. Department of Labor, Federal Office Building, 909 First Avenue, Room 3048, WA 98174.

Equal Employment Opportunity Commission (EEOC)

For nearest EEOC office call 800 USA-EEOC

State Agencies
Labor Departments and Human Rights Commissions

Alabama: Department of Industrial Relations, Industrial Relations Building, Montgomery, AL 36130.

Alaska: Department of Labor, PO Box 1149, Juneau, AK 99802. Alaska State Commission for Human Rights, 800 A Street, Suite 202, Anchorage, AK 99501.

Arizona: Department of Labor, 800 W. Washington Ave., PO Box 19070, Phoenix, AZ 85005. Arizona Civil Rights Division, 1275 W. Washington, Phoenix, AZ 85007.

Arkansas: Department of Labor, 1022 High Street, Little Rock, AK 72202.

California: Department of Industrial Relations, 525 Golden Gate Avenue, PO Box 603, San Francisco, CA 94101. Department of Fair Employment and Housing, 1201 I Street, Sacramento, CA 95814.

Colorado: Department of Labor and Employment, 251 East 12th Avenue, Denver, CO 80203. Colorado Civil Rights Commission, 1525 Sherman, Room 600C, Denver, CO 80203.

Connecticut: Labor Department, 200 Folly Brook Boulevard, Wethersfield, CT 06109. Commission on Human Rights and Opportunities, 90 Washington Street, Hartford, CT 06106.

Delaware: Department of Labor, 820 N. French Street, Wilmington, DE 19801. (Includes anti-discrimination section.)

District of Columbia: D.C. Department of Employment Services, 500 C Street, NW, Washington, DC 20001. Commission on Human Rights, District Building, Washington, DC 20004.

Florida: Department of Labor and Employment Security, Berkeley Building, 2590 Executive Center Circle East, Tallahassee, FL 32301. Commission on Human Relations, 325 John Knox Road, Suite 240, Bldg. F, Tallahassee, FL 32303.

Georgia: Department of Labor, State Labor Building, 254 Washington Street, SW, Atlanta, CA 30334.

Guam: Department of Labor, Government of Guam, Box 23548, GMF, Guam, M.I. 96921.

Hawaii: Department of Labor and Industrial Relations, 830 Punchbowl Street, Honolulu, HI 96813. Department of Labor and Industrial Relations, Labor Law Enforcement (for discrimination complaints), 888 Mililani Street, Room 401, Honolulu, HI 96813.

Idaho: Department of Labor and Industrial Services, Room 400, Statehouse Mail, 317 Main Street, Boise, ID 83720. Commission on Human Rights, 450 W. State, 1st Floor, Boise, ID 83720.

Illinois: Department of Labor, 1 West Old Capitol Plaza, Springfield, IL 627801-1217. Department of Human Rights, 100 West Randolph Street, Chicago, IL 60601.

Indiana: Department of Labor, Room 1013, State Office Building, 100 N. Senate Avenue, Indianapolis, IN 46204. Civil Rights Commission, 32 West Washington Street, Indianapolis, IN 46204-3526.

Iowa: Division of Labor, 1000 East Grand Avenue, Des Moines, IA 50319. Civil Rights Commission, 211 East Maple Street, c/o State Mailroom, Des Moines, IA 50319.

Kansas: Department of Human Resources, 401 Topeka Avenue, Topeka, KS 66603. KS Commission on Civil Rights, 214 Southwest 6th Street, Liberty Bldg., 5th Floor, Topeka, KS 66603.

Kentucky: Labor Cabinet, U.S. 127 South Building, Frankfort, KY 40601. Commission on Human Rights, 832 Capitol Plaza Tower, Frankfort, KY 40601.

Louisiana: Department of Labor, 1045 State Land and Natural Resources Building, PO Box 44094, Baton Rouge, LA 70804.

Maine: Department of Labor, 20 Union Street, Augusta, ME 04330. Human Rights Commission, State House-Station 51, Augusta, ME 04333.

Maryland: Division of Labor and Industry, 501 St. Paul Place, Baltimore, MD 21202. Commission on Human Relations, 20 East Franklin Street, Baltimore, MD 21202.

Massachusetts: Department of Labor and Industries, State Office Building, 100 Cambridge Street, Boston, MA 02202. Commission Against Discrimination, 1 Ashburton Place, Suite 601, Boston, MA 02108.

Michigan: Department of Labor, Leonard Plaza Building, 309 N. Washington, PO Box 30015, Lansing, MI 48909. Department of Civil Rights, 303 W. Kalamazoo, Lansing, MI 48913.

Minnesota: Department of Labor and Industry, 444 Lafayette Road, St. Paul, MN 55101. Department of Human Rights, 5th Floor Bremer Tower, 7th Place and Minnesota Street, St. Paul, MN 55101.

Mississippi: Workmen's Compensation Commission, PO Box 5300, Jackson, MS 39216.

Missouri: Department of Labor and Industrial Relations, 1904 Missouri Boulevard, PO Box 599, Jefferson City, MO 65102. Commission on Human Rights, 315 Ellis Blvd., PO Box 1129, Jefferson City, MO 65102-1129.

Montana: Department of Labor and Industry, PO Box 1728, Helena, MT 59624. Human Rights Commission, 1236 6th Avenue, PO Box 1728, Helena, MT 59624.

Nebraska: Department of Labor, 550 S. 16th Street, Box 94600, State House Station, Lincoln, NE 68509. Equal Opportunity Commission, 301 Centennial Mall, South, P.O. Box 94934, Lincoln, NE 68509-4934.

Nevada: Labor Commission, 505 East King Street, Room 602, Carson City, NV 89710. Equal Rights Commission, 1515 E. Tropicana, Las Vegas, NV 89158.

New Hampshire: Department of Labor, 19 Pillsbury Street, Concord, NH 03301. Commission for Human Rights, 61 South Spring Street, Concord, NH 03301.

New Jersey: Department of Labor, PO Box CN 110, Trenton, NJ 08625. Division on Civil Rights, 1100 Raymond Boulevard, Newark, NJ 07102.

New Mexico: Labor Department, PO Box 1928, Albuquerque, NM 87103. Human Rights Commission, 930 Baca Street, Suite A, Santa Fe, NM 87501.

New York: Department of Labor, State Campus Building 12, Albany, NY 12240. Division of Human Rights, 55 West 125 Street, New York, NY 10047.

North Carolina: Department of Labor, Labor Building, 214 West Jones Street, Raleigh, NC 27603.

North Dakota: Department of Labor, State Capitol, 5th Floor, Bismarck, ND 58505.

Ohio: Department of Industrial Relations, 2323 W. 5th Avenue, Columbus, OH 43215. Civil Rights Commission, 220 Parsons Avenue, Columbus, OH 43215.

Oklahoma: Department of Labor, 1315 N. Broadway Place, Oklahoma City, OK 73103-4817. Human Rights Commission, Room G11, Jim Thorpe Building, 2101 North Lincoln Blvd., Oklahoma City, OK 73105.

Oregon: Bureau of Labor and Industries, State Office Building, 1400 SW Fifth, Portland, OR 97201. (Includes civil rights division.)

Pennsylvania: Department of Labor and Industry, 1700 Labor and Industry Building, 7th & Forster Streets, Harrisburg, PA 17120. Human Relations Commission, 101 South Second Street, Suite 300, PO Box 3145, Harrisburg, PA 17105.

Puerto Rico: Department of Labor and Human Resources, 505 Munoz Rivera Avenue, GPO Box 3088, Hato Rey, PR 00918. (Includes antidiscrimination unit.)

Rhode Island: Department of Labor, 220 Elmwood Avenue, Providence, RI 02907. Commission for Human Rights, 10 Abbott Park Place, Providence, RI 02903-3768.

South Carolina: Department of Labor, 3600 Forest Drive, PO Box 11329, Columbia, SC 29211. Human Affairs Commission, Post Office Drawer 11300, Columbia, SC 29211.

South Dakota: Department of Labor, 700 Governors Drive, Pierre, SD 57501.

Tennessee: Department of Labor, 501 Union Building, Nashville, TN 37219. Commission for Human Development, 208 Tennessee Building, 535 Church Street, Nashville, TN 37219.

Texas: Department of Labor and Standards, PO Box 12157, Capitol Station, Austin, TX 78711. Commission on Human Rights, PO Box 13493, Capitol Station, Austin, TX 78711.

Utah: Industrial Commission, 160 East 300 South, PO Box 5800, Salt Lake City, UT 84110-5800. Antidiscrimination Division, 160 East 300 South, PO Box 5800, Salt Lake City, UT 84111-5800.

Vermont: Department of Labor and Industry, State Office Building, Montpelier, VT 05602.

Virginia: Department of Labor and Industry, PO Box 12064, Richmond, VA 23241. Human Rights Council, c/o Office of the Secretary of Administration, PO Box 1475, Richmond, VA 23212.

Virgin Islands: Department of Labor, PO Box 890, Christiansted, St. Croix, VI 00820.

Washington: Department of Labor and Industries, General Administration Building, Olympia, WA 98504. Human Rights Commission, 402 Evergreen Plaza Building, FJ-41, Olympia, WA 98504-3341.

West Virginia: Department of Labor, Capitol Complex, 1800 Washington Street, East, Charleston, WV 25305. Human Rights Commission, 215 Professional Building, 1036 Quarrier Street, Charleston, WV 25301.

Wisconsin: Department of Industry, Labor and Human Relations, 201 East Washington Avenue, PO Box 7946, Madison, WI 53707. Equal Rights Division, PO Box 8928, Madison, WI 53708.

Wyoming: Department of Labor and Statistics, Herschler Building, Cheyenne, WY 82002. Fair Employment Commission, Herschler Building, 2nd Floor East Wing, Cheyenne, WY 82002.

Appendix B

Glossary

Note: For legal terms not listed in this glossary, the reader may refer to *Black's Law Dictionary* or *Cochran's Law Dictionary* in the reference section of most libraries.

adjustable rate mortgage (ARM): A loan with an interest rate that changes with market conditions on predetermined dates.

administration: The legal process in which the court supervises the inventory of the decedent's estate, the payment of debts, and the distribution of the remaining property.

administrator: A person appointed by the court to administer the estate of a person who died without a will (*intestate*).

adverse impact: Disadvantage to members of the protected class resulting from a substantially different rate of selection in hiring, firing, promotion, or other employment decisions.

affidavit: A written statement of facts, signed and sworn to before an official with the authority to administer oaths.

affirm: To ratify or approve the judgment of a lower court or an administrative decision.

agent: A person with the authority to do an act for another.

ancillary administration: The administration of a decedent's property that is located in a state other than the state in which the person was domiciled at the time of his or her death.

annual percentage rate (APR): A term used to represent the percentage relationship of the total finance charge to the amount of a loan over the term of the loan. Do not confuse the APR with your quoted interest rate, which is used to determine your monthly principal and interest payment. The APR reflects the cost of your mortgage loan as a yearly rate. It will be higher than the interest rate stated on the note because it includes (in addition to the interest rate) loan discount points, fees, and mortgage insurance.

annuity: Payment of a fixed sum of money to a named person at regular intervals.

appeal: A request or application to a higher court to set aside or modify the decision or ruling of a lower court.

appellant: The party who initiates an appeal.

appellee: The party to a lawsuit against whom an appeal is taken.

appraisal: A report written by a qualified expert that states an opinion on the value of a property based on its characteristics and the selling prices of similar properties or comparable properties in the area.

arbitration: The act of submitting a dispute to the nonjudicial judgment of one or more disinterested persons, called *arbitrators.*

arbitration clause: A contract clause that outlines the procedures for handling a dispute, should one arise. Arbitration clauses often name a third party like the American Arbitration Association to be an impartial referee.

assign: To transfer rights to another party, called the *assignee.* The party who assigns the rights is called the *assignor.*

automated underwriting: A computerized method of reviewing home mortgage applications for loan approval.

autopsy: The examination of a body for the purposes of determining the cause of death.

basis of property: The value of the property used for tax computation purposes. In most cases, it is the original cost of the property plus any improvements added and adjusted for depreciation.

beneficiary: A person or organization who receives the benefits of a will, trust or insurance policy.

bequest: A gift of personal property under a will.

bona fide: In good faith, honesty, and without fraud.

bona fide occupational qualification (BFOQ): A good faith, honest, and without fraud preemployment qualification that is essential to establish the ability of the applicant to perform the necessary and required duties of the position in question. (For a discussion of this requirement, see Chapter 1.)

bond: A guarantee whereby a company or person agrees to replace any loss of property as the results of negligence or criminal conduct.

book value: The net worth of a business's assets, minus liabilities without considering any value for goodwill.

bridge loan: A loan that enables home buyers to get financing to make a down payment and pay closing costs on a new home before selling the home they currently own.

brief: A prepared statement of a party's position in a legal proceeding.

burden of proof: The duty of a party to present the evidence to establish that party's contentions or version of the facts. Failure to meet the burden of proof will result in a decision for the opposing party.

bypass trust: A trust used to prevent property of the first spouse to die from being included in the gross estate of the surviving spouse. The surviving spouse, however, is permitted to receive certain benefits from the property contained in the trust.

case law: Judicial precedent set forth in prior court opinions that will bind parties in future lawsuits.

caveat: A warning.

change order: A written order authorizing a change in the work, timeline, and/or price of a project.

circumstantial evidence: Evidence not directly proving the existence of a fact in question but tending to imply its existence.

Civil Rights Act of 1964: The civil rights act that forms the basis of most equal opportunity requirements. Title 42, U.S. Code, section 1447 et seq. (See Chapter 1.)

civil service commissions: Various groups of local, state, or federal officials that supervise public employees.

claimant: A person who makes a claim for benefits.

Clayton Act: The act that amended the Sherman Antitrust Act and that prohibits unlawful restraints on trade.

closing: The final step after a lender approves an application The home buyer and lender sign the security-agreement note for the mortgage loan, which states all the terms and conditions of the loan. The funds for the loan are turned over to the home buyer's closing agent.

closing agent: Usually an attorney or title agency representative who oversees the closing and witnesses the signing of the closing documents.

closing costs: The costs paid by the mortgage borrower (and sometimes the seller) in addition to the purchase price of the property These include the lender's fees, title fees, and appraisal costs.

codicil: An amendment to a will.

collective bargaining: The bargaining between management and labor unions regarding the terms and conditions of employment.

commerce clause: Article I, section VIII of the U.S. Constitution, which gives the U.S. Congress the authority to regulate trade between the states.

commitment letter: A binding, written pledge by the lender to a mortgage applicant to make a loan, usually under certain stated conditions.

common law: An ambiguous term used to describe the concept of law that relies on precedent (previous court opinions) and traditions.

community property: The legal concept of property ownership exists in eight states and provides that most property acquired during the course of a marriage from the earnings or efforts of each spouse is jointly owned by both spouses.

compensatory damages: The measure of actual damages or losses.

concurrent jurisdiction: The authority of two or more courts to entertain a particular lawsuit.

consequential damages: A measure of damages referring to the indirect injuries or losses that a party suffers.

conservator: A person or corporation appointed by a court to manage the affairs of a person incapable of managing his or her own affairs.

consideration: Something of value given in exchange for something of value by another. For a contract to be valid, there needs to be consideration from all parties.

conventional loan: A mortgage that is not insured or guaranteed by a government agency such as the FHA, VA, or Farmers Home Administration.

corpus of a trust: The original assets of a trust. The corpus doesn't include trust income.

credit report: A report issued by an independent agency which contains certain information concerning a mortgage applicant's credit history and current credit standing.

debt-to-income ratio: A formula lenders use to determine the loan amount for which you may qualify. Also known as the *back-end ratio*. Guidelines may vary, depending on the loan program.

decedent: The dead person.

defendant: The party against whom a lawsuit is initiated.

de novo: A new, fresh start.

deposition: Oral questions and answers reduced to writing for possible use in a legal proceeding.

devise: An early English term that refers to a gift of real estate in a will.

dictum: Statement in a judicial opinion which is not necessary to support the decision in that case and therefore not considered as precedence.

disclaimer: A refusal to accept a gift. Normally required to be in writing.

domicile: The state of a person's permanent residence.

donee: A person who receives a gift from another.

donor: A person who makes a gift to another or others.

down payment: A portion of the sale price paid to the seller by the home buyer to close the sales transaction. Also, the difference between the sale price and the home mortgage amount.

Equal Employment Opportunity Commission (EEOC): A commission established under the Civil Rights Act of 1964 to administer the act.

equity: Your ownership interest, or that portion of the value of the property that exceeds the current amount of your home loan. For example, if the property is worth $100,000 and the loan is for $75,000, then you have $25,000, or 25 percent, equity in your home.

escrow account: A holding account for the amount a mortgage borrower pays each month and which the lender uses to pay for the borrower's taxes, other periodic debts against the property, homeowners insurance, and, if applicable, mortgage insurance.

et seq.: Latin term meaning *and following parts.*

executor: The individual named in a will as the person to administer the estate.

Fair Labor Standards Act of 1938: An act designed to establish fair labor standards in employment involved in interstate commerce.

fee simple: Refers to ownership rights in real estate. A fee simple ownership is the highest form. It means that you own the total interest in the property.

FICO score: A numerical rating developed and maintained by Fair Issac and Company (FICO) that indicates a borrower's creditworthiness based on a number of criteria.

fixed-rate mortgage: A loan with an interest rate that remains the same for the entire repayment term.

float the rate: This term is used when a mortgage applicant chooses not to secure a rate lock, but instead allows the interest rate to fluctuate until the applicant decides to lock it in, usually no later than five days prior to closing.

formal will: A will that is typed or printed, signed by the testator, and witnessed by witnesses.

front-end ratio: Also known as the *housing expense-to-income ratio*, it compares your proposed monthly house payment to your total household gross monthly income.

funding fee: The amount charged on VA mortgages to cover administrative costs.

gift tax exclusion: An annual exclusion of $10,000 of gifts per year per donee from any one donor is exempt from federal gift taxes.

gift taxes: Taxes imposed by the federal government on gifts made during the donor's lifetime.

good faith: An honest and fair purpose without the intent to commit an unjust act.

good faith estimate: A document that tells mortgage borrowers the approximate costs they will pay at or before closing, based on common practice in the locality.

government loan: A mortgage insured by a government agency, such as the FHA, VA, Farmers Home Administration, or a state bond program. The loans are generally made by private lenders, such as Wells Fargo Home Mortgage.

grantor: The person who grants property to a trust. The person who establishes a trust.

hearsay evidence: Statements made by witnesses in legal proceedings regarding information obtained from a third person.

holographic will: This is a will that is written entirely in the handwriting of the person making the will. It is legal in most states without the requirement that the will be witnessed by witnesses.

homeowner insurance (also called *hazard insurance*): A real estate insurance policy required of the buyer protecting the property against loss caused by fire, some natural causes, vandalism, and so on. May also include added coverage such as personal liability and theft away from the home.

HUD-I settlement statement: A standard form used to disclose costs at closing.

index: Interest rate adjustments on adjustable-rate mortgage (ARM) loans are based on a specific "index" or treasury issue (bond) which is selected because it is a reliable, familiar financial indicator. Your monthly interest rate payment will be adjusted up or down in relation to this market indicator, plus the margin as specified in your note. See *margin.*

injunction: A court order directing a party to refrain from certain activity.

interest rate: A percentage of the mortgage amount that is paid to the lender for the use of the money, usually expressed as an annual percentage.

inter vivos trust: A trust created during the lifetime of the person creating the trust (settlor).

interim interest: The interest that accrues, on a per diem basis, from the day of closing until the end of the month.

interstate commerce: Any trade, transportation, or communication among the several states or with the District of Columbia. *Affecting interstate commerce* means involved in, having an impact on, burdening, or obstructing it.

intestate: Refers to a person who dies without a valid will.

issue: A term used to refer to children or direct descendants of the deceased.

job analysis: A detailed statement of work behaviors and other information relevant to a job.

job description: A general statement of the duties and responsibilities entailed in a job.

jurisdiction: The authority for a court or administrative body to hear and decide a dispute.

labor arbitration: A nonjudicial settlement of disputes between labor and management.

labor dispute: Any dispute under a labor contract between the employer and the labor union concerning the terms, conditions, or tenure of employment or concerning the representation of persons in negotiating, maintaining, or changing the terms or conditions of employment.

Labor-Management Relations Act of 1947 (LMRA): The Taft-Hartley Act, which amended the National Labor Relations Act, to provide additional facilities for mediation of labor disputes and place obligations on labor organizations similar to those earlier placed on management.

Labor-Management Reporting and Disclosure Act of 1959 (LMRDA): An act designed to ensure democratic procedures in labor unions and establish a bill of rights for union members.

labor organization: Any labor organization, committee, or group that is organized for the benefit of employees and subject to the provisions of the Civil Rights Act of 1964 or the federal labor management acts.

lien waiver: A signed document that says that a supplier or contractor has been paid and waives his or her right to file a claim against the property.

life estate: The ownership of the right to use and enjoy property during the life of a person.

living trust: A trust that is created during the lifetime of the person creating the trust (settlor). The terms *living trust* and *inter vivos trust* are interchangeable.

loan conditions: These are terms under which the lender agrees to make the loan. They include the interest rate, the length of the loan agreement, and any requirements the borrower must meet prior to closing.

loan payment reserves: A requirement of many loan programs that, in addition to funds for the down payment and other purchase-related costs, you have saved enough money to cover one or two months of mortgage payments after your closing.

loan settlement: The conclusion of the mortgage transaction. This includes the delivery of a deed, the signing of notes, and the disbursement of funds necessary to the mortgage loan transaction.

loan-to-value ratio: The ratio of the amount borrowed to the appraised value or sale price of real property expressed as a percentage.

margin: The number of percentage points added to the index to calculate the interest rate for an adjustable-rate mortgage (ARM) at each adjustment period. See also *index.*

mortgagee: The lender.

mortgage insurance (MI): An insurance policy that will repay a portion of the loan if the borrower does not make payments as agreed upon in the note. Mortgage insurance may be required in cases in which the borrower makes less than a 20 percent down payment on the home loan.

mortgagor: The borrower.

nationality: The status acquired by belonging or associated with a nation or state. It arises by birth or naturalization.

National Labor Relations Act of 1935 (NLRA): The Wagner Act, which established the NLRB and was designed to support unionism and collective bargaining.

National Labor Relations Board (NLRB): A commission established by the NLRA to enforce the rights of employees under the act.

nonconforming loan: A mortgage program that offers approval guidelines which are not industry standards. It may, for example, have loan limits that differ from limits of conforming loans, but may offer financing in conforming and jumbo amounts.

Norris-LaGuardia Act: An act passed by the U.S. Congress in 1932 designed to stop federal courts from issuing injunctions in labor strikes.

original jurisdiction. The court with the authority to first hear the case; the trial court.

origination fee: The amount collected by the lender for making a loan. It is generally equal to a percentage of the principal amount borrowed.

per stirpes: A phrase used in wills to indicate that the division of property will be such that the children of a deceased heir take their parent's share.

plaintiff: The party who initiates a lawsuit.

pleadings: The formal written statements of parties to a lawsuit which establish the basis of each party's contentions before the court.

points: One point equals 1 percent of the loan amount. Total points on a loan include origination points, used to offset the cost of making a loan and discount points, which can be paid to reduce the loan's interest rate.

pour-over will: A will that provides that property belonging to the decease go to a previously established trust.

preapproval: A written commitment from a lender, subject to a property appraisal and other stated conditions, that lets you know exactly how much you can afford to pay for a home purchase.

prejudice: A bias that interferes with a person's impartiality and sense of fairness.

prepaids: That portion of your loan closing costs which must be collected at closing to cover taxes, interest, and insurance.

principal: The amount of a loan, excluding interest; or the remaining balance of a loan, excluding interest.

private mortgage insurance (PMJ): A mortgage insurance policy on a conventional mortgage loan issued by a private insurance company.

rate cap: The limit of how much the interest rate may change on an ARM at each adjustment and over the life of the loan.

rate lock: An agreement in which the borrower and the lender agree to protect the interest rate, points, and term of the loan while it is processed.

retention clauses: A contract provision allowing the homeowner to hold back a portion of all payments until the project is finished.

revocable trust: A living trust created by a written document that during the settlor's lifetime may be revoked by the settlor.

right-to-work laws: State antiunion laws that prohibit labor contracts requiring all employees to join a union.

settlor: The person who created a trust, that is, the *trustor*.

Sherman Antitrust Act: An act, passed in 1890, designed to protect trade and commerce by prohibiting certain restraints of trade and monopolies. (See Title 15, U.S. Code, section 1 et seq.)

strike: An organized refusal to work by the employees that is designed to place economic pressure on the employer.

subprime loan: A home financing program that accommodates borrowers with special qualifying factors, including poor credit histories.

Taft-Hartley Act. See *Labor-Management Relations Act.*

testamentary trust: A trust created by a will.

total disability: A physical disability that prevents a person from performing all of the substantial acts necessary for the person's job or occupation.

trustee: The individual or institution that holds and administers property of a trust.

trustor: The person who established the trust, that is, the settlor or grantor.

truth-in-lending statement: Required by federal regulations, this statement tells purchasers the costs of financing their loan expressed as the annual percentage rate (APR). Do not confuse the APR with your interest rate, which is used to determine your monthly principal and interest payment.

underwriting: The process of a lender reviewing the application, documentation, and property prior to rendering a loan decision.

Wagner Act. See *National Labor Relations Act.*

Index of Forms

Pages in italics refer to material only appearing on the accompanying CD. Form numbers used in this book are in parentheses; form numbers of preprinted federal and other official documents are included in the name of the form.

General Index

Pages listed in italics refer to material appearing only on the accompanying CD.

About the Author

Cliff Roberson is authorized to practice law in Texas and California. He also has been admitted to practice before the U.S. Supreme Court and federal courts in Texas and California. He was a professor at Washburn University in Topeka, Kansas and now lives in Houston, Texas. Cliff is the author of numerous publications, including the following:

- *The Complete Book of Business Forms and Agreements*, McGraw-Hill
- *Fight the IRS and Win: A Self-Defense Guide for Taxpayers*, Liberty House
- *Hire Right—Fire Right: A Manager's Guide to Employment Practices That Avoid Lawsuits*, McGraw-Hill
- *The Businessperson's Legal Advisor*, Tab
- *The Small Business Tax Advisor: Understanding the New Tax Law*, Liberty House
- *The McGraw-Hill Tax Advisor*, McGraw-Hill
- *The Landlord's Book of Forms and Agreements*, McGraw-Hill

CD-ROM WARRANTY

This software is protected by both United States copyright law and international copyright treaty provision. You must treat this software just like a book. By saying "just like a book," McGraw-Hill means, for example, that this software may be used by any number of people and may be freely moved from one computer location to another, so long as there is no possibility of its being used at one location or on one computer while it also is being used at another. Just as a book cannot be read by two different people in two different places at the same time, neither can the software be used by two different people in two different places at the same time (unless, of course, McGraw-Hill's copyright is being violated).

LIMITED WARRANTY

Customers who have problems installing or running a McGraw-Hill CD should consult our online technical support site at http://books.mcgraw-hill.com/techsupport. McGraw-Hill takes great care to provide you with top-quality software, thoroughly checked to prevent virus infections. McGraw-Hill warrants the physical CD-ROM contained herein to be free of defects in materials and workmanship for a period of sixty days from the purchase date. If McGraw-Hill receives written notification within the warranty period of defects in materials or workmanship, and such notification is determined by McGraw-Hill to be correct, McGraw-Hill will replace the defective CD-ROM. Send requests to:

McGraw-Hill
Customer Services
P.O. Box 545
Blacklick, OH 43004-0545

The entire and exclusive liability and remedy for breach of this Limited Warranty shall be limited to replacement of a defective CD-ROM and shall not include or extend to any claim for or right to cover any other damages, including, but not limited to, loss of profit, data, or use of the software, or special, incidental, or consequential damages or other similar claims, even if McGraw-Hill has been specifically advised of the possibility of such damages. In no event will McGraw-Hill's liability for any damages to you or any other person ever exceed the lower of suggested list price or actual price paid for the license to use the software, regardless of any form of the claim.

McGRAW-HILL SPECIFICALLY DISCLAIMS ALL OTHER WARRANTIES, EXPRESS OR IMPLIED, INCLUDING, BUT NOT LIMITED TO, ANY IMPLIED WARRANTY OF MERCHANTABILITY OR FITNESS FOR A PARTICULAR PURPOSE.

Specifically, McGraw-Hill makes no representation or warranty that the software is fit for any particular purpose and any implied warranty of merchantability is limited to the sixty-day duration of the Limited Warranty covering the physical CD-ROM only (and not the software) and is otherwise expressly and specifically disclaimed.

This limited warranty gives you specific legal rights; you may have others which may vary from state to state. Some states do not allow the exclusion of incidental or consequential damages, or the limitation on how long an implied warranty lasts, so some of the above may not apply to you.